All Who Love Our Blessed Redeemer

Monographs in Baptist History

VOLUME 24

SERIES EDITOR
Michael A. G. Haykin, The Southern Baptist Theological Seminary

EDITORIAL BOARD
Matthew Barrett, Midwestern Baptist Theological Seminary
Peter Beck, Charleston Southern University
Anthony L. Chute, California Baptist University
Jason G. Duesing, Midwest Baptist Theological Seminary
Nathan A. Finn, North Greenville University
Crawford Gribben, Queen's University, Belfast
Gordon L. Heath, McMaster Divinity College
Barry Howson, Heritage Theological Seminary
Jason K. Lee, Cedarville University
Thomas J. Nettles, The Southern Baptist Theological Seminary, retired
James A. Patterson, Union University
James M. Renihan, Institute of Reformed Baptist Studies
Jeffrey P. Straub, Independent Scholar
Brian R. Talbot, Broughty Ferry Baptist Church, Scotland
Malcolm B. Yarnell III, Southwestern Baptist Theological Seminary

Ours is a day in which not only the gaze of western culture but also increasingly that of Evangelicals is riveted to the present. The past seems to be nowhere in view and hence it is disparagingly dismissed as being of little value for our rapidly changing world. Such historical amnesia is fatal for any culture, but particularly so for Christian communities whose identity is profoundly bound up with their history. The goal of this new series of monographs, Studies in Baptist History, seeks to provide one of these Christian communities, that of evangelical Baptists, with reasons and resources for remembering the past. The editors are deeply convinced that Baptist history contains rich resources of theological reflection, praxis and spirituality that can help Baptists, as well as other Christians, live more Christianly in the present. The monographs in this series will therefore aim at illuminating various aspects of the Baptist tradition and in the process provide Baptists with a usable past.

All Who Love Our Blessed Redeemer

The Catholicity of John Ryland Jr.

Lon Graham

☙PICKWICK *Publications* • Eugene, Oregon

ALL WHO LOVE OUR BLESSED REDEEMER
The Catholicity of John Ryland Jr.

Monographs in Baptist History 24

Copyright © 2022 Lon Graham. All rights reserved. Except for brief quotations in critical publications or reviews, no part of this book may be reproduced in any manner without prior written permission from the publisher. Write: Permissions, Wipf and Stock Publishers, 199 W. 8th Ave., Suite 3, Eugene, OR 97401.

Pickwick Publications
An Imprint of Wipf and Stock Publishers
199 W. 8th Ave., Suite 3
Eugene, OR 97401

www.wipfandstock.com

PAPERBACK ISBN: 978-1-6667-3267-2
HARDCOVER ISBN: 978-1-6667-2663-3
EBOOK ISBN: 978-1-6667-2664-0

Cataloguing-in-Publication data:

Names: Graham, Lon, author.

Title: All who love our blessed redeemer : the catholicity of John Ryland Jr. / by Lon Graham.

Description: Eugene, OR: Pickwick Publications, 2022 | Series: Monographs in Baptist History | Includes bibliographical references.

Identifiers: ISBN 978-1-6667-3267-2 (paperback) | ISBN 978-1-6667-2663-3 (hardcover) | ISBN 978-1-6667-2664-0 (ebook)

Subjects: LCSH: Ryland, John, 1753–1825. | Baptists–History. | Church.

Classification: BX6495.R9 G7 2022 (paperback) | BX6495.R9 (ebook)

08/24/22

To Mom and Dad

Contents

Acknowledgments | ix

1 Methodology and History of Ryland Studies | 1

2 Biography of Ryland | 29

3 Earlier Catholicities | 46

4 Catholicity in Action | 77

5 Theological Foundations | 128

6 Personal Foundations | 152

7 Conclusion | 176

Bibliography | 189

Acknowledgments

THIS BOOK BEGAN LIFE as a doctoral dissertation completed through the International Baptist Theological Study Centre and the Vrije Universiteit Amsterdam. Those I acknowledge here walked with me on the journey toward the finish line of the PhD.

This project was begun, carried on, and completed as a result of the encouragement, patience, trust, and help of many people. That I would have so many who love and support me is reason enough to be thankful. I am grateful to all of them, but several deserve special mention here.

My work on this topic began in one church context and ended in another. It began while I served as the pastor of Christ Community Church in Blaine, Washington. The people of that church encouraged me as I began the journey to earn a PhD, support for which I remain grateful. They loved me and my family for thirteen years, and I will always be thankful for them and the time we shared and served together.

The project was finished at The Woods Baptist Church in Tyler, Texas, where I serve as pastor. Though I came to them in the middle of the project, they took it on as though they had been there from the beginning, supporting me as I continued my doctoral studies and celebrating with me when I finally finished.

I also want to acknowledge the educational context in which the project took shape and was produced. IBTS Centre is a wonderful community of diverse and brilliant scholars who combine a robust faith with a commitment to sound scholarship. I am deeply grateful for my time at IBTS, as it has shaped me as a scholar and Christian in meaningful, lasting ways, and it has furnished me with life-giving relationships with colleagues around the world.

For my dissertation, I was blessed to have two of the best and most helpful supervisors a person could have, the late Anthony R. Cross and Henk Bakker. These two guided my research, gave insightful criticisms, and talked me down from a ledge or two. They were not only good supervisors; they proved to be excellent friends as well.

The various archives and libraries from which I have gathered my research have all been helpful. Several individuals are deserving of special mention: Emily Burgoyne at the Angus Library and Archive at Regent's Park College; Mike Brealey at Bristol Baptist College; Phil Dickinson at Broadmead Baptist Church; Mary Matter at the Whatcom County Library System; Jill Sweetapple at the American Baptist Historical Society; and, last but not least, Pieter van Wingerden (Pieter the Great) at the John Smyth Library at IBTS.

I also want to acknowledge the help that Dana Welch gave in reading through and offering editorial insight into this manuscript. She improved it greatly, and any deficiencies which remain are the fault of the author.

I could not have done any of this without my family. From my dad and his undying support for me to my kids understanding why I had to be gone for extended periods or needed to be left alone to write, they have been amazing this whole time. They all know more about John Ryland Jr. than they ever wanted to know, but they have graciously listened to me talk about him for years now.

At the center of my thankfulness for my family is my wife, Amy. I not only could not have done this without her, I could not have done much of anything I have done without her. She is the dearest of women, and I am grateful beyond measure that I get to be her husband.

Finally, I am thankful to God for the opportunity to pursue this research. I have learned much from Ryland about loving those whom God loves, and so, for me, this has been an exercise in discipleship as well as scholarship.

1

Methodology and History of Ryland Studies

THE PRESENT WORK WILL examine the sources, nature, and context of the catholicity of John Ryland Jr., a Particular Baptist minister who lived in the eighteenth and nineteenth centuries.[1] In this opening chapter, a working definition of catholicity will be offered, the need for the study will be outlined, and the methodology for discerning Ryland's catholicity will be presented.

Defining Ryland's Catholicity

In recent years, the term "catholicity," and its derivatives, has come into favor among many Baptists,[2] most notably through the movement called, variously, "Baptist catholicity,"[3] "Bapto-Catholicism,"[4] and "Catholic Baptists."[5]

---

1. While he was well-known in his own day, remembrance of Ryland is not as widespread two centuries later. For that reason, a brief biography of Ryland is presented in the next chapter.

2. "Catholicity" has come into favor among those who are not Baptists as well. See van Vlastuin, *Catholic Today*, 162–68. There is, of course, a sense in which restricting catholicity to one denomination betrays the ideals of catholicity itself. However, for the purpose of the present work, which has as its subject a Particular Baptist minister, such a limitation is helpful in providing focus.

3. Harmon, *Towards Baptist Catholicity*, xvii.

4. Jorgenson, "Bapto-Catholicism," 3–4.

5. Freeman, "Confession for Catholic Baptists," 83–97. Not being a formal project or intentional grouping of scholars, and possessing a wide variety of perspectives, it is difficult to classify; indeed, such a thing may well be impossible. In what is so far

Much of the discussion revolves around the work of Steven R. Harmon, especially his *Towards Baptist Catholicity: Essays on Tradition and the Baptist Vision*.[6] In that work, Harmon borrows his definition of catholicity from the Faith and Order Commission of the World Council of Churches, holding that it is "visible unity in one faith and one Eucharistic fellowship, expressed in worship and in common life in Christ."[7] This definition, while perhaps using vocabulary that Ryland himself would not have used,[8] moves in the direction of the catholicity which he practiced.

---

the most comprehensive overview of Baptist catholicity, Cameron Jorgenson compares Baptist catholicity to what he calls "the 'Radical Orthodoxy' project," which, he says, "describes itself as a 'sensibility' rather than a 'movement,' and extends its work through publications and the exchange of ideas at academic conferences" (Jorgenson, "Bapto-Catholic," 121–22). Moreover, within both Radical Orthodoxy and Baptist catholicity, there are those "whose works resonate with the themes of the project apart from any intentional identification with the group" (Jorgenson, "Bapto-Catholic," 122). "Project" may be suggestive of more formality of relationships between the scholars than is warranted, but Jorgenson's broader point regarding the resonation between the works of these scholars is worth noting.

6. In addition to *Towards Baptist Catholicity*, Harmon has written extensively on the subject. His other related works include: Harmon, "'Catholic Baptists' and the New Horizon of Tradition in Baptist Theology," 117–43; "*Dei Verbum* § 9 in Baptist Perspective," 299–321; "Scripture in the Life of the Baptist Churches," 187–215; "Why Baptist Catholicity, and By What Authority?" 386–92; "Free Church Theology," 420–42; *Baptist Identity and the Ecumenical Future*.

Harmon is far from the first to urge Baptists to adopt a more catholic stance with regard to other denominations and expressions of the Christian faith. Spencer Boersma has done the work of showing the relationship of McClendon's work to Baptist catholicity (Boersma, "Baptist Vision," 266–77). In addition to the works of McClendon that deal relatively directly with catholicity (McClendon and Yoder, "Christian Identity in Ecumenical Perspective," 561–80; McClendon, "What is a Southern Baptist Ecumenism?" 73–78), Boersma brings together the somewhat disparate thoughts of McClendon on catholicity scattered throughout his other works, including all three volumes of his *Systematic Theology*, into a coherent whole.

7. World Council of Churches, Faith and Order Commission, "Appendix 12: Bylaws of Faith and Order," 101. Cf. Harmon, *Towards Baptist Catholicity*, 202. Harmon also outlines seven marks of Baptist catholicity (Harmon, *Towards Baptist Catholicity*, 7–17): 1) tradition is recognized as a "source of authority" (7) in theological reasoning; 2) the creeds are given a place in the life of the church; 3) the liturgy of the church is seen as the primary context by which tradition forms believers; 4) the faith community is understood as the "locus of authority" (11) for understanding the tradition; 5) there is an emphasis on sacramental theology; 6) tradition is engaged critically for contemporary theological discourse; and 7) there is a desire for a "thick ecumenism," by which Harmon means "a common commitment both to deep exploration of the ancient ecumenical tradition and to deep exploration of the particularities of the respective denominational traditions" (16).

8. "Eucharist/Eucharistic" is not a word commonly found in his writings.

The burden of this work, however, is to discern catholicity *as understood and practiced by John Ryland Jr.* Before offering a definition of catholicity, a difficulty must be acknowledged and overcome. The difficulty is the term "catholicity" itself. Because it has become a popular term, it has taken on a variety of meanings.[9] It might be argued, therefore, that another term, such as ecumenism or one of its variants, would be more helpful and less prone to being misunderstood. However, "catholic" and its variants has a better claim to being the most appropriate term for explaining Ryland's thought and practice. Not only was "ecumenism" and its variants not in use during Ryland's lifetime, "catholic" was a word that he himself used to describe his own understanding of the relationship of Christians to other Christians outside of their own tradition.[10] In a letter to a friend, Ryland writes of his understanding of the statement found in the Apostles' Creed: "I believe [in] the catholic church, the communion of saints."[11] He interprets the clause thus: "I believe that expression most properly belongs to all who are really written in heaven and renewed by the Holy Spirit; and I infer that no man is sound in the Apostles' Creed who does not believe himself more truly akin to all them that he himself expects to meet in heaven, than any external form can make him to be related to those that he does not and cannot hope to meet there."[12] He says that he does not believe that the Creed was actually written by the apostles, but it is, nevertheless, apostolic.[13] He elaborates more plainly on his understanding of what it means to be "catholic," saying,

> I trust I do believe that all who are really sanctified have one common interest, and are, indeed, living members of one common body, of which our blessed Emmanuel is really the head, and are really animated by one Spirit. I should think myself, at best, a most diseased member of the body of Christ, if I had not

9. Van Vlastuin has shown how the term and concept has been understood throughout church history. See, especially, van Vlastuin, *Catholic Today*, 162–75.

10. It was a term that Particular Baptists used quite often to refer to openness to and love for others. For the use of "catholic" in this sense by two of Ryland's contemporaries, see Fuller, *Strictures on Sandemanianism*, 237–38; and Hall, *On Terms of Communion*, 128. It is also used in article twenty-six of the Second London Baptist Confession (1677) and the church covenant of the New Road Baptist Church, Oxford (Turner, *Charity the Bond of Perfection*, 22).

11. Ryland, "Letter to Stephen West," March 31, 1814, 180–81.

12. Ryland, "Letter to Stephen West," March 31, 1814, 181. This indicates that, for Ryland, the catholic church precedes the communion of saints, as it is to those who are truly members of the catholic church that Ryland feels compelled to extend Christian love and acceptance. The claims of the church come before the claims of the individual.

13. He does not specify what he means by apostolic. It is possible that he means something like "authoritative," though less so than the Scriptures.

a fellow-feeling for every one who really loves and resembles him, which no outward agreement on things concerning which truly regenerate men can differ would in any wise equal.[14]

This contention of Ryland helps to move toward a working definition of his catholicity. It will be less concerned with institutional unity and historic practice and more focused on spiritual harmony.[15] Those elements of Christian relationships that focus on the spiritual unity of believers are where Ryland drew his understanding and practice of catholicity. This being the case, Ryland offers some help toward a definition of his catholicity in his sermon entitled "The Communion of Saints."[16] He writes that the object of his sermon is "to deepen your conviction that all good men, who are going the same way (for there is but one way) to the same heaven, ought to have fellowship—cordial and intimate fellowship—one with another."[17] Ryland goes on to stress that it is union with Christ, and no other qualification, that unites Christians in the most intimate of fellowship: "But so far as we can obtain evidence of godly sincerity, and a cordial union with Christ, we ought to take pleasure in the communion of faith, by the acknowledging of every good thing which is in our brethren toward Christ Jesus."[18] For Ryland, there is a catholic spirit or impulse that draws Christians toward one another in unity.[19] It is important to realize as well that Ryland is not asking

---

14. Ryland, "Letter to Stephen West," March 31, 1814, 181. He promises West that he is committed to act "on this plan" and "guard against every [thing] that would really savor of another spirit" (Ryland, "Letter to Stephen West," March 31, 1814, 181).

15. Predecessors of this way of understanding catholicity may be found in the Puritans, most notably John Owen, who writes, "Firſt, as therein, and among the Members of it, is comprized that *real living and ſpiritual body of his*, which is firſtly, peculiarly and properly the *Catholick Church* militant in this world. Theſe are his Elect, Redeemed, juſtified, and ſanctified ones, who are ſavingly united unto their Head, by the ſame quickning and ſanctifying Spirit, dwelling *in him in all fulneſs*, and communicated *unto them by him*, according to his Promiſe. This is that *Catholick Church* which we profeſs to believe, which being hid from the eyes of men, and abſolutely inviſible in its Myſtical Form, or ſpiritual ſaving Relation unto the Lord Chriſt, and its Unity with him, is yet more or leſs always viſible, by that *Profeſſion of Faith* in him, and obedience unto him, which it maketh in the world, and is always obliged ſo to do" (Owen, *Discourses Concerning Evangelical Love*, 39). It is important to notice that, for Owen, while spiritual may mean "invisible" in a sense, the unity of Christians is nevertheless expected to be seen in some form. The same is true of Ryland. For more on Owen's catholicity, see van Vlastuin, *Catholic Today*, 119–27.

16. Ryland, "Communion of Saints," *Pastoral Memorials*, 2:277–84.

17. Ryland, "Communion of Saints," *Pastoral Memorials*, 2:280.

18. Ryland, "Communion of Saints," *Pastoral Memorials*, 2:280.

19. It is this spirit that leads Ryland, and those who thought similarly, to deem certain issues, which others construed as central, as minor issues. The most obvious of

for mere polite niceties among good men. Rather, his catholicity is built upon the love that a Christian ought to have for other Christians. He writes:

> I am not pleading for mere compassion, and disinterested benevolence, such as ought to be shown to all men . . . But I plead for cordial esteem, for that love of complacency which is due to all who wear the image of Christ. Whether men follow with us, or not, we should rejoice that they follow Christ, and that they are owned by him in advancing his kingdom, and promoting the salvation of souls.[20]

Based on the foregoing, then, Ryland's understanding of catholicity may be described as visible unity in Christ and in intimate fellowship, expressed in life and service together for Christ. His catholicity is, fundamentally, an openness of welcome and cooperation with a spectrum of Christians broader than those who would have typically been embraced by his Baptist contemporaries. This definition will be the lens through which this work examines Ryland's thought on Christian union and communion. Subsequent chapters will demonstrate that this is the kind of catholicity Ryland practiced, albeit imperfectly, as well as show the roots of his catholicity. It will also be the definition of catholicity which is applied to the Particular Baptists predecessors of Ryland. There are, of course, other ways of construing "catholicity," as evidenced by Harmon's definition given at the beginning of this chapter. However, it is the present author's contention that this is how Ryland understood what "catholic" meant, and it reflects how he practiced "catholicity." The burden of the rest of this book is to demonstrate and examine the lived catholic spirit of Ryland in his context.

That being said, while this is not a work on Baptist catholicity, it is hoped that its findings might contribute material for that ongoing discussion. The work of Aaron James is an example of what the present work seeks to accomplish. James describes his work as "not a book *on* Baptist Catholicity, it is a book *from* Baptist Catholicity."[21] The present work is very much in line with that understanding: this is not a contribution to the ongoing discussion of Baptist catholicity but is sympathetic to the movement and may be used as a historical resource for those writing on the subject. David Mark Rathel's article on John Gill as a "case study in Baptist catholicity"[22] may also be seen as another example of this approach.

---

these is baptism. As will be discussed below, this kind of catholicity among Baptists found expression in the adoption of open communionism.

20. Ryland, "Communion of Saints," *Pastoral Memorials*, 2:280.
21. James, *Analogous Uses of Language*, 24.
22. Rathel, "Case Study in Baptist Catholicity," 109.

Why This Study

This study is necessary and urgent for three major reasons. First, as will be shown in the section reviewing the secondary literature on Ryland, there has been a recent revival of interest in Ryland.[23] Those who have written about Ryland in recent years have noted the importance of his catholicity, but no one has dedicated sustained attention to it. The present work will fill this existing lacuna. Second, Ryland was remembered by those who knew him for his broadmindedness. In his funeral sermon for Ryland, Robert Hall Jr. mentions Ryland's catholicity quite prominently, saying,

> Though a Calvinist, in the strictest sense of the word, and attached to its peculiarities in a higher degree than most of the advocates of that system, he extended his affection to all who bore the image of Christ, and was ingenious in discovering reasons for thinking well of many who widely dissented from his religious views. No man was more remarkable for combining a zealous attachment to his own principles with the utmost liberality of mind towards those who differed from him; an abhorrence of error, with the kindest feelings towards the erroneous. He detested the spirit of monopoly in religion, and opposed every tendency to circumscribe it by the limits of party.[24]

Those who knew him best believed his catholicity to be a major aspect of his life and practice. A study of it, therefore, is warranted. Third, while there are some Baptists through the centuries who have had a similar catholic outlook,[25] Ryland stands out in his era for the breadth of his catholicity and openness to those outside of his denominational tradition.[26] A century prior

---

23. See "The Ongoing Recovery of Ryland" later in this chapter.

24. Hall, "Sermon Occasioned by the Death of Ryland," *Works of Hall*, 1:218. Hall goes on to make mention of Ryland's extensive correspondence in relation to his catholicity: "He whose removal from us we so deeply regret, was too thoroughly imbued with the spirit of Christ, to expose him to that snare; his love of good men of every nation, sect, and party, was fervent and disinterested, nor was it confined to the bounds of his personal knowledge; it engaged him in a most affectionate and extensive correspondence with eminent persons in remote quarters of the globe, whose faces he never saw; so signally was he prepared for sitting down with Abraham, Isaac, and Jacob, in the kingdom of heaven, where the whole assembly of the church of the first-born will be convened before the throne of God and the Lamb" (218).

25. Some of the more important of these will be examined below to show how Ryland fit into the context of Particular Baptist catholicity.

26. This is not to say that Ryland is the sole example of such a catholicity. Daniel Turner and the New Road Baptist Church in Oxford could also be adduced as illustrative of this kind of broad sympathies (see Turner, *Charity the Bond of Perfection*, 21–22; Fiddes, "Daniel Turner and a Theology of the Church Universal," 116–18). Ryland's

to Ryland, Benjamin Keach, a man whose influence upon Particular Baptists continued long after his death, wrote of the dangers of "the wilderness" that is the world.[27] The only sanctuary from this wilderness is the church:

> Some part of a wilderness hath been turned into a garden or fruitful vineyard: so God hath out of the people of this world, taken his churches and walled them about, that none of the evil beasts can hurt them: all mankind naturally were alike dry and barren, as a wilderness, and brought forth no good fruit. But God hath separated some of this barren ground, to make lovely gardens for himself to walk and delight in.[28]

Closer to Ryland's own time are the words of John Gill, who says, "And the church is like an 'enclosed' garden; for distinction, being separated by the grace of God, in election, redemption, effectual calling and for protection, being encompassed with the power of God, as a wall about it; and for secrecy, being so closely surrounded, that it is not to be seen nor known by the world."[29] This has led to the "enclosed garden" understanding of Particular Baptist identity, exemplified in the work of Michael A. G. Haykin, who has shown that, for many Particular Baptists in the seventeenth and

---

successor, Robert Hall Jr., might also be seen as an example of this kind of catholicity (Hall, *On Terms of Communion*, 126–29), though he could easily be seen as one influenced by Ryland. The presence of similar thinkers, however, does not diminish the importance of Ryland's catholicity.

27. Keach, *Gospel Mysteries Unveiled*, 2:330. Keach warns, "A howling wilderness is no fit place for mankind to inhabit, it is therefore forsaken of the inhabitants: so the godly cannot live amongst, but separate themselves from the people of the world" (2:330).

28. Keach, *Gospel Mysteries Unveiled*, 2:332. And the true church, according to Keach, is one that consists only of baptized believers (Keach, *Glory of a True Church*, 5). The Church of England, then, would not be classified as a true church; indeed, Keach says that that whole Church is largely "apostatized . . . from their ancient doctrine! Their people are unacquainted with this righteousness, because their teachers generally are ignorant of it" (Keach, *Gospel Mysteries Unveiled*, 3:76).

29. Gill, *Exposition of the Old Testament*, 4:662; cf. Haykin, *One Heart and One Soul*, 20. The image of an enclosed garden was used in other ways by less strict churches. College Lane Baptist Church, Northampton, used it in their "Gospel Rules for Church Members" to refer to the keeping of the church's secrets: "We do promise to keep the Secrets of our Church jointly without divulging them to any that are not Members of this particular Body though they may be otherwise near and far to us for we believe that the Church ought to be as a Garden enclosed and as a Fountain sealed" (J. C. Ryland, "College Lane Church Book, 1737–1781," 91). The 1737–1781 church book for College Lane is, strictly speaking, anonymous, but it is written in the handwriting of the senior pastor, John Collett Ryland, so he is credited here as the author.

eighteenth centuries, the church was understood as an "enclosed garden."[30] He writes of the development of this idea, saying,

> This image of an enclosed garden, though, had about it an inevitable air of insularity. It could easily become a picture of refusal to engage with what was outside the garden. So it was that far too many sectors of the Particular Baptist community in the eighteenth century were inward-looking and insular, closeting themselves within their meeting-houses and limiting their horizons to the maintenance of church life and their own distinct worship. The image of the 'enclosed garden,' which had been such a positive image in the seventeenth century, became a picture of stagnation in the following century.[31]

This examination of Ryland's catholicity will seek to demonstrate that the situation is more complex than the picture of the enclosed garden might allow.

Sources for the Present Work

Because the research question of this work has to do with the catholicity of John Ryland Jr., the main area of research will focus on the extant written sources from Ryland and those with whom he had contact.[32] His works may be subdivided into two groups: public and private.

---

30. Haykin, "Garden Inclosed," 2–4.

31. Haykin, "Garden Inclosed," 3.

32. Some of Ryland's public and private works are thought to be lost. Among his published works that are no longer extant are his *Evidences of Christianity, in Verse* (written before 1773) and *Eight Important Querys, Seriously and Earnestly Addressed to You* (written before 1773). Reference to these is made in *The Faithfulness of God in His Word Evinced*, 88. They are early works of Ryland's, and it is possible that they were never even published. His lost unpublished works include all of his letters to John Newton, many of his letters to Jonathan Edwards Jr., and his correspondence with Richard Furman. He also makes reference to destroying his diaries: "And if I should be removed suddenly, I do very earnestly request and charge my dear Wife or Children, to burn my old Diaries, without fail, if I should not have done it myself" (Ryland, *Autograph Reminiscences*, 2). Since Ryland was not "removed suddenly" but saw his health decline over several months, it is reasonable to assume that he himself destroyed those diaries, though there is a curious publication of "Extracts from the Diary of the Late Rev. Dr. Ryland" in an 1832 edition of the *New Baptist Miscellany*. Unfortunately, no information is given as to their provenance, and these diaries are not found elsewhere.

Ryland's Public Works

Ryland's public works encompass the whole of his published material, which includes printed sermons, poems, circular letters, prefaces to the works of others, articles, and books. During his lifetime, he published over one hundred such works, beginning when he was just thirteen years old. Most of these works have not been reprinted since they were first published in the late-eighteenth and early-nineteenth centuries, and very few of them have been subjected to rigorous critical examination.[33] One of the contributions of this work will be to bring attention to and examine these largely overlooked works.

A significant potential limitation of using Ryland's published material is its occasional and popular nature. Ryland was not a systematic theologian.[34] His writings most often deal with a pressing issue or theme, and his audience was most often the person in the pew rather than the academy.[35] Ryland, however, was a remarkably logical writer.[36] Though his published works are

---

33. Jonathan Yeager reprinted a portion of Ryland's "Confession of Faith" in Yeager, *Early Evangelicalism*, 293–99. Several of Ryland's works are available as reproductions from print-on-demand services, such as Palala Press and Gale ECCO, but these are not typically considered as true republications of the material. Champion has examined briefly some of Ryland's work in two articles ("Theology of John Ryland: Its Sources and Influences," 17–29; and "Evangelical Calvinism and the Structures of Baptist Church Life," 196–208). Haykin's work with Ryland will be delineated below, as will that of Christopher Crocker and Ryan Griffith, both of whom have made Ryland the subject of extended academic study.

34. While Ryland was a rational thinker, his objective in his published writings was not to provide a systematic understanding of his overall theology. The aim of his ministry, including his writings, is revealed in his advice to the young men training at the Stepney Academy: "The object of his Desire, who is separated to the work of the Ministry, should be the good of souls, precious, immortal souls; that have been exposed by sin to eternal death, to the torments of hell; that are perishing for lack of knowledge, that are plunging themselves into endless perdition. He should be actuated by the desire of opposed error and sin; of rescuing from mental bondage those who are led captive by the prince of darkness, and of bringing them to enjoy the glorious liberty of the children of God" (Ryland, *Advice to Young Ministers*, 7–8).

35. That his published writings are most often sermons is proof of this, though it is not to say that Ryland did not address nor have concerns about the academy. As the principal of Bristol Baptist Academy, he was invested in the work of scholarship, but even that investment had a pastoral emphasis: he was training pastors and other ministers. When he addressed the academy, his concern for them was ultimately pastoral. See his *Advice to Young Ministers*, which gives practical instruction to the potential ministers/ministerial students, geared less to their acquisition of knowledge and more to the formation of their character.

36. This is unsurprising, as one of the many subjects which Ryland taught at the Bristol Baptist Academy was logic (Moon, *Education for Ministry*, 28).

meant for popular consumption, he nevertheless makes a logical case for his assertions and understands his beliefs to stand consistently in a larger framework of theological commitments. In "The Use of Reason in Matters of Religion,"[37] Ryland demonstrates his belief in the necessity of reason and logical formulations in understanding and expounding religious truth. Ryland holds that reason "determines that we may depend on these [sources of information from the senses, memory, testimony, and tradition] as sources of knowledge, and then admits a variety of truths on each of these grounds."[38] Ryland understands reason, then, as the arbiter of knowledge, accounting for what qualifies as a sufficient source of knowledge and then putting that knowledge into its proper place. Ryland's high view of reason is seen in an admonition he gave in an evangelistic sermon, in which he chastises those who are indecisive and uncertain with regard to the Christian message, saying, "I fear your indecision is chiefly owing to want of attention, diligence, and earnestness in your researches."[39] If they but used the reason which they possessed in earnest, diligent research, they would come to believe in the message he preached. Thus, Ryland's writing, while not containing a body of divinity, assuredly came from a man who held to a body of divinity.[40] The drawback of such occasional writing is that it may not represent the fullness of what a particular author believes. In particular, Ryland never wrote specifically on his catholicity. However, if catholicity has to do with visible unity in Christ and in intimate fellowship, expressed in life and service together for Christ, then Ryland had much to say about it, even if the name itself is

---

37. Ryland, "Use of Reason in Matters of Religion," *Pastoral Memorials*, 2:19–25.

38. Ryland, "Use of Reason in Matters of Religion," *Pastoral Memorials*, 2:21.

39. Ryland, "On Indecision in Religion," *Pastoral Memorials*, 1:48.

40. The Western Association, in which Ryland served several times as moderator (during the years 1795, 1796, 1798, 1800, 1805, 1810, 1811, 1818, 1820, and 1823) and for which he composed two association letters (1797 and 1804), annually read some "Preliminaries," which contained, as a matter of first importance, a statement in which they "agree in opinion with one another" concerning the truth "judiciouſly and ſcripturally ſtated, in the confeſſion of faith, put forth by the Elders and Brethren of our denomination, who met, in the city of London, in the year 1689" (Western Association Letter, 1798, "Preliminaries," 14, although Anthony R. Cross points out that the Western Association was reformed under Bernard Foskett with the 1699 3rd ed. of the Second London Confession; see Cross, *Useful Learning*, 51). The letter goes on to lay out its expectation that "every aſſociating church" will "expreſs their approbation of the ſame" (Western Association Letter, 1798, "Preliminaries," 14). One may reasonably assume, therefore, that Ryland held to that particular body of divinity and understood all his sermons and writings to be consonant with it. Christopher Crocker has shown that, at the very least, Ryland's confession of faith delivered at his ordination is not only compatible with but in many places quite similar to the Second London Confession (Crocker, "Life and Legacy of John Ryland Jr.," 247–48).

not used. The chapters which follow will show, through the discernment of emphases in separate writings throughout his career, that Ryland's catholic practice was central to his public ministry and private life.

Ryland's Private Works

Ryland's private works include correspondence, autobiographical reminiscences, and church records. Ryland was a prolific letter writer, and the extant letters, scattered throughout archives in the Great Britain, Canada, and the United States, bear testimony to this. His list of correspondents reveals some of the leading religious figures of his day, including Jonathan Edwards Jr., William Wilberforce, Samuel Hopkins, John Erskine, John Newton, and even the Emperor of Russia. The vast majority of Ryland's correspondence remains unpublished and unstudied.[41] That material will be examined in order to establish Ryland's theology and practice of catholicity. The utilization of this material constitutes another of the unique contributions of the present work.

The limitations of using such private works are obvious. First, there is much that is lost. For example, it is known that Ryland carried on a long correspondence with Jonathan Edwards Jr.,[42] in which Ryland was, at times, unusually open about his personal life and feelings.[43] Unfortunately, there

41. A few of Ryland's letters have been published. Several letters to Stephen West were published in "Letters of Ryland to West," *Bibliotheca Sacra*, 178–87. In addition to the letters to West, Daniel T. Weaver and Michael Haykin published a letter of Ryland to Samuel Hopkins that is held by a private collector in "A Significant Letter from John Ryland to Samuel Hopkins," 29–33. Correspondence to Ryland has proven more popular, as Geoffrey F. Nuttall published a summary of Robert Hall Jr.'s letters to Ryland in "Letters from Robert Hall to John Ryland 1791–1824," 127–31, and Grant Gordon published the extant collection of John Newton's letters to Ryland in *Wise Counsel*. Very little critical study of Ryland's correspondence has been done. Crocker also utilized some of it in his "Life and Legacy of John Ryland Jr." Haykin has also used some of Ryland's correspondence in his works on Ryland. There is much that is left understudied at best and unstudied at worst.

42. Jonathan Edwards Jr. was the son of the celebrated Jonathan Edwards who was the pastor of the church in Northampton, Massachusetts. Because both father and son will appear several times, effort must be taken to distinguish between the two. The son will always be referred to as "Jonathan Edwards Jr." or "Edwards Jr.," while the father will simply be "Jonathan Edwards" or "Edwards."

43. In one letter, one of the first Ryland wrote to Jonathan Edwards Jr., he lays bare his pain at the loss of his wife, who died only five months prior. After giving details of her passing, Ryland says to Edwards Jr., "Do pray for me! I can pray but seldom with a degree of proper feeling, but if it will induce you to remember one who so much needs your prayrs, I can truly say, I do at many times mention you by name in private among others whom I pray and hope the Lord will blefs greatly" (Ryland, "Letter to Jonathan Edwards Jr.," June 29, 1787). Such openness is not typically found in Ryland's published material.

is little remaining of the letters sent from Ryland to Edwards Jr., though there are many from Edwards Jr. to Ryland. In addition, Ryland's regular correspondence with Fuller, in which Ryland himself stated that it was rare for two weeks to go by without a letter from his friend,[44] is incomplete. The second limitation of using Ryland's private works is the same limitation attached to any use of private material: the researcher is peering into places his subject never intended to be seen. Thoughts may be underdeveloped or largely unformed. Despite this, the fact is that the material exists, it is part of the corpus of extant Ryland material, and both the correspondents and the subject matter are revealing.

Deeds of Ryland

Because catholicity involves the practice of an individual,[45] and because Ryland was a man of great activity in life,[46] another source for this work will be evidence of Ryland's extensive catholic practice. This includes his involvement with mission societies aside from the Baptist Missionary Society, his ministry in non-Baptist and non-Calvinist churches, his broad-minded friendships, and his promotion of the works of non-Baptist authors such as Jonathan Edwards. Much of this material has not been studied, especially his involvement with non-BMS mission societies and his ministry in non-Baptist and non-Calvinist churches. However, it has the potential to shed needed light on Ryland's actual practice of catholicity.

In order to examine this aspect of Ryland's life, several sources will be consulted. First, contemporary accounts of non-BMS missionary society meetings, which show Ryland's presence and contribution, will be utilized. These include newspaper accounts as well as minutes from these meetings.[47]

---

44. In his memoir of Fuller, Ryland writes, "Most of our common acquaintance are well aware, that I was his oldest and most intimate friend; and though my removal to Bristol, above twenty years ago, placed us at a distance from each other, yet a constant correspondence was all along maintained; and, to me at least, it seemed a tedious interval, if more than a fortnight elapsed without my receiving a letter from him" (Ryland, "Preface," *Work of Faith*, vi–vii). Ryland and Fuller were friends for thirty-nine years. If Ryland's estimate of their correspondence is even half correct, then the two men exchanged hundreds of letters, of which only a fraction remains.

45. The definition outlined above includes practice. It is *visible unity expressed* in life and service together for Christ.

46. In many of his letters, especially in later years as his responsibilities grew, he asks for forgiveness in writing briefly but says he has no choice because of his many engagements.

47. Ryland was well-known in his day, and his name appears quite often in newspaper accounts, especially in Bristol and the surrounding areas, though not limited to those places. In fact, Ryland's preaching tours into Scotland in 1811 and 1816 were

Second, Ryland's "Text Book," housed at the Northamptonshire Record Office, in which he recorded every time he ever preached, will be examined to show that Ryland's preaching ministry extended well beyond the Calvinistic Baptist sphere.[48] Third, Ryland's own words about and contributions to Edwardsean literature will be used to demonstrate his promotion of those ideas. Finally, as mentioned above, Ryland's correspondence with those outside of his theological tradition will be explored.

Secondary Literature: Early Memories of Ryland

Attention will also be given to the small corpus of Ryland studies, which include obituaries, entries in larger works, articles, and doctoral dissertations. By the time of his death, Ryland had exercised an extensive ministry: over 400 were baptized under his ministry at Broadmead, over 200 students had gone through training at Bristol Baptist Academy, he had begun a thriving (if troubled[49]) missionary society, and he had published numerous writings and engaged in a voluminous international correspondence. Unsurprisingly, then, monuments to his memory began to be erected immediately after his death in the form of obituaries in magazines and journals on both sides of the Atlantic, which show a well-known man who had proven exceedingly useful in his life and ministry.[50]

The first biography of Ryland was the funeral sermon given for him by Robert Hall Jr.[51] The first part of the sermon functions as a defense against the accusation that the gospel does not inculcate true friendship and patriotism, while the second half is a brief biographical reminiscence.[52] The

---

considered newsworthy events in the Scottish newspaper *Caledonian Mercury*. See *Caledonian Mercury*, June 22, 1811, 3, and July 27, 1816, 3.

48. This is a bound, handwritten document that purports to be "a List of all the Texts preach'd upon by J.R.j. with the Time & Place wherein he has ever preach'd f^m. them." It contains a wealth of information about Ryland's preaching ministry, beginning with sermons written and left unpreached in 1766 and continuing to his last preached sermon on January 30, 1825. It has rarely been used in previous research, but it is an invaluable artifact and important piece of the puzzle for discerning how Ryland practiced his beliefs about catholicity (among other aspects of his life and thought).

49. From the time of Fuller's death until well after Ryland's death, the BMS was in danger of pulling itself apart from internal divisions. See Ivimey, *Letters on the Serampore Controversy*; Hall Jr., "Letter to the Committee of the Baptist Missionary Society," *Works of Hall*, 2:444–46; Stanley, *History of the Baptist Missionary Society*, 57–61.

50. On Ryland's "usefulness," see Cross, *Useful Learning*, 362–65; Crocker, "Life and Legacy," 2–11.

51. Hall, "Sermon Occasioned by the Death Ryland," *Works of Hall*, 1:203–24.

52. For his sermon, Hall was both lauded and criticized in the press. The review

material dedicated to Ryland is skeletal, highlighting his many ministerial labors and their positive reception. Hall focuses on Ryland's piety, saying that it was "his distinguished characteristic, which he possessed to a degree that raised him inconceivably beyond the level of ordinary christians."[53]

After the initial flood of remembrances,[54] Ryland's memory was kept alive by his younger son, Jonathan Edwards Ryland, who edited a two-volume edition of his father's sermons and essays and included a memoir of his father.[55] This memoir became the basis for many subsequent Ryland biographical notices. The portrait painted is clearly biased, which is understandable, considering it was written by a son for his beloved and recently-deceased father.[56] Focusing chiefly on the positive characteristics and contributions of Ryland, it portrays Ryland as he was no doubt remembered

---

in *The Monthly Repository of Theology and General Literature* is a specimen of both criticism and praise. The reviewer praises Hall's elegance of words, writing of his "excellent sense and . . . felicity of language" (Anonymous, "Review of *A Sermon*," *Monthly Repository of Theology and General Literature*, 172), yet he also calls certain passages "reprehensible" because of Hall's use of a story about the apostle John recounted by Eusebius (Anonymous, "Review of *A Sermon*," *Monthly Repository of Theology and General Literature*, 176). The reviewer for *The Spiritual Magazine* would have agreed with the latter judgment, as he ended his review thus: "We lay it before our readers for the exercise of their own judgment, only remarking, in conclusion, that if the highly-talented preacher *must* appear as an opposer of Jehovah's purpose and grace, let him, hereafter, from the abundant stores of his own acquirements adopt such terms for the expression of his sentiments, as will cast a thick veil over the errors he attempts to hide" (Anonymous, "Review of *A Sermon*," *The Spiritual Magazine*, 219).

53. Hall, "Sermon Occasioned by the Death of Ryland," *Works of Hall*, 1:214. So important was Ryland's piety to Hall that he goes so far as to question "whether the success of our mission is most to be ascribed to the vigour of Fuller, the prudence of Sutcliff, or the piety of Ryland" (223).

54. Periodicals which contained remembrances of Ryland included the August 1825, October 1825, and August 1826 editions of *The American Baptist Magazine* and the August 1825 and January 1826 editions of *Baptist Magazine*. Even the Bristol city newspaper made mention of the funeral service, writing that the "remains of this truly good man were interred on Thursday last," with a ceremony it deemed "highly impressive" and at which those present "seemed to consider that he had lost a friend who was dear to him" (Anonymous, *The Bristol Mirror*, June 4, 1825, 3).

55. J. E. Ryland, "Memoir," *Pastoral Memorials*, 2:1–56.

56. John Ryland's affection for his family, and theirs for him, is something that has been missed in previous biographies of Ryland. He wrote poems to his children, grandchildren, and wife (see Ryland, *Poems by John Ryland Junr, Vol. 1* (1778–1821); and *Poems by John Ryland Junr, Vol. 2* [1783–1795], Bristol Baptist College Archives). In letters to Jonathan Edwards Ryland, Ryland refers to himself as "your affectionate father" and to Jonathan as his "dear son" (Ryland, "Letter to Jonathan Edwards Ryland," October 30, 1818; "Letter to Jonathan Edwards Ryland," December 10, 1819). On Ryland's love for and grief over his first wife, see Graham, "Dearest of Women Is Gone," 66–83.

by his friends and admirers.[57] J. E. Ryland punctuates his portrayal of his father with a variety of other testimonies, including those of John Newton, Robert Hall Jr., and even quoting Ryland himself in his diaries, letters, and printed works. The memoir presents the reader with an intimate picture of a man who did not always divulge himself to those around him by conveying the grief which seized him after his first wife's death, the challenges of being a prominent pastor, and the difficult health of his last years and final days. The memoir by his son is a vital piece of biographical information, but it must be understood as what it is: the biography of a father by a beloved son.[58] It is, therefore, a starting point which must be weighed against other

57. There were few detractors of Ryland who were left alive by the time he died. Indeed, he is portrayed in the literature as a man of few enemies, though in life he had detractors and opponents, most notably William Huntington (1745–1813) and two of Ryland's own assistants at Broadmead, Joseph Hughes (1769–1833) and Henry Page (1781–1833), both of whom were also tutors at the Academy. The controversy with Huntington was over the issue of the place of the law in the life of a believer (Tillman, "He Worked out His Salvation with Fear and Trembling," 41–66). Hughes resigned as Ryland's assistant and from the Academy in 1796 because he believed that he should be paid more (Ryland, "Original Manuscripts: Material related to the Departure of Joseph Hughes," Bristol Baptist College; cf. Crocker, "Life and Legacy of John Ryland Jr.," 172–76). He and Ryland seemed to have mended their friendship, as Hughes participated in the funeral service for Ryland (Foster, "Letter to Rev. Josiah Hill," *Life and Correspondence of Foster*, 2:70). Page resigned in 1817 for reasons that are not completely clear but most likely have to do with a clash of personalities and possibly of theology between him and Ryland (Ryland, "Original Manuscripts: Material related to the Departure of Henry Page," Bristol Baptist College; cf. Crocker, "Life and Legacy of John Ryland Jr.," 205–8).

58. Ryland's relationships with his two sons, John Tyler Ryland and Jonathan Edwards Ryland, the older and younger respectively, have been the source of scholarly discussion and confusion. Elizabeth gave birth to John Tyler Ryland on December 9, 1786, but she died forty-five days later on January 23, 1787. Stella Read, former librarian at Bristol Baptist College, ignited a debate over Ryland's parental care for his sons when she published an article in which she called into question Ryland's affection for his older son. She said that "subconsciously he [Ryland, the father] blamed the baby for her death and was never able to forgive him for it," and so treated him poorly (Read, "Further Information on the Ryland Family," 203). This is a troubling accusation, though one not borne out by further investigation. Read not only got some of the factual information incorrect (e.g., Elizabath Ryland died on January 23 not January 28, as Read asserts), but researchers have proven her quite incorrect with regard to Ryland's relationships with his sons (see Hayden, "John Tyler Ryland, 1786–1841: A Further Assessment," 120–27; and Whelan and Hayden, "John Tyler Ryland, 1786–1841: A Postscript with Two Additional Manuscripts," 120–28). Additionally, Ryland's handwritten book of *Poems*, housed at the Bristol Baptist College Archives, contain poems written to John Tyler every year on the child's birthday. They display Ryland's affection for his son in ways that contradict the idea that he was cold toward him or could not forgive him. In Read's defense, Ryland perhaps had more in common with Jonathan Edwards Ryland, at least in terms of academic interests. In a letter to his nephew, William, Ryland writes but one sentence

sources of information about Ryland, including his own works, writings of his opponents, and later biographies.

On the heels of the publication of the second volume of *Pastoral Memorials*, reviews appeared of the work which functioned as delayed eulogies.[59] The most notable of these was from the pen of John Foster, the celebrated essayist.[60] Foster was a friend and admirer of Ryland's, as his review of *Pastoral Memorials* shows.[61] He spends so much of his allotted space extolling the virtues of Ryland that he spares little for actually reviewing the two volumes, a fact of which he was keenly aware: "But we are conscious of having departed too far from the proper business of our profession, in dilating so much in general observations, and on the character of the revered author of these volumes; and have reduced ourselves to the necessity of being very brief in the notice of their contents."[62] It seems as though part of his reason for publicly admiring Ryland was that, even at such an early stage, he was being forgotten.[63] One of Foster's motives, then, is to bring his friend to the remembrance of a later audience. This sort of bias toward Ryland proves to be an issue for many Ryland studies: the man was and is admired by people, and the historiography surrounding him is almost universally favorable to him.

---

about John Tyler, remarking that he is "set up in business at Plymouth Dock," and then devotes the next five sentences to his younger son's academic pursuits (Ryland, "Letter to William Ryland," October 25, 1808). Nevertheless, the evidence available suggests that both John Tyler and Jonathan Edwards were both beloved of their father.

59. See, for example, Anonymous, "Memoir of Richards and Ryland," 205–24.

60. Foster, "Ryland's *Pastoral Memorials*," 537–44. For more on Foster, see Everts, "Life, Character, and Writings of John Foster," 5–53; Foster, *Life and Correspondence of John Foster*; and Foster, *Critical Essays Contributed to the Eclectic Review*.

61. He summarizes Ryland's career: "Dr. Ryland was a man highly and honourably distinguished, during a long period of time, within a sphere which, though it may be denominated local or provincial, was of considerable compass" (Foster, "Ryland's *Pastoral Memorials*," 541).

62. Foster, "Ryland's *Pastoral Memorials*," 543.

63. Foster writes, in a sobering passage, "A pensive and somewhat mournful sentiment is often excited, in seeing how the memory of good men fades away in the places, and the portions of the community, where they may have been very considerably distinguished for piety, ability, and usefulness. This sentiment is felt especially by those few of their survivors who may have been nearly their co-evals, who had the longest known and valued them, and have lingered behind them a considerable number of years. The less and less frequent mention of them in the social circles, the diminishing number of sentences, the easy despatch, in recalling and dismissing their characters and actions, the indications in various ways how transient the regrets have been for their loss, awaken in the minds of these survivors, at some moments, a disconsolate reflection, how easily even a valuable human being can be spared" (Foster, "Ryland's *Pastoral Memorials*," 537–38).

Problems in the Literature: Ryland's Name Used to Further Particular Agendas

One of the major problems in the secondary literature about Ryland is seen in how he came to be used simply to further later agendas. This is evidenced in a variety of contexts,[64] two of which will suffice here. First, there was the appropriation of Ryland's work by Strict Baptists, who claimed to hold to the high Calvinism of John Gill and John Brine.[65] While Ryland himself never disavowed Gill or Brine, he distanced himself from their high Calvinist tendencies, especially as it relates to the free offer of the gospel and the Modern Question.[66] It is interesting, then, that Ryland would be appropriated by the Strict Baptists, as the brand of theology to which Ryland held most of his

---

64. Ryland's name continues in newspaper accounts decades after his death to justify or validate a particular cause, usually the cause of missionary activity. In an article about the BMS in the *Bristol Mercury* in 1840, Francis Augustus Cox (1783–1853) is recorded as celebrating his connection to Ryland: "He had the honour and happiness to be a student in the college, now so efficiently conducted, and which was then under the care of a man whose name was not only distinguished in Bristol but held in remembrance throughout the whole Christian church—the venerated Dr. Ryland (applause). His was truly a missionary name" (Anonymous, "Baptist Missionary Society," *Bristol Mercury*, May 16, 1840, n.p.). A similar veneration of Ryland as a missionary genius is found two years later in the same publication, calling on people to support the Home Missionary Society as much as the BMS and using Ryland's name to garner support: "If we love the Foreign Missionary Society we should love the Home Missionary Society too; the Home Missionary Society boasts the same fathers as the foreign—Fuller and Sutcliffe, Pearce and Ryland were the men who first originated both institutions" (Anonymous, "Baptist Home Missionary Society," *Bristol Mercury*, November 5, 1842, 6).

65. High Calvinism was a branch of traditional Reformed theology developed among Particular Baptists by men such as John Gill and John Brine. For the theology of Gill, see Rathel, "Was John Gill a Hyper-Calvinist?" 47–59; and Daniel, "Hyper-Calvinism and John Gill." For more on Brine, see Garrett, *Baptist Theology*, 92–93; and Toon, "John Brine, 1703–1765," 557–71.

66. The Modern Question had to do with whether or not it is the duty of all people to believe the gospel. Matthias Maurice, a Welsh Independent minister, who started the controversy with his *A Modern Question Modestly Answer'd*, framed the question like this: "Whether the Eternal God does by his Word make it the Duty of poor unconverted Sinners, who hear the Goſpel preach'd or publiſh'd, to believed in Jeſus Chriſt?" (Maurice, *Modern Question Modestly Answer'd*, 3). This would, of course, involve other issues, such as whether the gospel may be rightly said to be an offer to sinners. Ryland modified the question slightly, outlining it as, "Whether it be the duty of all men to whom the gospel is published, to repent and believe in Christ" (Ryland, *Work of Faith*, 6). Ryland, along with his friends and colleagues Andrew Fuller and John Sutcliff, answered this query in the affirmative. See Ryland's history of and answer to the Modern Question in *Serious Remarks*, 2:8–26. For more on the Modern Question, see Nuttall, "Northamptonshire and 'the Modern Question,'" 101–23; Cross, *Useful Learning*, 112–19; Priest, "Andrew Fuller, Hyper-Calvinism, and the 'Modern Question,'" 43–73.

adult life was considered an aberration by that tradition.⁶⁷ However, earlier in Ryland's life, he held to high Calvinistic theological emphases, and the Strict Baptists limited their appropriation of Ryland to his earlier works. One such work, entitled *Serious Essays on the Truths of the Glorious Gospel, and the Various Branches of Vital Experience, for the Use of True Christians*, was re-published in a "revised" edition "with a preface and many illustrative notes" by John Andrew Jones in 1829, four years after Ryland's death.⁶⁸ In a preface, Jones points out that Ryland's sentiments on some points contained in *Serious Essays* changed as he came of age, a change due to his imbibing the theology of Jonathan Edwards as well as his affirmative answer to the Modern Question.⁶⁹ Such a change, according to Jones, is lamentable, as he says "that any *material* departure from the theological statements in this volume, must be *a departure from the truth*."⁷⁰ Nevertheless, Jones felt that, in the young Ryland at least, he had a theological ally against the corruptions in the theology of Fuller,⁷¹ and he used Ryland's name and work to further his theological agenda.

---

67. Ryland believed that the gospel is an offer made to sinners, to which they are obliged to respond. This was rejected by the Strict Baptists. See Toon, "English Strict Baptists," 30–36.

68. Jones was a Strict Baptist pastor and disseminator of the works of high Calvinists such as Gill and Brine (Shaw, "Jones, John Andrews," 135–36; cf. Strict Baptist Churches of the United Kingdom, "Circular Letter," 68–69). At the time of the publication of the revised edition of Ryland's book, Jones was the pastor of the Baptist church in Brentford, Middlesex; he afterwards moved to London, to the Baptist church in Mitchell Street, St Luke. For more on Jones, see Slim, *My Contemporaries of the Nineteenth Century*, 166.

69. Jones, "Editor's Preface," iv–v. Jones makes this admission, he says, owing to a promise he made to the son of Andrew Fuller to do so (Jones, "Editor's Preface," v). Ryland and his friends were aware of the criticisms of drawing too much from Edwards. In his funeral sermon for his friend Andrew Fuller, Ryland quoted the last letter that Fuller wrote to him, in which Fuller said, "We have some, who have been giving out of late, that 'If Sutcliff and some others had preached more of Christ, and less of Jonathan Edwards, they would have been more useful.' If those who talk thus, preached Christ half as much as Jonathan Edwards did, and were half as useful as he was, their usefulness would be double what it is" (Ryland, *Indwelling and Righteousness of Christ*, 34).

70. Jones, "Preface," v (italics in original).

71. Jones, "Preface," v. He quotes William Button approvingly: "I am sorry to find, what is advanced in Mr. Fuller's treatise seems to gain so much ground; as it appears to me to be opposite to scripture and experience, and tends to overthrow the distinguishing and glorious doctrines of the Gospel." The irony of such a conclusion should not be lost on the reader: Ryland was a fervent supporter of his friend Fuller's theology. An additional irony is provided in the fact that Jones also republished Ryland's *Salvation Finished*, the funeral sermon for Robert Hall Sr., who influenced Ryland in the direction of an affirmative answer to the Modern Question. Jones retitled it as *Memoirs of the Rev. Robert Hall of Arnsby*.

On the other end of the Calvinistic theological spectrum from Jones was Charles Haddon Spurgeon (1834–1892), who also used Ryland in a similar manner to further his own agenda rather than offer a critical assessment of Ryland's thought.[72] Spurgeon refers several times to Ryland throughout his works. For example, he uses a story involving Ryland and his first wife, Elizabeth, who Spurgeon calls Betty.[73] The story revolves around her illness and eventual death and has her seeking consolation in her husband. She expresses to Ryland that she has no hope for heaven and expects to go to hell. According to Spurgeon, Ryland asks her what she intends to do there; when she gives no answer, he asks her if she intends to pray, to which she replies, "Oh, John . . . I would pray anywhere; I cannot help praying!" He then assures her, "Well, then . . . they will say, 'Here is Betty Ryland praying here in hell. Throw her out! We won't have anybody praying here! Throw her out!'"[74] Spurgeon made further references to Ryland in other sermons and works.[75]

72. Spurgeon also shows the use of Ryland in popular matters rather than academic discourse (see below). It was in the popular mind that Ryland was remembered, not necessarily in the academy and its ongoing conversations.

73. Ryland called his wife Betsy (Ryland, "Letter to Jonathan Edwards Jr.," June 29, 1787).

74. Spurgeon, "Raven's Cry," *Spurgeon's Sermons on Prayer*, 27. The stories are memorable and effective in getting Spurgeon's point across, but it should be said that the first time they appear in print is in Spurgeon's own sermons. In fact, there is evidence from Ryland's own hand that this is not how his wife's illness progressed. To Jonathan Edwards Jr., he writes, "She died very sweetly! I never saw anybody die beside. I had hold of her hand all the while. God took away all her fears . . . She had had better health the last two years than I ever knew her before—& her natural spirits better—She seem'd to have little anxious fear of death during her pregnancy" (Ryland, "Letter to Jonathan Edwards Jr.," June 29, 1787). This is not to call Spurgeon a liar, but it is to suggest that he passed on an anecdote for which he did not find proper sources.

75. In another story involving Ryland's wife and her death, she asks him if he will know her in heaven, and he responds, "Why . . . I know you here; and do you think I shall be a bigger fool in heaven than I am on earth?" (Spurgeon, "Resurrection of the Dead," *Sermons of Rev. C. H. Spurgeon of London*, 272). That seems to have settled the matter. Spurgeon also demonstrates a knowledge of Ryland's biography of Andrew Fuller (Spurgeon, *Feathers for Arrows*, 170; cf. Ryland, *Work of Faith*, 68–69). He also introduces a poetic quotation from Ryland in a sermon entitled "Wheat in the Barn" as being from "good old father Ryland" (Spurgeon, "Wheat in the Barn," *Farm Sermons*, 323). Interestingly, the quotation is from a "poetical letter" that Ryland composed as a young boy of eleven. J. C. Ryland had written a letter to William Christian, and, before it could be sent, the young Ryland added his own poetry to it (see Ryland, "Letter in Rhyme by Rev. John Ryland," Bristol Baptist College Archives; Ryland, "Ryland's Poetical Letter," 327–29). Finally, in Spurgeon's sermon notes, he includes a quotation from Ryland about those in hell returning to the sin that sent them there if given the opportunity (Spurgeon, *My Sermon-Notes*, 153). I have not been able to find this quotation in Ryland's works, and it may, in fact, have been a saying of John Collett Ryland that has been confused with John Ryland Jr. (Scraggs, *Instructive Selections*, 1:192–93).

Spurgeon's most abundant use of Ryland material, however, comes in *The Treasury of David*, in which Ryland is quoted throughout. Spurgeon's usage of Ryland here demonstrates an awareness of a variety of Ryland material, and he seems to have had access to Ryland's *Pastoral Memorials*, from which he quoted extensively in his coverage of Pss 77,[76] 81,[77] and 119.[78] Spurgeon also makes use of Ryland's poetry in his commentary on Pss 57[79] and 118.[80]

In both of these cases, and in others like them, Ryland is cited for different reasons but for similar aims: to validate a certain position. Ryland's name was known, but he was increasingly unknown as an individual and used merely to give credence to particular causes.[81]

Fading Historical Memory

Ryland's fame was still sufficient enough in the late-nineteenth century to earn him a place in the *Dictionary of National Biography*.[82] Although the brief article leans heavily on J. E. Ryland's memoir of Ryland as well as Hall Jr.'s funeral sermon,[83] it does offer some insight into the origins of several paintings and engravings of Ryland.[84] He was seen by the editors as being important enough to be included in the *Dictionary*, but the article

---

76. Spurgeon, *Treasury of David*, 3:420–21; cf. Ryland, "Meditation on the Divine Dispensations," *Pastoral Memorials*, 1:89–93.

77. Spurgeon, *Treasury of David*, 4:32–33; cf. Ryland, "Enlarged Desires Satisfied," *Pastoral Memorials*, 1:93–97.

78. Spurgeon, *Treasury of David*, 6:168–69; cf. Ryland, "The Desirableness of a Spiritual Taste," *Pastoral Memorials*, 1:113–18.

79. Spurgeon, *Treasury of David*, 3:51; cf. Ryland, *Serious Essays on the Truths of the Glorious Gospel*, 133.

80. Spurgeon, *Treasury of David*, 5:328; cf. Ryland, "Sovereign Ruler of the Skies," *Selection of Hymns*, Hymn 545.

81. This need not be a nefarious thing. At times, Ryland's name was used in positive contexts merely to show a person's or institution's continuity with the past. For example, in the funeral sermon for Ryland's successor, T. S. Crisp, Edward Steane invoked Ryland as a part of a heavenly welcome for Crisp: "May we not conceive that one of his former associates in the ministry of this congregation, or perhaps all of them, met him as he passed through the pearly gates, and welcomed him to the abodes of the blessed? . . . And shall it be deemed extravagant if I venture still further to suggest that they have introduced him to the more intimate of their own former friends? Has not Ryland brought him to Pearce, to Fuller, and to Carey?" (Steane, *Address Delivered at the Funeral of the Rev. Thomas Steffe Crisp*, 8–9). Thanks to Anthony R. Cross for bringing this reference to my attention.

82. Courtney, "Ryland, John," 50:55–56.

83. The funeral sermon is quoted directly, although without attribution.

84. Courtney, "Ryland, John," 50:55–56.

demonstrates that Ryland's works were relatively unknown by that time. For example, among his "chief works" are listed several of his earliest works, including *The Plagues of Egypt*, a poem he wrote and published when he was only thirteen years old,[85] and which he wished to be forgotten.[86] While it is up for debate as to which of his works should be named "chief," his fame during his lifetime rested not on his early poetic attempts but on his later theological and pastoral works.

As the decades wore on, Ryland continued to appear in historical works, though the entries tend to grow shorter.[87] The fleeting references in Armitage's *History of the Baptists*, published in 1887 and only dealing with Ryland in relationship to William Carey and the BMS,[88] pale in comparison to the lengthy entry in Chapman's *Brief Memorials of Departed Saints*,[89] published in 1842 and consisting of over 3,500 words.[90] The last major appearance of Ryland in a historical work comes in 1897 in James Culross's *Three Rylands*,

85. Courtney, "Ryland, John," 50:56.

86. Ryland, *Autograph Reminiscences*, 2.

87. They not only decreased in length, they also reveal that Ryland was less and less known and was increasingly confused with his father. The confusion began as early as the mid-nineteenth century. For example, in a newspaper article about William Jay, Jay's friendship with "Rev. John Ryland, of Northampton" is mentioned as being especially meaningful to him (Silvester, "Two Famous Bath Preachers," 6). That Jay had a close friendship with and admiration of John Collett Ryland is surely true, according to Jay's *Autobiography* (Jay, *Autobiography of William Jay*, 1:323–35). However, the article goes on to refer to this friend of Jay as "Dr. Ryland," and it asserts that Jay was this same Ryland's amanuensis for his *Life of James Hervey*. John Collett Ryland was never known as "Dr. Ryland." Moreover, it was John Collett Ryland who wrote the *Life of Hervey*. Silvester is not alone in confusing the two, for several authors attribute J. C. Ryland's famous rebuke of William Carey at the Northamptonshire Baptist Association meeting to John Ryland Jr. (see, for example, Vedder, *Short History of the Baptists*, 176; and Seelye, *Christian Missions*, 123), a practice that continues to the present (Riddell and Cotterell, *Islam in Context*, 124). By the mid-twentieth century, the publications of the son were confused with those of the father. For this, see Starr's attribution of J. C. Ryland's *An Essay on the Dignity and Usefulness of Human Learning* to John Ryland Jr. (Starr, *Baptist Bibliography*, 20:183).

88. Armitage, *History of the Baptists*, 579–581.

89. Chapman, *Brief Memorials of Departed Saints*, 208–21. Chapman's work is deeply indebted to that of Robert Hall Jr., from whom he quotes extensively with attribution (211–15; cf. Hall, "Sermon Occasioned by the Death of Ryland," *Works of Hall*, 1:214–17), and J. E. Ryland, from whom he borrows without attribution (Chapman, *Brief Memorials*, 217–20; cf. J. E. Ryland, "Memoir," *Pastoral Memorials*, 2:35–37).

90. In answer to the objection that these two works have different aims and, thus, cannot be compared in this way, it is admitted that the two works do indeed have different goals, but the disparity of attention paid to Ryland in the earlier versus the latter is stark enough to warrant attention. In the earlier work, he is considered worthy of what amounts to a short essay, while in the latter he is a mere bit player in a much larger story in which Carey is the unquestioned star.

in which Ryland is included along with his father and son.[91] Culross provides a relatively brief, positive, yet not flattering, portrait of Ryland.[92] In an era when his accomplishments were being forgotten or relegated to that of a supporting role, Culross shows Ryland to have played an important part in Baptist history.[93] Though he is dependent in some respects on J. E. Ryland's "Memoir," he also includes original research, particularly with regard to the living memory of Ryland.[94]

In 1862, Ryland was again subject of a memoir in an edited volume, *Hymns and Verses on Sacred Subjects*, which reveals a surprising way in which Ryland came to be remembered in the late-nineteenth century: for his hymns. Ryland was a prolific writer of poems and hymns during his lifetime,[95] but he does not seem to have been well-known for them until after his death.[96] Thirty-four years after Ryland died, he was included in Joseph Belcher's *Historical Sketches of Hymns, Their Writers, and Their Influence*, in which Belcher recounts the origins of two of Ryland's hymns, "In

---

91. Ryland is also included in the *Baptist Encyclopedia*, but the entry, like others in the encyclopedia, is short and contributes little to Ryland studies except to show that he was still remembered as an important person in Baptist history. Indeed, the *Baptist Encyclopedia* refers to his labors among the Particular Baptists as a kind of a bishop: "for a long time he exercised by common consent a kind of episcopal supervision over a large number of churches" (Anonymous, "Ryland, John, D.D.," *Baptist Encyclopedia*, 1018).

92. His lack of flattery is indicated in his introduction of his subject, whose chapter is placed after that of John Collett Ryland: "[W]e are passing from a man of original talent and temperament to one of a more ordinary type" (Culross, *Three Rylands*, 69). In describing Ryland's preaching, Culross notes, "[O]f rhetorical art or oratorical grace he had nothing" (82).

93. When describing his ministry in Northampton, Ryland is called the "Baptist bishop," a title that Ryland himself likely would have rejected (Culross, *Three Rylands*, 76). Culross also points out that Ryland's name appears at the head of the list of original subscribers to the BMS as well as the list of the first five committee members (79). Culross also relates the story of Ryland's influence on the formation of the London Missionary Society through his friendship with David Bogue and James Steven, saying that "Ryland, and he alone, was privileged to have part in forming two of the great missionary societies of modern days" (87).

94. His description of a preaching visit from Ryland is informative, painting a picture of an immensely popular attraction whose visits were remembered three-quarters of a century after his death (Culross, *Three Rylands*, 84). It seems, then, that despite his "ordinary type" and lack of "rhetorical art or oratorical grace," Ryland could command and hold the attention of an audience.

95. Hundreds of his hymns and poems are housed at the Bristol Baptist College Archives.

96. While he wrote many hymns and poems, Ryland is rarely, if ever, referred to as a hymn writer until after his death. In life, he was known as a pastor, preacher, and denominational leader.

All My Lord's Appointed Ways" and "Lord, Teach a Little Child to Pray."[97] A generation after Belcher, Ryland was remembered by Edwin Francis Hatfield in his *Poets of the Church*.[98] Finally, at the end of the nineteenth century, Ryland was included in John Julian's *Dictionary of Hymnology*, where Julian notes that several of Ryland's hymns are still in circulation in hymnals, but, because of their "plain and simple" style which lacks "poetry and passion," they are "not likely to be largely drawn upon for future hymnals."[99]

In all of this, whether references to him by the Strict Baptists, Spurgeon, or elsewhere, Ryland was not studied or appropriated critically. He is a name plucked from history, adduced because there is likely some remnant of affection associated with him. As memory of him continued to fade, however, Ryland came to be appreciated by historians chiefly for the parts that he played in larger movements and organizations, usually the BMS and Bristol Baptist College.[100] In the first half of the twentieth century, there were a few scattered articles dedicated to Ryland. H. Wheeler Robinson published Ryland's own account of his conversion.[101] J. Stuart published a letter of Robert Hall Jr. concerning the printing of the sermon Hall gave for Ryland's funeral.[102] A letter of Ryland's to the father of James Mursell concerning Mursell's coming to Bristol Baptist Academy was published as "Mursell's Preparation for College."[103] An interesting commonality among these is the fact that they are not critical interactions with Ryland's work but, rather, transcriptions of hitherto unpublished material by or about him.

---

97. Belcher, *Historical Sketches of Hymns*, 231–34. The former hymn was supposedly composed as a guest preacher preached, and, at the end of the sermon, the new hymn was sung (233). The latter hymn was written for Andrew Fuller's daughter, who lay dying (233–34). Edwin McKean Long borrowed heavily from Belcher's work (Long, *Illustrated History of Hymns and Their Authors*, 350–53).

98. Hatfield, *Poets of the Church*, 520–24.

99. Julian, "John Ryland," 984.

100. He is mentioned several times by Ivimey, *History of the English Baptists*, 4:119, 281, 417, 436, 609; Cox, *History of the Baptist Missionary Society*, 1:288–90; Marshman, *Life and Times of Carey, Marshman, and Ward*, 2:105–37, 189–205; Taylor, *History of College Street Church*, 29–39; Swaine, *Faithful Men*, 185–302; and Moon, *Education for Ministry*, 27–39.

101. Robinson, "Experience of John Ryland," 17–26. Ryland refers to this account in his *Autograph Reminiscences*, 15.

102. Stuart, "Printing Ryland's Funeral Sermon," 145–47.

103. Ryland, "Mursell's Preparation for College," 74–76.

The Ongoing Recovery of Ryland

Beginning in 1977, with Champion's article "The Letters of John Newton to John Ryland,"[104] historians and theologians began to take an interest in Ryland's own life and theology.[105] Champion followed up his initial article with another entitled "The Theology of John Ryland: Its Sources and Influences,"[106] a work that remains the only one dedicated to the theology of Ryland as a whole. Champion showed in brief form the influence of Jonathan Edwards on Ryland, the nature of Ryland's evangelical (or moderate) Calvinism, and the influence Ryland had on Baptist missions. In an article published a year later, entitled "Evangelical Calvinism and the Structures of Baptist Life," Champion produced further research demonstrating the importance of Ryland in shaping the ethos of Particular Baptist life. In summarizing the driving forces behind the new "evangelical Calvinism" espoused by Ryland and his contemporaries, Champion attributes the polemical force to Andrew Fuller and the visionary practice to William Carey. To Ryland, and particularly to his preached and published sermons, he attributes the "most systematic and integrated statement of this total theological position."[107] He goes on to show how Ryland's sermons served to advance the cause of evangelical Calvinism in four significant ways: 1) promotion of the doctrine of the sovereignty of God; 2) the priority of grace in salvation, to which a person must respond in faith; 3) the responsibility of believers to conform their lives to the revealed will of God in the Scriptures; and 4) the call of God to take the gospel to all people in the world.[108]

Champion's insight into Ryland is helpful for situating Ryland into his context and showing his importance in Baptist history, but there is little mention of his catholicity, which is out of step with the earliest biographies of Ryland, written by those who knew him in life. As shown above, remembrances of Ryland pointed to his catholicity as an important aspect of his temperament and ministry,[109] an emphasis that was lost in succeeding

---

104. Champion, "Letters of John Newton to John Ryland," 157–63.

105. This is not to say that Champion began a Ryland renaissance. There has been a general resurgence of interest in Ryland's era. See Finn, "Renaissance in Andrew Fuller Studies," 44–61. Though Finn focuses on Andrew Fuller, he also demonstrates that there has been a broader interest in Fuller's time and associates, including Ryland. Champion was merely the first, in more modern times, to focus solely on Ryland.

106. Champion, "Theology of John Ryland," 17–29.

107. Champion, "Evangelical Calvinism," 199.

108. Champion, "Evangelical Calvinism," 199.

109. In addition to Hall Jr.'s remembrance, John Foster remembered Ryland's broad affections, writing, "He was uniformly, during more than half a century, conspicuous in the most genuine zeal to serve the cause of religion; a zeal remarkably clear of every

biographies. Recent academic works on Ryland have begun to recover the importance of his catholicity;[110] the present work will, therefore, meet the need of investigating an aspect of Ryland's thought that has been seen as important from the earliest biographies to recent academic works but which has not been the subject of a lengthy academic study.

Since Champion's initial article, Ryland has been the subject of shorter entries in larger works[111] and a mainstay in popular historical writing,[112] though not discernably more than other Baptist figures of his era. In terms of academic study, there have been several authors who have featured Ryland more prominently and through whom an understanding of his life and thought has been advanced. Timothy Whelan's *Baptist Autographs in the John Rylands Library of Manchester, 1741-1845* features many of Ryland's letters. Whelan has also produced articles that highlight Ryland's relationships with Samuel Taylor Coleridge[113] and William Wilberforce.[114] Bruce Hindmarsh's *The Evangelical Conversion Narrative* features Ryland in a large, though supporting, role.[115] Jonathan Yeager has brought Ryland's correspondence with John Erskine to light in his recent work.[116] Anthony R. Cross has also included Ryland in his *Useful Learning*, in which he effectively places Ryland in his historical context of the growth of the moderate

---

thing like egotism and display; and so free from the acrid taint of bigotry, that he commanded the respect, and a still kinder feeling, of persons of all sects and denominations. His benevolence, in whatever mode he could exert it, was promptly and most unostentatiously manifested on all occasions" (Foster, "Ryland's *Pastoral Memorials*," 541).

110. Haykin sees it as an essential part of Ryland's pneumatology (Haykin, "Sum of All Good," 343–48). Crocker understands it as a vital part of Ryland's legacy (Crocker, "Life and Legacy," 331–60).

111. See, for example, Gordon, "John Ryland (1753–1825)," 2:77–95; Garrett, *Baptist Theology*, 166–73; Brackney, *Genetic History of Baptist Thought*, 168–70; and Dray, *Proper Old Confloption Down Penzance*, 38–46.

112. Leonard, *Baptist Ways*, 101–5; McBeth, *Baptist Heritage*, 182–84; Betteridge, *Deep Roots, Living Branches*, 75, 87, 89, 124, 131.

113. Whelan, "S. T. Coleridge, Joseph Cottle, and Some Bristol Baptists, 1794–96," 99–114.

114. Whelan, "Evangelical Anglican Interaction," 56–85.

115. Hindmarsh, *Evangelical Conversion Narrative*, 307–320. Hindmarsh offers significant, critical insight into Ryland's account of his own conversion, as told in his *Autograph Reminiscences*. Ryland also figures in Hindmarsh's *John Newton and the English Evangelical Tradition*, 142–59.

116. Yeager, *Enlightened Evangelicalism*, 150–53, 193–96. As mentioned above, Yeager also reprinted a portion of Ryland's "Confession of Faith" (Yeager, *Early Evangelicalism*, 293–99), though he did not publish the whole confession. It is, however, noteworthy as the first time even a large section of that work has been made available for a wider audience.

Calvinism espoused in Robert Hall Sr.'s *Help to Zion's Travellers* as well as Ryland's relationship to the others who played similar roles to his among the Particular Baptists.[117]

Haykin has also contributed significantly to the recent rediscovery of Ryland. He has written about Ryland's pneumatology and the role it played in his catholicity and understanding of missions,[118] his educational philosophy and the influence it had on the Baptist world through the Bristol Baptist Academy,[119] and his friendships with John Sutcliff and Andrew Fuller and the impact they had on nineteenth-century Baptist history.[120] Prior to the work of Griffith and Crocker, noted below, Haykin had done the most to recover Ryland and the contribution he made to Baptist life.[121]

Interest in Ryland's correspondence, which began with Champion in 1977, has continued, with Geoffrey F. Nuttall producing an account of Robert Hall Jr.'s letters to Ryland[122] and Grant Gordon publishing the letters of John Newton to Ryland in *Wise Counsel*. As helpful as these studies are, they are limited in that they are interested in Ryland only inasmuch as he interacts with other, more well-known persons. They, therefore, do not examine Ryland on his own terms, despite the fact that he was an important leader within the Particular Baptist movement and, thus, worthy of singular consideration.

In terms of graduate-level academic research devoted to Ryland, three recent works are worth noting. Keith Tillman produced a master's thesis on the spirituality of Ryland as seen in the antinomian controversy with William Huntington.[123] One of the unique contributions of Tillman's work is to show Ryland as a controversialist. While Ryland was not known for

---

117. Cross, *Useful Learning*, 268–373. Cross also has access to and uses resources not often found in other works, such as an undated letter of Ryland's found in Gifford Sr.'s "Remains," Ryland's "Hebrew Notes on Psalms 1 and 23" (meant for the instruction of Andrew Fuller in the Hebrew language), and a letter of Ryland to Jonathan Edwards Jr., dated June 29, 1787. Cross also covers Ryland's views of education in his *To Communicate Simply You Must Understand Profoundly*.

118. Haykin, "Sum of All Good," 332–53.

119. Haykin, "John Ryland, Jr. (1753–1825) and Theological Education," 173–91.

120. Haykin, *One Heart and One Soul*, 69–84.

121. See also his "John Ryland Jr.—'O Lord, I would delight in Thee:' The Life and Ministry of John Ryland, Jr.," 13–20.

122. Nuttall, "Letters from Robert Hall to John Ryland," 127–31.

123. Tillman, "'He Worked Out His Salvation with Fear and Trembling.'" For more on the kind of controversy that accompanied Huntington, see Whelan, "For the Hand of a Woman, Has Levell'd the Blow," 431–54.

controversy,[124] he was at times drawn into it. The most notable and public of these controversies was that with Huntington.

Two doctoral dissertations on John Ryland and his thought have recently been completed. At the Southern Baptist Theological Seminary, Ryan Griffith writes about the influence of Jonathan Edwards on John Ryland.[125] Griffith sets Ryland's biography of Andrew Fuller, *The Work of Faith and Labour of Love*, in the context of Edwardsean biography, seen most clearly in Edwards's *Diary of David Brainerd*, but also in other examples such as Samuel Hopkins's *The Life and Character of the Late Reverend Mr. Jonathan Edwards* and *The Life and Character of Mrs. Susanna Anthony*. At Bristol Baptist College, Christopher W. Crocker has produced a critical biography of Ryland, with special emphasis on his "usefulness" in the context of the nineteenth century. Crocker's dissertation makes the most extensive use of Ryland's public and private works to date. He also includes a chapter on Ryland's catholicity, but it is merely an overview and is, as such, suggestive of the need for further research.

Conclusion

This chapter offered a working definition for the catholicity of John Ryland Jr., which is visible unity in Christ and in intimate fellowship, expressed in life and service together for Christ. It has shown the importance of Ryland as well as that of his catholicity. The study will now proceed by an examination of primary sources related to Ryland, including his sermons, letters, church books, diaries, and notebooks. These have been collected from archives in the United Kingdom, United States, and Canada, and many of them have not been utilized in prior academic research. Subsequent chapters will investigate both how Ryland related to those outside of his tradition as well as why he did so. Though he never produced a work specifically addressing his catholic theology and practice, he repeatedly stated his reasons for

---

124. Hall Jr. remarked on Ryland's sensitive nature and aversion to controversy: "His extreme susceptibility of feeling, combined with his gentleness and timidity, necessarily exposed him to be wounded whenever he encountered harsh and unfeeling manners; and from the same cause, he was liable to be hurt by every symptom of unkindness, even where none was intended. His sensitive mind was impressed with every variety of temper in those with whom he conversed; and if his peace was less frequently invaded from this quarter than might have been expected, it is to be ascribed to that reverence which his character so universally inspired. It seemed a sort of sacrilege to trespass upon so much innocence and piety" (Hall, "Sermon Occasioned by the Death of Ryland," *Works of Hall*, 1:216).

125. Griffith, "Promoting Pure and Undefiled Religion.'"

his catholicity. The present work will focus on those statements and works, with a view to establishing the theological framework within which Ryland's catholicity operated. It will also show that Ryland's catholicity was not unprecedented, nor did he develop his catholicity in a vacuum but, rather, was moved in that direction by personal as well as theological influences. It will, finally, seek to demonstrate that, at least in the case of one of its leading lights, Baptist self-identity in the eighteenth and nineteenth centuries is more complex than the image of the "walled garden" suggests.

A chief limitation of this study will be the connections drawn between historical data and the theological interpretations of that data. As the work will show, Ryland's catholicity was deed-oriented, so that it manifested itself chiefly in his actions rather than in theological explanations of those actions. Additionally, Ryland did not write a treatise on catholicity, which means that the reconstruction of his theology of catholicity presented in this work is just that: a reconstruction. One is left to deduce a theology based on various publications, private writings, and meaningful actions. Moreover, the personal influences that led to Ryland's catholic practice have been identified through similarities between Ryland and those influences, as well as Ryland's own statements about the people who influenced him. He never stated explicitly from whom he learned his catholicity. Conclusions will, therefore, be the present researcher's interpretation of the data, open to correction and refinement by future research.

A note about spelling and punctuation: the spelling and punctuation in primary source material will be preserved as much as possible. This includes Ryland's inconsistent abbreviations as well as the long "s" common prior to 1800.

2

Biography of Ryland

IN THE ANGLICAN PARSONAGE house in the town of Warwick,[1] on January 29, 1753, Elizabeth (Frith) Ryland gave birth to a son, John, named after his father.[2] John Ryland Sr. had become the pastor of the Baptist church in Warwick on July 26, 1750, and he married Elizabeth soon thereafter.

---

1. The Anglican rector, whom Ryland Jr. calls "Dr. Tate" (this is, perhaps, Edward Tait, DD, who was both rector of St. Mary's and master of Lord Leycester Hospital in Warwick at the time), rented his house to Ryland Sr., who was then the pastor of the church meeting in the Back-hills area of Warwick. When he was criticized for seemingly helping the "anabaptist preacher" (a title Ryland Sr. would have expressly denied), the rector commented, "What would you have me do? I have bro't the man as near to the church as I can, but I cannot force him into it" (Ryland, "Autograph Reminiscences," 12). The story is retold in many histories and biographies of J. C. Ryland. See Newman, *Rylandiana*, 6–7; Ivimey, *History*, 4:609; Betteridge, *Deep Roots, Living Branches*, 75; Culross, *Three Rylands*, 25; Jay, *Autobiography*, 1:335.

2. Today, the father is known as John Collett Ryland, though, in life, he was usually referred to without the middle name or initial. Indeed, when he signed his own name, he signed it, simply, "John Ryland" or "John Ryland, Pastor." Ryland Jr. notes that his father was named by his parents with the middle name "Collett" and, in the father's earliest manuscripts, he used all three names, but, in print, he did not use the middle name (Ryland, "Autograph Reminiscences," 9). In print and when referred to by others, the father was known variously as "John Ryland, AM," "John Ryland, snr," and "Mr. Ryland," distinguished from his son, on whom had been conferred a doctorate from Brown University in 1792 and who became known as "Dr. Ryland." In order to avoid confusion, I will refer to the father as "J. C. Ryland" and "Ryland Sr." When necessary, the son will be referred to as either "Ryland Jr." or "Dr. Ryland."

Together, they had four children in addition to John: Elizabeth, James, Herman Witsius,[3] and Rebecca.[4]

Early Years

Ryland Jr. spent his first six years in the town of his birth, where his preparation and education for the ministry that would be his life's work began. He was taught the alphabet by the family maid, who took him to the church cemetery to point out the letters on the gravestones.[5] His early religious education was conducted by his mother, who taught him "a great deal of scripture history" through the Dutch tiles that made up the chimney in the house in Warwick.[6] The chief influence in his early years, however, was his father, who was a committed educationalist and schoolmaster. More will be said of J. C. Ryland's influence on his son in a later chapter, but it must be noted here that he inculcated in his son a desire for learning and deep devotion to the life of the mind, which was evident in Ryland Jr. at an early age. There is a well-known story of the five-year-old Ryland meeting James Hervey, the celebrated Anglican priest, and reading Ps 23 for him in

---

3. This son was named for the Dutch theologian Herman Witsius, one of J. C. Ryland's favorite writers. Ryland Jr. followed his father in the convention of naming sons after favorite theologians: his second son was named Jonathan Edwards Ryland.

4. Rebecca died at five years of age, *pace* Culross, who asserts she died in infancy (Culross, *Three Rylands*, 25). Ryland Jr. gives an account of her death in his "Autograph Reminiscences" (32). James was converted under Ryland Jr.'s ministry (Ryland, "Autograph Reminiscences," 45), and John sought to help his brother throughout James's life (see Newton, "Letter to John Ryland," April 23, 1803; cf. Gordon, *Wise Counsel*, 397). Elizabeth married Joseph Dent, a deacon in the church at College Lane (see the brief memoir of Elizabeth in *Baptist Magazine* 13 [May 1821], 185–88). Herman Witsius migrated to Canada, where he entered government service, eventually becoming Secretary to the Governor and a member of the Upper House of the Legislature. For more on Herman Witsius Ryland, see Christie, *History of the Late Province of Lower Canada*, 6:iii–xi.

5. Ryland, "Autograph Reminiscences," 12.

6. Ryland, "Autograph Reminiscences," 13. For an interesting account of the use of Dutch tiles in educating children in religion, see *Dutch Tiles: Being the Narratives of Holy Scripture*. The book begins with what seems like an allusion to Ryland's own upbringing: "It is mentioned in the life of an excellent man, that when a little boy he acquired the knowledge of a great part of Scripture history by means of some Dutch tiles which were in the fire-place of the room in which his mother usually sat" (Anonymous, *Dutch Tiles*, 1). It is later clarified that Philip Doddridge was the "excellent man," but the similarities between the stories indicates either that the author mixed them up and applied the wrong story to Doddridge or that the practice of teaching Scripture through Dutch tiles was widespread in England at the time. If the latter is the case, Ryland received a rather typical religious education.

Hebrew.[7] Though Ryland Jr. never completed a college course, he could read Greek, Hebrew, and Latin,[8] and his son, Jonathan Edwards Ryland, notes in the memoir for his father that he taught "a course of reading on Theology, Ecclesiastical History, Jewish Antiquities, and Rhetoric."[9]

The time spent in Warwick would ultimately be short-lived, however, as, in October 1759, J. C. Ryland took a new position as the pastor of the College Lane Baptist Church in Northampton.[10] Northampton became home for Ryland Jr. for the next thirty-four years. While Warwick was formative in many important ways, Northampton shaped Ryland into the man he would become. Most notable for present purposes, it was in Northampton that Ryland Jr. underwent a religious conversion and experienced a call to pastoral ministry, both of which were critical events in his life.

Conversion and Call to Ministry

For Ryland, religious conversion was less about changing religions and more about a deepening of religious conviction and experience in the religion in which he was raised.[11] He writes about the beginning of his awakening,

---

7. Ryland, "Autograph Reminiscences," 13. This story is recounted in many biographical accounts of Ryland Jr. For a small sampling, see Cross, *Useful Learning*, 353; Culross, *Three Rylands*, 69; Hatfield, *Poets of the Church*, 521; Anonymous, "Ryland, John, D.D.," *Baptist Encyclopedia*, 1018; Summers, "John Ryland, D.D.," *Quarterly Review*, 751.

Ryland himself seems to be the source of the story, as he recounts it in his "Autograph Reminiscences," saying that he remembered the event. While it is possible that he is exaggerating, there is evidence that indicates that the child Ryland was especially gifted with intellectual capabilities. His father, John Collett Ryland, in his private papers, records the following, "John is now eleven years and ſeven months old; he has read Geneſis in Hebrew five times through; he read through the Greek Teſtament before nine years old. He can read Horace and Virgil. He has read through Telemachus in French! He has read through Pope's Homer, in eleven volumes; read Dryden's Virgil, in three volumes. He has read Rollin's ancient hiſtory, ten volumes 8vo. And he knows the Pagan mythology ſurpriſingly" (cited in Rippon, *Gentle Dismission of Saints from Earth to Heaven*, 43).

8. Ryland's achievements in these languages were significant. In his sermon notes, written for the pulpit, the biblical text was written in its original language. He also composed at least one poem partially in Latin (Ryland, *Poems*, 2:67).

9. Ryland, "Memoir," *Pastoral Memorials*, 2:51. He also notes that Ryland taught Hebrew as well as the Latin Classics.

10. The church is referred to by various names throughout its history: the church in College-lane (or Colledge-lane), College Lane, and College Street. For more information on this church, see Taylor, *History of College Street Church, Northampton*. In this work, it will be referred to as "College Lane," as that is what Ryland Jr. called it.

11. He was raised on the catechism of Isaac Watts, and, when he was very young, even before the move from Warwick, Ryland "was very fond of reading Bunyan's Holy War" (Ryland, "Autograph Reminiscences," 13) and would weep while reading parts of

sometime prior to 1766, "I was persuaded that all would go to Hell, who died without conversion; and my conscience was sometimes alarm'd with a sense of my own danger."[12] This alarm was often short-lived, but it returned with some permanence in 1766 after the death of a friend and the religious conversion of several others.[13] Through them, Ryland came to his own awakening, which was accompanied by many fears, assurances, uncertainties, and renewals of faith; recounting that period, he writes, "Many complaints of dullness often occur, and many seasons of fear and distress."[14] On September 23, 1766, however, the temporary religious convictions that he had felt became permanent,[15] and Ryland came to feel personally the truths which his parents had taught him, writing, "Yes, I felt it now; tho' I knew, in some manner, before that it was so, yet I did not habitually lay it to heart. Those who know how I was educated may well suppose I cou'd not have been destitute of a speculative acquaintance with evangelical truths; but I now began to feel more deeply affected with it, than I had ever been before."[16] This concept of faith being more than a speculative acquaintance with religious truth became his paradigm for understanding not only conversion but the heart of the Christian faith. Later, he would write, "True religion is internal, and consists primarily in holy affections, and devout exercises of the heart. But if these be genuine, they will, in proportion to their strength, show themselves externally, and influence the whole conduct."[17] The experience of faith proves to be vital to Ryland's understanding of catholicity.

Daniel Defoe's *Family Instructor* (Ryland, "Autograph Reminiscences," 14).

12. Ryland, "Autograph Reminiscences," 14. For more on Ryland's conversion, see Hindmarsh, *Evangelical Conversion Narrative*, 301–20.

13. Ryland, "Autograph Reminiscences," 15–16.

14. Ryland, "Autograph Reminiscences," 23. He writes the following which seems to typify his experience during this time of his life: "I now began, however, to be watchful over the frame of my mind, and kept a Diary, wherein I set down its various fluctuations, as to my earnestneſs or barrenneſs in prayer, and noticed the workings of pride or other sins of the ♥" (Ryland, "Autograph Reminiscences," 22; cf. 24, 26, 27, 30). A note about the heart icon: it was Ryland's universal custom to draw a heart rather than write the word. This was the case even if "heart" was only part of the word, so that "disheartened" becomes "dis♥ened." His practice has been retained here.

15. Ryland, "Text Book," September 13, 1766: "My first lasting Conviction began Sept. 23. 1766."

16. Ryland, "Autograph Reminiscences," 17.

17. Ryland, "Obedience the Test of Love for God," *Pastoral Memorials*, 2:291. Elsewhere, he connected inner spiritual experience with outer renewal: "The fear of God is not a mere outward form, or show; nor yet a mere tormenting dread of punishment; but an internal, reverential regard for God, arising from a just acquaintance with his moral character, a sincere approbation of the whole of it, a conviction of his relation to us, and a cordial submission to his authority; which will be only increased by a sense of

Ryland's desire for the ministry came even before his religious awakening.[18] However, this seems to have been a passing fancy, as he later writes, "I find by a memorandum in Nov.ʳ [1767] that I began to think I might hereafter be employ'd in the work of the ministry."[19] He writes that on February 2 of the following year, he first preached from a text of Scripture.[20] According to his "Text Book," he preached many times over the next two years to what he calls "our Society," the group of boys from his father's school who sought to strengthen their newfound faith.[21] Ryland first preached "in public" at College Lane from the "Table Pew"[22] at the Thursday evening meeting, May 3, 1770. The frequency of his preaching only increased after that, such that the following year Ryland preached some 138 times.[23] College Lane affirmed his call to the ministry on March 10, 1771; ten years later, on June 8, 1781, the church ordained and called him as co-pastor with his father.[24]

---

his goodness, and especially by beholding his concern to discountenance sin in the very mode of granting pardon to sinners" (Ryland, "Fear of God a Preservative from Sin," *Pastoral Memorials*, 1:51). One may see Ryland's reliance upon the theology of Jonathan Edwards in his recounting of his experience, as Edwards defined "true religion" as consisting "in the affections" (Edwards, *Religious Affections*, 3). For more on Edwards's influence on Ryland, see Griffith, "Promoting Pure and Undefiled Religion," 45–60.

18. Ryland, "Autograph Reminiscences," 14–15. He even wrote two sermons during this time, on Eccl 12:1 and Gal 1:4–5 (Ryland, "Text Book," September 10 and September 13, 1766).

19. Ryland, "Autograph Reminiscences," 30.

20. Ryland, "Autograph Reminiscences," 31. He writes that he does not remember the text on which he preached (Ryland, "Text Book," February 2, 1768), an unusual admission from someone who was so steadfast in notetaking.

21. Ryland records that he preached nineteen times to the Society from February 2, 1768 through May 3, 1770, which was the first time he preached in public at College Lane. He notes, however, that "probably I have not set down quite all the times I spoke to our Society either before or after this time. I have since found an old list of 29 texts, before I preached in publick" (Ryland, "Text Book," May 1, 1768).

22. Taylor describes the Table Pew: "The Table . . . was a long wooden affair, occupying the greater part of the 'Table Pew' which was over the baptistry. It contained inside, under the top, several shelves . . . for the reception of a number of volumes, chiefly Dr. Gill's Commentaries" (Taylor, *History of College Street*, 30).

23. Ryland, "Text Book," End Pages.

24. J. C. Ryland, "College Lane Church Book, 1737–1781," 273; cf. Ryland, "Text Book," June 8, 1781. The church had extended a call to Ryland to co-pastor the church with his father, a call which Ryland answered on April 8, 1781 (J. C. Ryland, "College Lane Church Book, 1737–1781," 272).

Ministry at College Lane

His time and ministry at College Lane proved significant for his own life and ministry. In terms of Ryland's personal life, it was during his time at College Lane that he met, married, and lost his first wife, Elizabeth Tyler,[25] who died several weeks after giving birth to a son, John Tyler Ryland.[26] He afterward married a second wife, Frances Barrett,[27] and, together, they had at least nine children, four of whom survived into adulthood.[28] It was while at College Lane that Ryland honed his skills as a preacher and religious leader. He notes in his "Text Book" that he preached over 4,000 times while living in Northampton, and he did so in churches throughout the region and country.[29] He also helped lead the Particular Baptists[30] at this time, as he was a participant at several ordinations, Association meetings,

---

25. Elizabeth was the eldest daughter of Robert and Elizabeth Tyler of Banbury. They were married on January 12, 1780, and she died on January 23, 1787. See Anonymous, *England and Wales, Non-Conformist and Non-Parochial Registers, 1567–1970*, 80.

26. The *Northampton, College Street (Baptist), 1786–1837, Record of Non-Conformist and Non-Parochial Registers* contains an unexpectedly intimate look into the period of Ryland's life when he gained his first son and lost his wife. It is merely a register of deaths and births, written in a formulaic style and recorded by the minister of the church, which was Ryland himself. On the left page, he records the birth of his son, in which he added the names of not only the boy's parents but his grandparents and signs it "Registerd the sixteenth day of December 1786 by me his Father," signing his name with unusual flourish. On the facing page, again written by Ryland, he records the death of his wife. Ryland was devastated by the death of Elizabeth and seems to have undergone something like a crisis of faith. See Graham, "Dearest of Women Is Gone," 66–83.

27. Frances Barrett was born June 3, 1761. Her father's name was William Barrett (Anonymous, *Northamptonshire, England, Church of England Baptisms, Marriages and Burials, 1532–1812*); her mother is unknown. Frances and John were married June 18, 1789 (Anonymous, *Northamptonshire, England, Church of England Marriages, 1754–1912*). She died on May 15, 1840 (*Bristol Mercury*, Saturday May 16, 1840, 8). Her diary is held by the Bristol Baptist College Archives and was published in Frances Barrett Ryland, "The Diary of Frances Barrett Ryland," *Nonconformist Women Writers*, 8:307–97.

28. The surviving children were Jonathan Edwards (1797–1866), Elizabeth Barrett (1798–1875), Frances Barrett (1800–1832), and Mary (1803–1865).

29. Ryland, "Text Book," *passim*. He regularly preached at College Lane as well as Kingsthorpe, Bradwin, and his father's school. He also made repeated trips to London, Birmingham, and Bristol (among many others) in order to preach, and he preached at the churches of such Baptist luminaries as John Gill, Abraham Booth, and Andrew Gifford.

30. The Particular Baptists were a denomination of chiefly Calvinistic Baptist churches in England and Wales. They were loosely organized nationally but had a more organized associational connection. It was through the associational life of the Particular Baptists that Ryland exercised leadership.

and openings of new meeting houses for the Baptists.³¹ Ryland's role in the Northamptonshire Baptist Association grew significantly during this time. He is first mentioned in the Association minutes in 1779 as praying at the service,³² and he was appointed Moderator the next year and preached at the evening service.³³ Thereafter, he is mentioned as regularly fulfilling a variety of roles in the meetings: he prayed at the 1779, 1782, 1786, 1790, 1791, and 1793 meetings; preached at the 1780, 1783, 1785, 1787, 1788, 1789, 1792, and 1794 meetings; moderated the 1785 and 1792 meetings; and wrote the circular letter for the 1784 and 1792 meetings.³⁴

It is also important to note that, while Ryland was initially co-pastor with his father and only later sole pastor, it seems that, in his father's later years at College Lane, the bulk of the pastoral responsibilities fell to the son alone, so that, while he bore the title co-pastor, he was, *de facto*, the sole pastor of the church.³⁵

31. It is hard to overstate the amount of work that Ryland did for the Particular Baptists of this region during his time at College Lane. He was titled the co-pastor of the church at College Lane, but his "Text Book" reveals that he also functioned as a kind of "interim pastor" for several churches, including Kingsthorpe and Bradwin. For significant periods before 1785, when his father left Northampton and Ryland officially became the sole pastor at College Lane, he preached almost as much in those churches as he did his own, often preaching at one meeting in the morning and another in the afternoon or evening.

32. Anonymous, Northamptonshire Baptist Association, Circular Letter, 1779, 14. It is quite likely that Ryland was active in the Association well before this, for the 1774 Circular Letter makes reference to "Brother *Ryland*, ſenior" (Anonymous, Northamptonshire Baptist Association, Circular Letter, 1774, 8), whereas before he had been referred to without the title "ſenior," which indicates that "junior" was both present and well-known enough to require the clarification.

33. Anonymous, Northamptonshire Baptist Association, Circular Letter, 1780, 9.

34. In addition to the official Association meetings, Ryland notes in his "Text Book" (e.g., May 3, 1774, April 19, 1775, October 25, 1775, April 10, 1776, October 1, 1777, November 11, 1777) that he preached at several "meeting[s] of Ministers" in the region, as early as 1774, which indicates an early recognition of his leadership capabilities.

35. According to the "Text Book," Ryland appears to have taken on the bulk of the preaching burden at College Lane from the death of his mother on October 2, 1779 until his father's departure from Northampton November 11, 1785. Other notes in the "Text Book" show that he performed many of the funerals that occurred in the church (e.g., December 30, 1779, March 26, 1780, April 23, 1780, October 22, 1780, October 21, 1781). In addition, Ryland's official call from College Lane to serve as co-pastor indicates that Ryland Sr. had not been keeping up his duties as pastor as well as they could have hoped: "we have great reason to lament the Abatem^t of that Vigor and Zeal in the ways of God, that glowed with greater Force among us some years back. Among the Causes that have contributed to this spiritual Disease (as well as others amongst us) we cannot but reckon the want of more Watchfulness over ourselves and over one another, and the want of more Christian Communion with our Minister and with one another also. Our pastor, by the daily Attention to his numerous Family which he hath

For present purposes, two observations about Ryland's time at College Lane are worth making. First, Ryland's preaching ministry during the College Lane years was not confined to Particular Baptist churches. He preached in Independent, Presbyterian, Methodist, and General Baptist churches as well. More will be said of this in a later chapter, but it is important to realize that the basic ideas relating to catholicity were taking shape and even somewhat formed at this early stage. Second, College Lane was a mixed-communion church, welcoming both Baptists and paedobaptists to Lord's supper fellowship and membership. The church covenant for College Lane reads:

> And whereas we differ in our Judgments about Water Baptiſm; We do now ſolemnly declare That <u>we</u> who are for Infant Baptiſm do not hereby, and will not, impoſe on the Conſciences of any of our Brethren or Siſters that are amongſt us, that are for Baptiſm upon Profeſſion of Faith: So on the other Hand, WE who are for Believers Baptiſm, do not, and will not, impoſe on the Conſciences of any of our Brethren or Siſters that are amongſt us, that are for Infant Baptiſm.[36]

In the College Lane Church Book, 1737–1781, there are also three separate essays inserted defending their mixed-communion practice.[37] Mixed communionism was not incidental to their life as a church; it was central. While it is not possible to know exactly how that position impacted Ryland Jr., it is significant that the practice he would adopt was substantially that of College Lane. This indicates that, at the very least, there was some degree of influence between the church and its pastor.

While serving as pastor in Northampton, Ryland met some of the men with whom he would shape the future of the denomination, including

---

in charge, is much hindered from visiting the families and individuals of his Flock, his Strength he has often declared, is decaying so that he is incapable of performing the whole work himself; & from this cause, as well as from the providential Call of his Absence from us two or three months in the year, he stands in need of Assistance in the Administration of the Sacraments, as well as in preaching and other Ordinances of the Gospel" (J. C. Ryland, "College Lane Church Book, 1737–1781," 274–75).

36. J. C. Ryland, "College Lane Church Book, 1737–1781," n.p. For more information on College Lane and mixed-communionism, see Taylor, *History of College Street*, 5.

37. J. C. Ryland, "College Lane Church Book, 1737–1781," 99–116; 157–79; 201–15. The first two of the essays appear to have been written by J. C. Ryland, as they are in his handwriting and contain arguments similar to those found in Ryland's *A Modest Plea for Free Communion at the Lord's Table; between True Believers of all Denominations*. The third is also in Ryland Sr.'s handwriting, but it is clearly labeled as having been written by John Geard, pastor of the Baptist church in Hitchin. For more on these writings, see Graham, "John Collett Ryland, Daniel Turner, and A Modest Plea," 34–42.

Andrew Fuller,[38] John Sutcliff,[39] and William Carey.[40] All four men took part in the Northamptonshire Baptist Association, from which Association meetings came the impetus to form the Particular Baptist Society for the Propagation of the Gospel Amongst the Heathen, or, as it came to be known, the Baptist Missionary Society. Carey eventually went to India as a missionary, leaving Fuller, Sutcliff, and Ryland behind to be the driving forces for the BMS at home in its formative years.[41] Shortly after the Society's inception, Ryland removed to Bristol, so that it was from Bristol that Ryland exercised his leadership for the Society. From there, he raised funds,[42] carried

---

38. Andrew Fuller (1754–1815) was the pastor of the Baptist church in Soham and later Kettering. Ryland met Fuller in 1776, most likely as a result of their participation in the Northamptonshire Baptist Association (Ryland, *Work of Faith*, 56).

39. John Sutcliff (1752–1814) was the pastor of the Baptist church in Olney. He initiated the famous "Prayer Call" of 1784. Ryland met Sutcliff on July 22, 1773, when Sutcliff came to visit J. C. Ryland and preached at College Lane (Ryland, "Autograph Reminiscences," 47).

40. Ryland met Carey when Carey was first converted to Christianity and desired to be baptized. Carey first applied to Ryland's father for baptism but was sent by him to Ryland Jr., who baptized Carey on October 5, 1783 in the River Nene where College Lane regularly held its baptismal services. Ryland later remembered the event: "On October 5, 1783, I baptized in the river Nen, a little beyond Dr. Doddridge's meetinghouse, at Northampton, a poor journeyman shoe-maker, little thinking that before nine years had elapsed, he would prove the first instrument of forming a Society for sending missionaries from England to preach the gospel to the heathen" (Ryland, "Zeal of the Lord of Hosts," 25).

41. Along with the Serampore Trio of William Carey, William Ward, and Joshua Marshman, Fuller, Sutcliff, and Ryland constituted a "home trio" for the BMS (Morden, "Andrew Fuller and the Baptist Missionary Society," 149; cf. Hall Jr., "Sermon Occasioned by the Death of Ryland," *Works of Hall*, 1:223).

42. This is seen most clearly in two places. First, Ryland's correspondence repeatedly references the raising of funds. In one example of many that could be adduced from his letters, Ryland writes to John Saffery, "Your Acct^s. are very satisfactory, & whatever you judge right to give your Supplies &c. we shall fully approve. I have within these few days rec^d. some Money for the Society, or if more be wanting I can draw on M^r. King, so you may refer Franklin to me if you chuse, or draw on M^r. King for what is necessary, & send Bro^r Pearce notice" (Ryland, "Letter to John Saffery," September 9, 1796). Second, Ryland himself went on tours in order to raise funds for the Society. A contemporary newspaper account from Scotland testifies to this, saying, "To-morrow *forenoon*, Dr. Ryland will preach in *Richmond Court Chapel.*—The money received on this occasion will be given—to assist in defraying the *expences incurred by travelling to preach the Gospel in India, and to circulate the Sacred Scriptures among the Natives*" ("Mission in India," *Caledonian Mercury*, June 22, 1811, 3). John Sutcliff joined Ryland on this particular trip. A similar account is given of a Scottish tour in 1816 featuring Ryland, Saffery, and John Dyer ("To the Friends of Christianity in Scotland. Baptist Missionary Society," *Caledonian Mercury*, July 25, 1816, 3).

on correspondence with and about missionaries,[43] planned mission work,[44] and eventually served as secretary after the death of Andrew Fuller.[45]

Ministry at Broadmead

Ryland seems to have been quite happy at College Lane;[46] he certainly was not looking to move to a new position. However, an event occurred in August 1791 that, unbeknownst to Ryland, would set in motion a series of events that would lead to his removal from Northampton. That month, Caleb Evans, the pastor of Broadmead Church, Bristol, and President of Bristol Baptist Academy, died.[47] By virtue of the combined role of pastor and president in one of the larger cities in England, Evans's successor would inherit an influential ministry. It was this prospect of usefulness in such a ministry that compelled Ryland to consider leaving his home of thirty-three years. It was not, however, an easy decision for him. Broadmead initially extended a call to Ryland on April 29, 1792, and he declined. They offered again on June 24, 1792, and, again, Ryland declined. His hesitancy had to do with three obstacles. First, he felt a genuine love for the people at College Lane, which is understandable, considering that it was at that church that he first believed, was baptized, first took the Lord's Supper, first preached, was called to the ministry, was twice married, and saw his first children born. It was not an insignificant place for him.[48] This leads to the second obstacle:

43. Ryland regularly corresponded with the missionaries sent by the BMS, including William Carey, William Ward, and Christopher Kitchin. Many of these letters, both to and from Ryland, may be found in the Angus Library Archives at Regent's Park College and the Isaac Mann Collection at the National Library of Wales.

44. The Isaac Mann Collection at the National Library of Wales contains many letters from Ryland to Christopher Kitchin (d. 1819), BMS missionary to Jamaica, which outline the planning of the Jamaican mission.

45. Fuller died in 1815, and the mantle of leadership fell upon Ryland and James Hinton, who served as co-secretary for two years. Afterward, John Dyer, at first appointed as assistant secretary, became the full-time secretary, with Ryland serving as something like a Secretary Emeritus. For more information on this period of BMS history, see Stanley, *History*, 31–33.

46. This is so in a general sense. Ryland experienced no small amount of hardship while in Northampton, especially after the departure of his father. See Crocker, "Life and Legacy," 123–30; Tillman, "Spirituality of John Ryland," 41–66.

47. Ryland makes note of Evans's passing in his "Text Book," writing on the date of August 21, 1791, "D^r. Evans's fun^l. Serm. was pr^d. at B^l [preached at Bristol] this Day by D^r. Stennett—little did I think then of being called to succeed him!!!" (Ryland, "Text Book," August 21, 1791).

48. In a letter to an unknown person about Broadmead, Ryland seems to have cleared away every other obstacle but this one: he cares too deeply for the people. He

he did not want to leave College Lane without a pastor. He knew that the church's views on mixed communion left it with fewer possibilities than the average church,[49] and he did not want to expose them to the prospect of a lengthy period of searching for a new minister.[50] Expressing his reservations to John Harris, Ryland writes, "At present I know of no one at Liberty, whom either they w^d. like for themselves or I shou'd like for them."[51] Third, Ryland felt himself inadequate for the task of taking on the pastorate of Broadmead and the presidency of the Bristol Baptist Academy. Ryland wrote of Bristol and "the Distrust I have of my Compentence to that Station."[52] Eventually, each of these obstacles fell, and Ryland moved his family to Bristol on December 4, 1793.[53]

The church at College Lane exemplified Ryland's catholicity in its open communion views, and the church at Broadmead did so as well, though in a slightly different manner. Indeed, the very phrase "the church at Broadmead" is somewhat misleading, as Ryland was not the pastor of one church that met at Broadmead chapel but two: a Baptist congregation and a paedobaptist congregation.[54] While the Baptist congregation was the main one,

---

writes, "I know of nothing material in the Way, except what every one is aware of, the mutual pain of parting with my dear old friends at Northampton. We scarsely know how to act, nor who must begin. For in fact our feelings are much like those of a person who is required to draw a tooth, that does not ach, out of his own head." (Ryland, "Letter to Unknown about Broadmead," n.d.). The feeling was mutual, as evidenced by the letter of dismissal from College Lane, which offers a brief sketch of Ryland's ministry in Northampton and concludes, "When we reflect on these things, you will excuse us if we feel a pang, and drop a tear at parting with you" (John Ryland Jr., "College Lane Church Book, 1781–1801," 150). As with the 1737–1781 church book, this edition is anonymous, but it is written throughout in the handwriting of John Ryland Jr., so he is credited as the author.

49. See Ryland, "Letter to John Harris," n.d.

50. It is possible that Ryland's caution here was due to the history of College Lane, which included the church disbanding for a time after the death of one of its ministers (Taylor, *History of College Street*, 14; cf. J. C. Ryland, "College Lane Church Book, 1737–1781," 1–2).

51. Ryland, "Letter to John Harris," n.d.

52. Ryland, "Letter to John Harris," n.d.

53. Ryland's ministry at College Lane was hardly over in 1793, however. He continued to preach there occasionally until June 15, 1823 (Ryland, "Text Book," June 15, 1823), helped the church choose their deacons as late as 1801 (Ryland, "College Lane Church Book, 1781–1801," 169), and continued to update the church book for College Lane periodically until the same year (Ryland, "College Lane Church Book, 1781–1801," 169).

54. Broadmead was once a mixed-communion church, but, by the time Ryland had assumed the pastorate, it had renounced mixed-communion sentiments and was a Baptist church, though it allowed the paedobaptist congregation to meet in its building

and certainly the larger one,[55] both churches sent a call to the pastorate to Ryland. Ryland pastored both congregations for thirty-one years, ending only in his death on May 25, 1825.

Ryland's time at Bristol would prove to be his most fruitful, for it is through his labors at Broadmead, at Bristol Baptist Academy, and with the BMS that he is most remembered. With respect to Broadmead, Ryland baptized 441 people during his time as pastor,[56] increased both the quality and quantity of his literary output,[57] and was again deeply involved in the life and leadership of the local Baptist association, called the Western Baptist Association.[58] Ryland's time at Broadmead, however, was not without hardship and controversy which tested his catholic spirit. Ryland experienced dissension with two of his assistants, Joseph Hughes and Henry Page, that could have led to his departure from Bristol.

Hughes had been called as the assistant to Caleb Evans in 1792, and he was kept on when Ryland came. In time, Hughes learned that his salary

---

(see Ryland, "Letter to Levi Hart," January 18, 1808).

55. The paedobaptist congregation, also known as "the Little Church," was formed on December 23, 1757, with Hugh Evans administering the Lord's Supper to them for the first time two days later (Anonymous, "Records of the Independent Church at Broadmead, 1757–1818," Bristol Record Office, 2–5; pace Hall and Mowvley, Tradition and Challenge, 19, who place all the events on Christmas Day). As the nickname indicates, it was a smaller body. The scant records available from its history, however, show that the Little Church was a vital, independent faith community (see Anonymous, "Records of the Independent Church at Broadmead, 1757–1818," and Anonymous, "Records of the Independent Church at Broadmead, 1830–1853").

56. Ryland, "Caleb Evans and John Ryland, Personal Notebook," n.p. These included two celebrated missionaries, Joshua Marshman and William Knibb. Knibb was baptized on March 7, 1822 and went on to serve as a missionary in Jamaica (Catherine Hall, Civilising Subjects: Metropole and Colony in the English Imagination 1830–1867 [Chicago: University of Chicago Press, 2002], 174–208; Hinton, Memoir of William Knibb, 9–11; Stanley, History, 76–84). Marshman, baptized on June 4, 1794, was among the first people baptized by Ryland at Broadmead. He was sent to India as a missionary along with William Carey and William Ward. As mentioned earlier, Ryland also baptized Carey, which means that he baptized two of the three men who made up the famous "Serampore Trio."

57. Ryland published more than twice as much in Bristol as he did in Northampton, and he seemed happier with the quality of his later output, as it was not among the works that he asked in his diary never to be republished (Ryland, "Autograph Reminiscences," 2).

58. From his first coming to Bristol and the Western Baptist Association in 1794 until its dissolution in 1823, Ryland served as moderator ten times (1795, 1796, 1798, 1800, 1805, 1810, 1811, 1818, 1820, and 1823), preached sixteen times at the meeting itself (1794, 1795, 1796, 1798, 1800, 1801, 1803, 1805, 1807, 1812, 1813, 1816, 1818, 1821, 1822, 1823), preached twice at an ordination held during the meeting (1804 and 1822), and wrote the circular letter twice (1797 and 1804).

was much lower than that of Ryland, a situation which he felt was unjust. A series of letters were exchanged between Hughes, Ryland, and the church, whose tone begins with acrimony and only descends from there, with Ryland threatening to return to Northampton[59] and Hughes accusing Ryland of a lack of concern for Hughes's own well-being.[60] Eventually, the deacons of the church determined that the rift between Hughes and the church as a whole, in which a large proportion disliked Hughes, had grown so large that a continuing relationship was not possible.[61] They urged him to resign to spare himself the embarrassment of being dismissed by a large majority of the church. He did so and eventually settled at Battersea. Ryland and Hughes eventually reconciled, however, as they worked together on ministerial projects and Hughes participated in Ryland's funeral service.[62]

After a six-year span with Ryland as sole minister at Broadmead, the church called Henry Page as assistant in 1802, and he served in that capacity for sixteen years. The relationship of Ryland and Page was strained for several years before their parting. In 1814, they endured a sharp disagreement with regard to people giving written experiences rather than an oral account of their faith in Christ. At Broadmead, some people had experienced significant anxiety about recounting their religious experience before such a large congregation. Page believed strongly that people had to give an oral account of their conversion, and he spoke harshly to those who disagreed with him.[63] For Ryland's part, he believed equally strongly that barring written experiences was unbiblical and undesirable.[64] The relationship between the two men was not strengthened by trial. Theological disagreement also plagued their relationship, as, according to Ryland, Page opposed Ryland's

59. He goes so far as to lay out a plan for doing so, complete with the selling of furniture, the reacquiring of his wife's school from his sister, and his brother-in-law, Joseph Dent, offering to repay the expenses of the Bristol church up to £500 (Ryland, "Material Relating to the Departure of Joseph Hughes," n.p.).

60. Hughes, "Material Relating to the Departure of Joseph Hughes," n.p. This is a handwritten copy by Ryland's hand. According to Ryland, Hughes wrote, "I am clearly convinced that my Comfort is wth. you a matter rather of general Wiſh than of serious Concern."

61. Ryland and Hughes, "Material Relating to the Departure of Joseph Hughes," *passim*.

62. Crocker, "Life and Legacy," 176; J. E. Ryland, "Memoir," *Pastoral Memorials*, 2:25.

63. Ryland, "Respecting Written Experiences," 1.

64. Part of the controversy related to Ryland's own daughter, who was anxious about speaking in front of the congregation. While Ryland attempts to keep some emotional distance from the situation, it is clear that his fatherly heart has been stoked by the issue. Prior to Ryland's tenure at Broadmead, it had been the practice of the church to bar written experiences, but Ryland had managed to overturn the prohibition. Of this achievement, he wrote, "Next to the suppression of False Calvinism, nothing gave me more satisfaction than this, since I came to Bristol" (Ryland, "Respecting Written Experiences," 4).

affection for and advocacy of Edwardsean theology. After the departure of Page and arrival of a new assistant, T. S. Crisp, Ryland wrote to Daniel Sutcliff of his relief, saying, "My new Colleague, Mr. Crisp is one of the most amiable men on Earth. He has no such antipathy to American Divinity as his predecessor, who w^d. hardly allow me the right of private judgement."[65]

Their relationship would continue to deteriorate to the point that, in 1817, Page resigned his position both as assistant minister at Broadmead and tutor at Bristol Baptist Academy. The letters written during this controversy, between Ryland and Page as well as the two men and the church and academy, reveal a relationship that seems broken beyond repair.[66] So calamitous was the disturbance between the two men that Ryland offered to leave his ministerial post of twenty-three years if the church so desired.[67] Eventually, Page left and moved to the Baptist church in Worcester, and Ryland continued in his post. The only known communication between the two men after this point comes several years later when Page sent Ryland a letter recommending a young man named Henry Birt to the church in Bristol.[68]

---

65. Ryland, "Letter to Daniel Sutcliff," August 12, 1818. Daniel Sutcliff was the brother of Ryland's friend John Sutcliff. This aspect of Ryland and Page's disagreement puts a new light on a letter Ryland wrote to Levi Hart in 1805. Ryland and Page's relationship was still quite amiable at that point, with Ryland telling Hart, "I have much Comfort in my Colleague, who was I trust born again in our house." However, Ryland goes on to say that a "M^r. Martin of London" had "lately told Bro^r Page (my Colleague) that he could not encourage the Subscriptions for our Academy, because I had embraced several of president Edwards's peculiarities" (Ryland, "Letter to Levi Hart," August 10, 1805). This most likely refers to John Martin, who was a Baptist pastor in London who opposed the teaching of Jonathan Edwards and his followers, including Ryland's friend Andrew Fuller (Martin, *Some Account of the Life and Writings of John Martin*, 74–75, 119–20). It is possible that Martin's influence on Page led to Page's opposition to Edwardseanism and Ryland's adherence to it.

66. In a letter to the congregation, Ryland writes, "But without wishing to enter into any complaints, I am now compelled to confess that Bro^r Page's natural disposition is so uncongenial with my own, that I must despair of our being thoroughly happy together" (Ryland, "Material Relating to the Departure of Henry Page," 6).

67. Ryland, "Material Relating to the Departure of Henry Page," 7: "If therefore the Church should prefer his ministry to mine, I beg leave to give up my station wholly to him."

68. This letter is copied into a letter from Ryland to John Dyer, undated but most likely written in 1824, as it mentions William Knibb's preparation to go to Jamaica, for which he departed on November 5, 1824 (Ryland, "Letter to John Dyer," 1824[?]). Page served the church in Worcester until 1827. He eventually left his wife and children behind to go to France, where he died in 1833 (Whelan, *Baptist Autographs*, 428).

Bristol Baptist Academy

Ryland's work at Bristol Baptist Academy also proved to be decisive for the future of the Baptists in Britain. His father had instilled in him an appreciation for learning, and he came to believe strongly that ministers should be educated. In an address to the young ministers at Stepney, he outlines his belief in an educated ministry, saying that a minister must have a "thirst for knowledge" if he is to be fit for the evangelical ministry.[69] Ministerial training is meant to satisfy this thirst, and, in Ryland's mind, it is meant to be "a Season of Seclusion from the World,"[70] in which the young minister does not indulge in relationships or courtships with the opposite sex, does not associate much with those outside of the ministerial profession, and is satisfied with the friendships he makes with those at school.[71] The point of ministerial education, according to Ryland, is not to make ministers; it is, rather, to "*make* young *Ministers* better *Scholars*."[72] This was his personal charter, and it was the charter of Bristol Baptist Academy, as the Academy only accepted men who "have been recommended by our Churches, as possessing, in the judgement of charity, genuine piety and promising talents."[73]

Over 200 students passed through Bristol Baptist Academy during Ryland's thirty-one years as president.[74] Many of these served faithfully in Baptist churches throughout England, Scotland, and Wales. Though most achieved no great fame in their service, and few would be remembered today,[75] the ministries of these men formed the foundation of

---

69. Ryland, *Advice to Young Ministers*, 5. Ryland went on to say that "though we readily allow it to be unnecessary for every minister to possess much of what is commonly called learning, yet, in the present day, when the advantages of education are more common among our hearers, we think it at least highly expedient that every large body of Christians should possess some learned ministers and the greater their numbers and attainment the better" (Ryland, *Advice to Young Ministers*, 18–19). Part of this quotation is cited in Moon, *Education for Ministry*, 28, though the first part is cut off, which renders it, in the Moon citation, a kind of programmatic statement for education. As it is in its context, it is a kind of missional concession.

70. Ryland, *Advice to Young Ministers*, 10.

71. Ryland, *Advice to Young Ministers*, 13. Later, he says that one's fellow ministers-in-training are meant to be supports to one's spirituality: "[W]hile you kindly assist each other in the pursuit of literary knowledge, let each strengthen the other in God, and stir him up to ardent piety" (Ryland, *Advice to Young Ministers*, 25).

72. Ryland, *Advice to Young Ministers*, 17.

73. Ryland, *Advice to Young Ministers*, 17.

74. The information in the following paragraph has been gleaned from Dissenting Academies Online (http://www.qmulreligionandliterature.co.uk/research/the-dissenting-academies-project/dissenting-academies-online/).

75. This is not in any way to diminish the role that they played. It is, rather, to show

nineteenth-century Baptist life in Britain. Many of the changes, positive or negative, happened through the labors of Bristol Baptist Academy students, as several went on to serve in key roles in Baptist life during the nineteenth century. These include people such as Joshua Marshman as one-third of the Serampore Trio; William Belsher in his London pastorates and service on the Baptist Board; Christopher Anderson in his important role in the Baptist Missionary Society as well as the Edinburgh Bible Society; Thomas Blundell Jr. in Northampton as Ryland's successor; John Howard Hinton in his long stint as Secretary of the Baptist Union;[76] and Eustace Carey in his promotion of the work of the BMS. Many served on the mission field, including the aforementioned Marshman and Carey in India as well as John Rowe and Joshua Tinson in Jamaica and Thomas Swan and John Mack, also in India.[77] Still others went on to shape future ministers and leaders in other academic institutions, among them James Acworth as president at Horton Academy, Francis Augustus Cox as a tutor at Stepney College, Charles Daniell as a tutor at Horton Academy, and Solomon Young as a tutor and president at Stepney College.[78] The theological outlook and spirituality of these men were shaped by the institution led by Ryland, and it is not going too far to say that, through them, Ryland influenced generations of Baptists in Britain and beyond.[79]

Conclusion

John Ryland lived during a time of transition for the Particular Baptists of England.[80] The denomination that had been in decline was beginning to see

---

that some of Ryland's students took on a strategic role that many of them did not.

76. Former students of Bristol Baptist Academy played a key role in the early years of the Baptist Union, including Francis A. Cox, James Hinton, and Thomas Thomas (Moon, *Education for Ministry*, 38). Edward Steane, another student of Ryland's, also served as secretary of the Union.

77. In all, twenty-six students under Ryland went as missionaries with the BMS (Moon, *Education for Ministry*, 35).

78. Another academic may be added to this list: Robert Aspland, who went on to found the Hackney Unitarian College. He departed from the faith of the Particular Baptists, and so played no role in the history thereafter, but he is worth mentioning as a student who studied directly under Ryland while in Bristol.

79. Ryland's correspondence reveals a tutor whose work with his students did not end when they left the school. In his letters, he is found seeking settlements for students, offering advice to them, and, in the case of William Adam, calling them back from perceived error (Ryland, "Letter to William Adam," 1–8).

80. For more information on this transitional period, see Nuttall, "Northamptonshire and 'The Modern Question,'" 101–23; Hayden, "Evangelical Calvinism among

some measure of awakening and was changing into a more mission-minded organization, largely through the influence of men such as Ryland, Fuller, and Sutcliff. Ryland's biography, briefly recounted here, sheds light on his place in those changing times as well as how he came to and expressed his catholic views. His upbringing with his father in Northampton shaped his understanding of theology and especially of catholicity, as his father still held to the older, high Calvinism but practiced a broad-minded acceptance of others outside his tradition. Moreover, the two churches that Ryland served as pastor exemplify Ryland's openness to those who disagreed with him, with the church at College Lane practicing mixed communion and the Broadmead church being composed of Baptist and paedobaptist churches, both of which Ryland served as pastor. It remains now to examine the context, practice, theological foundations, and personal influences of Ryland's catholicity.

Eighteenth-Century British Baptists," 305–65.

3

Earlier Catholicities

THE EXPANSIVENESS OF RYLAND's catholicity sets him apart from many of his contemporaries, but it is important to realize that his catholicity does not exist as an island in Northampton and Bristol, as there were others within the Baptist tradition who held similar convictions. While a full examination of all Baptists with views similar to Ryland would go far beyond the purpose of this chapter,[1] it will be helpful to demonstrate that while Ryland was exceptional in his catholicity, he was not alone in it. This chapter will show other people and institutions that held to similar convictions. Its purpose is not to provide an exhaustive account of Baptist catholicity in either the seventeenth or eighteenth centuries, but it is, rather, to provide a representative account of the position, which was a minority position, of Baptists who form a continuity of catholicity in which Ryland was situated.

Pursuant to that end, this chapter will focus on those Baptists who held to open communion and open membership views.[2] There is a potential objection to such an approach that should be countered: it could be argued that having a catholic view does not necessitate holding to open communion and open membership. In other words, the two are not the same.

---

1. This is an avenue for further research, as there are other people and institutions that held to similar views but which have not received much attention, such as Daniel Turner, New Road Baptist Church in Oxford, the Bristol Education Society and its openness to non-Baptists, and the general meetings of the Three Denominations in London and their Deputies.

2. These two views are distinct but related. Open communion refers to the practice of allowing those who have not been baptized as a believer to partake of the Lord's supper. Open membership is the practice of allowing into membership those who have not been baptized as a believer.

Two arguments may be raised against this assertion. First, Ryland believed that catholicity included having "cordial and intimate fellowship" with one another.[3] For him, this meant more than merely showing a general kindness to other people. It included participating in the Lord's supper together and welcoming them into the life of the local church, without regard to their position on or reception of baptism as a believer.[4] Catholicity and open communionism were inextricably linked in his thought and practice. Therefore, in understanding the continuity of catholicity in which Ryland exists, an examination of others holding to a similar view is needed. Second, while having a catholic view does not necessitate open membership and open communion, it should be understood that holding to open membership and open communion does involve some form of catholic understanding. The very essence of the two positions is that Christians ought to be bound together in love despite their disagreements. While it could be said that, for these people and institutions, baptism was merely a minor issue that they did not allow to divide them, and not a matter of catholicity, it should be understood that how a person assigns an important doctrine like baptism to the status of minor issue is very much related to their understanding of catholicity. Indeed, for the people and institutions in this chapter, it was their desire for visible unity in Christ that led them to treat baptism as they did. At their respective hearts, then, both open communion and open membership views encompass a catholic spirit. In light of this, it stands to reason to focus on those who held to an explicitly open communion and open membership position in order to discern a trail of catholic understanding within the Particular Baptist tradition.[5]

The burden of this chapter will be to discern catholic views and practices that can be seen as forerunners of Ryland. Because catholicity goes deeper than the mere vocabulary of catholicity (e.g., the word itself along with its cognates), this chapter will focus on the substance of catholicity,

---

3. Ryland, "Communion of Saints," *Pastoral Memorials*, 2:280.

4. In the preface to his work defending believer's baptism, he writes, "I wish mine [his candor, or kindness and love] to extend to all whom I believe to be conscientious, though I may think them erroneous in their judgment" (Ryland, *Candid Statement*, xi–xii). The context of this statement is a discussion of the open communion controversy and his decades-long practice of open communion. For Ryland, to extend kindness to other believers was to welcome them at the Table.

5. This focus means that other Baptist leaders and works, such as Thomas Grantham or the *Orthodox Creed*, will be left out of the discussion. Some work has been done on General Baptists and catholicity. On Grantham, see Thompson, "New Question in Baptist History," 51–72, and on the *Orthodox Creed*, see Harmon, *Towards Baptist Catholicity*, 77–80. The subject, however, calls for more research and continued attention which the present work is unable to give to it.

which, as defined in chapter one, is visible unity in Christ and in intimate fellowship, expressed in life and service together for Christ. The chapter will focus on four examples of such among the seventeenth-century Baptists: 1) Henry Jessey; 2) John Bunyan and the Bedford church; 3) Broadmead Baptist Church; and 4) the 1644 and 1677 *London Baptist Confessions*. Each one of these was chosen for a particular purpose: Jessey as a founding figure for the Particular Baptists;[6] Bunyan and Bedford both as evidence of Jessey's influence and as examples of a popular pastor holding to similar catholic views; Broadmead as an influential church, an indirect influence on Ryland, and the eventual place of his ministry; and the *Confessions* as formal documents of Particular Baptist belief that, in the case of the 1677 *Confession*, continued to exercise influence well into the eighteenth century.

Henry Jessey

The first Particular Baptist churches emerged in London in the 1630s.[7] By 1644, there were seven such churches in London, which issued a confession of faith in that year, with revisions published in 1646 and 1653. Aside from their shared Calvinistic theology, those seven churches had another thing in common: a relationship to a semi-separatist[8] church known as the Jacob-Lathrop-Jessey church.[9] The name derives from the first three pastors of the

---

6. This is not to say that Jessey was the founder of the Particular Baptist movement. Rather, it is to recognize the significant place he assumes in the early history of the Particular Baptists. As will be shown below, the church of which he was the pastor was a key place for the first Particular Baptists.

7. For more information on the early days of the Particular Baptists, see White, *English Baptists of the 17th Century*; Tolmie, *Triumph of the Saints*, 50–68; Bebbington, *Baptists Through the Centuries*, 45–64; Bustin, "Hanserd Knollys and the Formation of Particular Baptist Identity in Seventeenth-Century London," 3–21; Wright, *Early English Baptists*, 228–30; and Belyea, "Origins of the Particular Baptists," 40–67.

8. Due to the changing times, changes in leadership, differing styles of governance, and even evolving theological commitments, the ecclesiology of the JLJ church is somewhat difficult to identify. It was influenced by the Separatists, as Jacob defined the church: "A true Visible or Ministeriall Church of Christ is a particular Congregation being a spirituall perfect Corporation of Believers, & having power in it selfe immediately from Christ to administer all Religious meanes of faith to the members thereof" (Jacob, "Principles & Foundations of Christian Religion," in Burrage, "Lost Prison Papers of Henry Jacob," 505–6). Further, he held that a church is constituted by "a free mutuall consent of Believers" (Jacob, "Principles & Foundations," 506). However, Jacob denied being "one of the Separation," and he acknowledged "that in [the Church of] England are true Viſible Churches and Miniſters (though accidentally, yet) ſuch as I refuſe not to communicate with" (Jacob, *Declaration and Plainer Opening of Certain Points*, 5–6). For this reason, the term "semi-separatist" is used here.

9. Duesing, "Counted Worthy," 159. See also the more detailed discussion in Ian

church, Henry Jacob (1563–1624), John Lathrop (1584–1653), and Henry Jessey (1603–1663), hence the convention of calling it the JLJ church. For the purposes of this chapter, Jessey will be the only one considered.[10]

Of the three men who first led the JLJ church, Jessey served the longest. Jacob ministered to the church for six years (1616–1622), Lathrop for ten (1624–1634), and Jessey for twenty-six (1637–1663). When he came to the church, his belief with regard to baptism was that of his predecessors (e.g., infant baptism was a lawful, biblical practice). After many years of questioning and debate within the JLJ church itself, Jessey came to embrace believer's baptism[11] and assented to baptism as a believer.[12] With regard to baptism, in his catechism, Jessey affirms his commitment to Baptist doctrine in his response to the questions, "What is Baptiſme? and what is to be held out to us by it?" His answer is worth quoting at length:

> Baptiſme is an Ordinance of the Lord annexed to the Word of the Covenant; wherein perſons repenting, and believing in Jeſus

---

Birch, *To Follow the Lambe Wheresoever He Goeth*, 2–14.

10. Neither Jacob nor Lathrop could be considered Baptist or even baptistic. They were semi-separatists and, perhaps, Independents, but they both considered the proper subjects of baptism to be both believers and their children. For more information on Henry Jacob, see Brachlow, "Elizabethan Roots of Henry Jacob's Churchmanship," 228–54; Paul, "Henry Jacob and Seventeenth-Century Puritanism," 92–113; von Rohr, "Congregationalism of Henry Jacob," 107–17; Yarbrough, "Henry Jacob, a Moderate Separatist, and His Influence on Early English Congregationalism," 1972. Very little academic work has been done on John Lathrop; see Brachlow, "Lathrop, (or Lothrop, Lathorp), John (1584–1653)," 173–74.

11. Jessey writes of his change of mind: "And if upon your serch you stil judge otherwise, that then you may endeavor further to enforme me, yet I can be here, after nere a yeeres time, of serch about it, being first convinced about it with power in my Morning thoughts about it next after a day of Humbling ye soules before our God, and desiring to know the meaning of his rod." He writes, after a day of intense searching of the Scriptures with others in his church, "The very next morning was such a conviction against Paedobaptisme, upon my spirit, whilst I was pondering about it upon my bed, as I never had before; yea, such as I had no power against from such places of Scripture, & such grounds thence . . . and as I could never have resolution to the contrary thence to this day" (Anderson, "Letters of Henry Jessey and John Tombes to the Churches of New England, 1645," 36).

12. He was baptized on June 29, 1645 by Hanserd Knollys (Whitley, "Debate on Infant Baptism, 1643," 245, being an excerpt of the "Jessey Record" entitled "An Account of Divers Conferences"). For more contemporary witnesses to the baptism debates at the JLJ church, see Anonymous, "Records of the Jacob-Lathorp-Jessey Church, 1616–1641," 203–25; Anonymous, "Rise of Particular Baptists in London, 1633–1644," 226–36; Whitley, "Debate on Infant Baptism, 1643," 237–45; Anonymous, "Story of the Jacob-Jessey Church, 1616–1678," 246–50. Knollys had been a member of the JLJ church but left over his conviction with regard to believer's baptism. For more on Knollys, believer's baptism, and the JLJ church, see Bustin, *Paradox and Perseverance*, 79–80.

Chriſt, yielding up themſelves to him, in his Name, are ſolemnly dipt in water, and ariſe; ſignifying, repreſenting, and ſealing up to them, their Union with Chriſt; and their Communion with him in his Death, and Burial, and Reſurrection, (as alſo, their bodily Reſurrection, that it ſhall be) and the Remiſſion, and Waſhing away of their ſins, no longer to live in them, nor to themſelves; but as perſons raiſed from Death, and reſigned up, and engaged wholly to the Name of God the Father, and of the Son, and of the Holy Spirit; and theſe are to wait and pray for Chriſts Baptizing them in the Holy Spirit.[13]

Jessey's understanding of baptism is similar to that which is found among his contemporaries.[14] It signifies initial union with Christ as well as continuing communion with him in his death, burial, and resurrection. Further, it is a sign of the forgiveness of sins and the commitment not to live in them any longer but, rather, to be engaged in God's service and work in the world. Most notably, the proper subjects of baptism are those who have repented of their sins, believed in Jesus Christ, and submitted themselves to him.

While Jessey's writings on baptism strongly affirm that it is for believers alone, his understanding of church communion[15] is more open. His unwillingness to break church fellowship with those who differed with him sets him apart from other early Particular Baptists, many of whom defended

---

13. Jessey, *Miscellanea Sacra*, 128–29. While it is beyond the scope of this chapter, it is interesting that Jessey seems to believe in a further baptism of the Holy Spirit subsequent to belief and conversion.

14. For a discussion and comparison of Jessey with other Baptist confessions, see Duesing, "Counted Worthy," 169. Jessey's other definitions of baptism differ little from this one (cf. his definition in Jessey, *Storehouse of Provision*, 74–75, as well as his requirements for baptism on pp. 57–65). His "use of baptism" also departs little from the prevailing understanding of baptism among the Baptists. For Jessey, the use of baptism is threefold: 1) "to ſhew our *Love* to our God in all *Obedience* to his Wills"; 2) "to hold forth our *Conformity* to Jeſus CHRIST in all things"; and 3) "to hold forth our union with Chriſt, and our Communion with him" (Jessey, *Storehouse of Provision*, 76–77).

15. "Church fellowship," "church communion," and "communion" are all used in a variety of ways in the contemporary literature. They can refer to fellowship between individuals in a church community, the fellowship of the church taken as a whole, the Lord's supper, or all three interchangeably. Jessey himself does not draw a strong distinction between communion as fellowship between believers and communion in the Lord's supper. Speaking of his understanding of the ordinances, he lists three (hearing the word read, hearing the word preached, and praying), and then he says, "Fourthly, if then I know I muſt enjoy Communion of Saints. Fifthly, If then (being a believer,) that I ought to hold forth the Lords death, by the *Lords Supper*, in ſuch a Communion" (Jessey, *Storehouse of Provision*, 118–19). The Lord's supper is comprehended by Jessey within the overall communion of saints in church fellowship. "Communion" and related words, therefore, will refer to the fullness of Christian fellowship, including the Lord's supper, if possible. If that differs from what a particular writer has written, it will be made clear.

the position that people baptized as believers should not hold church communion with those who had not been so baptized.[16] In *Miscellanea Sacra*, he disassociates the life of the church in general from baptism. He asks, "What Communion have Saints, or ſhould Saints have?" He gives the answer, "All Saints have Communion with Jeſus Chriſt, their Head, (and ſo with the Father, and Holy Spirit;) And they ſhould ſeek to have Communion, as opportunities are, with Members of Chriſt, both publickly in his Churches, and privately amongſt Themſelves."[17] Moreover, a Christian church is defined by Jessey as "Chriſts Miſtical Body, called out of the World unto Communion with him, and with one another, in all his Holy Ordinances."[18] While this would seem to place an emphasis on agreement as to the ordinances as a prerequisite to church communion, Jessey goes on to define the "firſt" ordinances of the church as "ſupplications (to turn away deſerved judgements) and prayers (for undeſerved mercies) interceſſions (for others) and giving thanks, ſhould be made for all men, even for Kings, and for all that are in Authority (though they were then Perſecutors) that we may lead a quiet and peaceable life, in all Godlineſſe and Honeſty."[19] There is no mention in this answer of baptism as a prerequisite.[20]

16. Though he published his work after Jessey's death, William Kiffin's work against open communion would be indicative of the view of many Baptists at this time. While Kiffin does not deny "Love, Charity, and Chriſtian-Communion" to those who have not been baptized, he nevertheless maintains that such an unbaptized person is to be "exclude[ed] from immediate Church-fellowſhip" (Kiffin, *Sober Discourse*, 19). He goes on to make a distinction between "Chriſtian-Communion" and "Church-fellowſhip" that Jessey and others do not make, and he does so by appeal to order: those who are not baptized as believers are disordered, and so not fit for "Church-fellowſhip," which requires order and discipline (19–20). "Chriſtian-Communion," however, requires no such order and can be extended to those who are unbaptized as well as baptized: "we do not look upon Baptiſm to be ſuch a Wall of Diviſion, neither do we ſo practice it" (19).

17. Jessey, *Miscellanea Sacra*, 130.

18. Jessey, *Miscellanea Sacra*, 130. Note that the public communion of believers includes the Lord's supper, one of the "Holy Ordinances."

19. Jessey, *Miscellanea Sacra*, 131–32; *pace* Duesing's assertion that Jessey held to only two ordinances in the church (Duesing, "Counted Worthy," 169). Jessey believed that there are several ordinances, including preaching, reading the Scriptures, hearing the Scriptures preached, prayer, and corporate praise (Jessey, *Storehouse of Provision*, 119), though he does refer to baptism and the Lord's supper as the "Tokens of the New Covenant" (Jessey, *Miscellanea Sacra*, 127). He was not, however, concerned to maintain them as the only two ordinances of the gospel. Jessey is not unusual in this, as several other Baptists applied the word "ordinance" beyond baptism and the Lord's supper. See the discussion in Ward, "Pure Worship," 135–37. Philip Thompson has noted the distinction early Baptists made between ordinance, of which there may be many, and sacrament, of which there are two (Thompson, "Toward Baptist Ecclesiology in Pneumatological Perspective," 109n112; "People of the Free God," 240n87).

20. As seen above, Jessey did call baptism an ordinance, but it is not a "firſt"

Jessey's conviction is that those who had been baptized as believers, as well as those who had not been so baptized, should enjoy unhindered church fellowship with one another, including the ordinances. "Convictions" is a word specially chosen, since Jessey's ecclesiology has, at times, been seen less as an outgrowth of his settled theology and more of an expedient practice or a product of the inertia of tradition at the JLJ church. Jason Duesing's work on Jessey is an example of this: "The semi-separatist heritage Jessey received from the Jacob-Lathrop congregation, combined with Jessey's desire to maintain ties with the Independent and other movements of similar nature prevented him from aligning his church concretely with the Particular Baptists in London."[21] The assumption here is that Jessey lacked either the ability or will to think through his ecclesiology and come to a settled conviction on the issue. However, Jessey's ecclesiology was neither an expedient nor an example of the power of tradition. It was his conviction as to the essential nature of the church, founded on his interpretation of Scripture and theological principles.[22]

He clearly demonstrates his convictions in an answer to a question about unbaptized believers on a hypothetical deserted island. He is answering a question that has to do with two or three people who find themselves on "ſome Iſland, or other part of the world," where they are converted to Christianity. The question is, "what courſe to take about enjoying Baptiſme, or other Ordinances: what adviſe would you give them in ſuch a Caſe?"[23] Jessey answers that they should:

> beleive [sic] that he that brought them from the Kingdome of darkneſſe into his marvelous light . . . agree to pray together, for the *Spirit* of God, to guide and *lead them in all Truths* and ſo in this point . . . beleive, that if they be gathred together in Chriſts

---

ordinance performed in the church. According to Jessey, the definition of a "firſt" ordinance is rather obvious: it is the ordinance that a believer first knows and does (Jessey, *Storehouse of Provision*, 118–19).

21. Duesing, "Counted Worthy," 168.

22. It should be noted that Jessey's conviction is one tested in the fires of controversy. Repeatedly, debates raged in the JLJ church regarding baptism: the proper subjects, the proper mode, and its necessity prior to church membership. At times, groups would break off from the JLJ church to form their own particular assemblies, sometimes amicably, sometimes less so. For more information, see Anonymous, "Records of the Jacob-Lathorp-Jessey Church, 1616–1641," 203–25; Anonymous, "Rise of Particular Baptists in London, 1633–1644," 226–36; Whitley, "Debate on Infant Baptism, 1643," 237–45; Anonymous, "Story of the Jacob-Jessey Church, 1616–1678," 246–50. If Jessey's position on the matter is merely expedient and meant to avoid controversy, then he failed miserably in the attempt.

23. Jessey, *Storehouse of Provision*, 68.

Name, there Chrift is in the midft of them ... [and] fhould be gathered, and joined folemly together in his Name, that they may enjoy that gracious fpeciall prefence of Jefus Chrift.[24]

At this point, says Jessey, they are a "Chriftian Society or Church, endowed with the promife of God's fpeciall prefence, have power and priviledge from him by agreement to enjoy his Ordinances together."[25] Only after they have done these things, and entered into a church state together, does Jessey say that they may enjoy baptism. Therefore, in Jessey's thought, what constitutes a church is a shared faith and gathering in the name of Christ. A church may thus be present without baptism.

According to Jessey, a church is constituted when it has the correct "*matter* and *forme* ... the *Matter* of a true Church, to be Saints vifibly; the *Forme*, a gathering of thefe out of the world, and *joyning of them together* to worfhip the Lord in truth, fo far as they *know*, or fhall know; and edifie themfelves."[26] The duty of a congregation in a church state is to "*abound in love, to edifie one another, and comfort each other*."[27] It is this call to love, edify, and comfort, rather than conformity to the pattern of a ritual, that drives Jessey's ecclesiological practice. He writes that the desire for order, if left unchecked, would hinder the reception of any as a brother or sister, saying:

> But the Lord deals not fo with his People, but account LOVE the fulfilling of the Law, though they be ignorant in many things, both as to knowing, and doing; and receives them into Communion and Fellowfhip with himfelf, and would have others do the fame alfo: And if he would have fo much bearing in the Apoftle's dayes, when they had infallible helps to expound Truths unto them, much more now, the church hath been fo long in the Wildernefs and in Captivity, and not that his people fhould be *driven away in the dark day*, though they are fick and weak.[28]

He sees the community of the church, then, as an expression and extension of Christian love, which is itself an imitation of God's own love toward his children.

Jessey's beliefs on this issue are seen clearly in the grounds he gives for communion with other believers. His repeated standard of acceptance of a

24. Jessey, *Storehouse of Provision*, 68–69.
25. Jessey, *Storehouse of Provision*, 71.
26. Jessey, *Storehouse of Provision*, 102.
27. Jessey, *Storehouse of Provision*, 114–15.
28. Jessey, "Essay," 115. He says elsewhere in the essay that, so highly does God prize love among the brethren, He "would rather have a Duty omitted that is due to him, then [*sic*] Mercy to his Creatures omitted by them" (Jessey, "Essay," 109).

believer into church communion is seen in the following quotation: "That which the Lord limits, we muſt limit. And what he limits not, what are wee, that we ſhould limit?"[29] The Lord sets the Table, so to speak, and he sets the limits on who is invited to the Table, and the individual believer, and even the local church as a whole, cannot contradict his limitations. If the Lord has welcomed an individual in love, it is the duty of the local congregation to follow his lead in welcoming them in the same manner.[30] Jessey sought to take this mandate seriously, not limiting his communion to other Baptists or even other semi-separatists, but embracing Presbyterians, Independents, and Anglicans.[31]

At the very beginning of Particular Baptist life, then, we find a form of the catholicity later embraced by Ryland.[32] A question arises, however, concerning the catholicity found in the JLJ church: is the Jessey era just a temporary stop for the Particular Baptists on the way to their true conviction of

---

29. Jessey, *Storehouse of Provision*, 94; cf. 113.

30. Similar expressions may be found, such as, "Thoſe whom the Lord receives in our account, them he Commands us to receive" (Jessey, *Storehouse of Provision*, 96). And, "And as *God is Love*: So if *we dwell in Love, we dwell in God, and God in us*. (Joh 4.16.) And doe believe, that if we doe faile in this *Point* about *Communion*, or if in ſome *other* points, *any* of us *are otherwiſe minded*; that our *God* [in] his owne good time, *will reveal even this unto us*. (Phil. 3.15). And becauſe LOVE, is *a more excellent way*, then the enjoyments of *Apoſtles, Prophets, Teachers, workings of Miracles*; yea, then *all knowledge, all faith*; all gifts and Ordinances; (though all theſe are to be prized, and *earneſtly coveted*:) Therefore ſuch Believers, and ſuch Churches, as abound *more* in LOVE, ought to be prized *more*, then [sic] ſuch as abound in *all thoſe other things*, with leſſe Love" (Jessey, *Storehouse of Provision*, 129-30; the numbers on these pages are 119-20, but that is a misprint). Ecclesiological practice is driven by love as seen in the prior example of the Lord.

31. *Pace* Duesing, who says that Jessey was concerned only to commune with the Independent churches (Duesing, "Counted Worthy," 185). It is clear that Jessey had a far more catholic view than that, for, in his warning against judgmentalism, he groups Presbyterians, Independents, and Baptists together: "*Beware*, leaſt you charge any meer *Perſonall* ſinnes or faults, upon perſons in general, that are of the ſame *Opinion*, or Denomination: *For inſtance*: If one that is in the *Preſbyterian* way, or in the way of *Independants*, or *Anabaptiſts*, ſo tearmed: If one, or two, or divers of them be *Hypocrites*, or *proud*, or *deceitfull*, or *cruell*, &c. Do not thence ſay, *Theſe are your Preſbyterians*; or *This is an Independant courſe, &c*" (Jessey, "Epistle to the Reader," *Storehouse of Provision* [7–8; the pages are unnumbered, but these are the pages on which the quotation is found]).

32. This is not to say that they were the same nor is it to say that the reasons for such a catholic outlook were similar. There are significant differences between Ryland and Jessey, including how they came to their views and their practice of catholicity, but it is important to see that a catholic outlook was present from the beginning of the Particular Baptist movement.

separatism and the "walled garden"³³ of later years? On the surface, such an interpretation could make sense. After all, the JLJ church gave birth to other churches that embraced the idea of Baptist separation, such as that pastored by William Kiffin. Those who founded these churches saw themselves as being truly faithful to their Baptist principles (e.g., if baptism is only for believers, and if the church is to be made up of the baptized, then a church should only be made up of believers who have been baptized as believers).³⁴

However, such an interpretation would be mistaken, for at least two reasons. First, as was shown above, Jessey's belief on this count was not an expedient nor one enslaved to tradition; rather, it was a true conviction, founded on his reflection on Scripture and his own theological commitments. To say otherwise is to assume that Jessey did not know how to think through the implications of his own views, and it neglects the debates that surrounded the issue in Jessey's own church. It also does not reckon with the fact that Jessey, when confronted with evidence that his own view is wrong or deficient, was willing to change that view no matter the consequences, as he did in the case of believer's baptism.³⁵

Second, to say that the JLJ church cannot be used as an example of divergent views of catholicity among Particular Baptists does not acknowledge the role that that church played in the catholicity of other churches in England and Wales. While it would be well beyond the scope of this chapter to investigate the whole of that influence,³⁶ it will be helpful to show at least some of the ways that Jessey's catholicity showed up in later aspects of Baptist life and practice.

John Bunyan

Much like the JLJ church, John Bunyan's church in Bedford presents a unique ecclesiological case, though for different reasons. While the Bedford church could not be said to be a traditional Baptist church,³⁷ Bunyan

33. Haykin, "Garden Inclosed," 2–4, and Haykin, "Baptist Identity," 140–42.

34. See, e.g., Kiffin, *Sober Discourse*, in which he states and defends his position "to admit none into Church-Fellowſhip or Communion, that are Unbaptized" (2) with "Unbaptized" referring to "all perſons that either were never Baptized at all, or ſuch as have been (as they call it) *Chriſtned* or Baptized (more properly Sprinkled) in their Infancy" (9).

35. For more on this, see the "Jessey Records" published in Whitley, "Debate on Infant Baptism, 1643," 237–45.

36. More research is needed into the influence of Jessey on the Baptist and Congregational churches outside of London, especially in Wales and the West Country.

37. With Ebenezer Chandler, Bunyan's successor, the church in Bedford began to

himself held to Baptist principles on the issue of the subjects of baptism.[38] It might be questioned, then, what Bunyan and Bedford have to do with the question of Baptist catholicity.

Examining this particular church will be helpful for a couple of reasons. First, the Bedford church's convictions with regard to communion and membership were quite similar to those of the JLJ church. Moreover, the churches not only knew of one another but supported each other's ministry. Second, and more importantly, the church's most well-known pastor, John Bunyan, was influenced by the theology and practice of Henry Jessey and came to embody similar catholic principles.

The Bedford church was begun in 1650 through the efforts of John Gifford. There is no firm evidence of a relationship between Gifford and Jessey, nor is there evidence of influence from the latter to the former.[39] Richard Greaves, however, has produced two lines of circumstantial evidence pointing to Jessey's influence on the Bedford church. First, there is the issue of church membership requirements. When the Bedford church was formally organized, their requirements for membership were "faith in Christ and holiness of life, without respect to this or that circumstance or opinion in outward and circumstantiall things."[40] These were substantially the same as those found in the JLJ church under Jessey.[41] Second, interchanges between the two churches are revealing, as Greaves shows that the two churches had deep relational ties between them.[42] For example, when a member of the

---

baptize infants (Ban, "Was John Bunyan a Baptist?" 371).

38. Bunyan's baptistic convictions have been the source of some debate. Joseph Ban detailed the history of this debate (Ban, "Was John Bunyan a Baptist?" 367–76), which began with John Brown's questioning of Bunyan's Baptist commitments because of a supposed record of Bunyan's children having been christened at Bedford (Brown, *John Bunyan*, 237–41). Subsequent scholarship has called into question Brown's conclusions (Whitley, "Bunyan Christening," 263). Even if they had not, the matter need not be complicated, as it may be resolved fairly easily by reference to Bunyan's own words. Firstly, he refers to Anabaptists, and then says, "I go under that name myſelf" (Bunyan, *Heavenly Foot-man*, 15). Second, he writes that a person "muſt be a viſible Saint before, elſe he ought not to be baptized" (Bunyan, *Confession of My Faith and a Reason of My Practice*, 76). The term "viſible Saint" is an important one for Bunyan and will be examined below. Suffice it to say here that it means that a person must demonstrate themselves to be a Christian before baptism, which is the traditional Baptist position.

39. Greaves maintains that a traceable line of influence extends from Jessey to Gifford and the founding of the Bedford church to Bunyan (Greaves, *Glimpses of Glory*, 63). Unfortunately, the evidence for personal influence is slim.

40. Tibbutt, *Minutes of the First Independent Church*, 111, cited in Greaves, *Glimpses of Glory*, 63.

41. Greaves, *Glimpses of Glory*, 63.

42. Greaves, "Conscience, Liberty, and the Spirit," 35. Jessey was intentional about

Bedford church desired to move to London, the church in Bedford took "special care" to find and recommend a like-minded congregation, with the JLJ church being one of those that the Bedford church recommended.[43] There was, at the very least, a knowledge of and understanding between the two churches in which the Bedford church saw in Jessey and the JLJ church a kind of kindred theological and ecclesiological spirit.

The lines of influence and relationship are much clearer when it comes to Gifford's successor, John Bunyan. Bunyan self-consciously relied upon and marshaled the authority of Jessey in his debates over baptism and communion.[44] Not only did Bunyan append a work of Jessey to his *Differences in Judgment*,[45] he refers to Jessey ("honest and holy Mr. Jesse"), his work, and his authority several times in *Peaceable Principles and True*.[46] It will

---

fostering relationships between churches. In 1653, he went on a tour of thirty-six congregations through the country, preaching his understanding of open communionism (Anonymous, "Jacob-Jessey Church," 247).

43. Greaves names four churches in addition to the JLJ church as recommended by Bedford: those led by George Griffith, Anthony Palmer, George Cokayne, and John Owen. To this list, Anne Dunan-Page adds the churches of John Simpson, Richard Taylor, Matthew Meade, John Nesbitt, and Robert Traill to the Bedford London network (Dunan-Page, "Bunyan and the Bedford Congregation," 62). Lending credence to Dunan-Page's additions, Ebenezer Chandler had been a member of Taylor's church, and the letters between the two churches regarding his call evidence mutual affection (Blyth, *History of Bedford*, 266–67).

Greaves points out that, of the five he names, only Jessey was a self-professed Baptist, which, he argues, indicates that the Bedford church in general and Bunyan in particular showed more affinity for broadly Congregational churches than Baptist churches (Greaves, "Conscience, Liberty, and the Spirit," 35). This may be, but the reason for that is unclear. Was it that Bunyan's ecclesiology put him that much at odds with other Baptists? Or, was it because of personal animus between Bunyan and other Baptists? The latter is certainly possible, especially in light of Bunyan's treatment by other Baptists. For example, see Bunyan's account of John Owen's acceptance, then refusal, to append a work to his *Differences in Judgment*. Bunyan attributes Owen's eventual refusal to "the earneſt ſolicitations of ſeveral of you" (Bunyan, *Peaceable Principles and True*, 1:109). "You" in that quotation refers to Baptists who disagreed with Bunyan's open communionism.

44. Greaves also makes an intriguing suggestion that Bunyan, briefly freed from jail, went to London in October 1661 to visit Jessey (Greaves, *Glimpses of Glory*, 150). The evidence is scant and inconclusive, but it is distinctly possible.

45. Jessey did not compose the work specifically for Bunyan. Bunyan came by it and felt it appropriate to insert it, since Owen had declined the invitation to provide an addendum to Bunyan's work. Bunyan says of Jessey's essay, "I have alſo preſented thee with the Opinion of Mr. Henry Jeſſe, in the Caſe, which providentially I met with, as I was coming to London to put my Papers to the Preſs, and that it was his Judgment is Aſſerted to me, known many years ſince to ſome of the Baptiſts, to whom it was ſent, but never yet Anſwered; and will yet be Atteſted if need ſhall require" (Bunyan, *Differences in Judgment*, 4).

46. Bunyan, *Peaceable Principles and True*, 1:108, 111, 114.

help here to outline Bunyan's view of baptism and church membership in order to show the affinities between him and Jessey as well as illustrating the broader stream of catholicity in Particular Baptist history.

While Bunyan's *Differences in Judgment about Water Baptism—No Bar to Communion* (1673) presents an obvious target when examining Bunyan's understanding of the ordinance, his *Confession* (1671) proves to be just as fruitful a text for research, as it places his understanding of baptism and its relationship to the church and church membership within the context of his overall theology. This chapter, thus, will focus on his *Confession*, using *Differences in Judgment* as a supplementary text.

Bunyan wrote his *Confession* in the fall of 1671.[47] In the work, he outlines his theological convictions, showing himself to be a traditional Calvinist with regard to the particularity of grace[48] and a Baptist with regard to the proper recipients of the baptismal rite.[49] Much of the work, however, is taken up with an explanation of his open communion views. He writes, "Touching my Practice as to Communion with vifible Saints, although not Baptized with water; I fay, it is my prefent Judgement fo to do."[50] He then explains why and how he has come to this conviction.

His open communion understanding of church fellowship is founded on the belief that Christian fellowship rests on a person's relationship with and acceptance by God: "Now him that God receiveth and holdeth communion with, him you fhould receive and hold communion with."[51] Like Jessey,

---

47. Greaves, *Glimpses of Glory*, 271.

48. While there is some debate as to whether Bunyan held to a traditional Calvinistic understanding of the extent of the atonement (Wenkel, "John Bunyan's Soteriology," 333–52), Bunyan assuredly holds to other Calvinist soteriological convictions, as evidenced in the following statements: "I believe, we being finfull Creatures in our felves, that no good thing done by us, can procure of God the imputation of the righteoufnefs of Jefus Chrift. But that imputation is *an act of grace*, a free gift without our deferving" (Bunyan, *Confession*, 19); "I believe, that the faith that fo doth [trust in Christ] is not to be found with any but thofe, in whom the Spirit of God by mighty power doth work it; all others being fearfull and incredulous, dare not venture their fouls and eternity upon it" (23); "I bilieve [sic], that this faith is effectually wrought in none, but thofe which before the world, were appointed unto Glory" (23–24); and "I believe that this decree, choyce or election, was before the foundation of the world; and fo before the elect themfelves, had being in themfelves" (26).

49. Bunyan, *Confession*, 76.

50. Bunyan, "To the Reader," *Confession*, [7; the pages are unnumbered; these are the pages on which the quotation is found].

51. Bunyan, *Confession*, 102 [92; the pages are numbered incorrectly; the pages not in brackets are the correct page numbers, while the pages in brackets are what is found on the page itself]. "Communion" most likely includes the Lord's supper, because, for Bunyan, the Lord's supper was a corporate, visible display of the unity of Christians. Along with baptism, Bunyan understood the Lord's supper as "not the fundamentals of

Bunyan felt that, if God accepts and communes with someone, then he has no right to deny the same to that person; his standards of communion are not higher than God's.[52] The question that Bunyan is eager to answer, then, is how one knows that another person is accepted by God. He answers both negatively and positively.

Negatively, one's knowledge of another's acceptance with God is not founded on the other person having submitted to the proper church ritual. Bunyan contrasts baptism and circumcision in this regard, saying that, while circumcision was the ordinance that initiated a person into the old covenant community, such that without it one would be cut off from the people, this is not true of baptism and the new covenant community: "To think that becauſe in time paſt, Baptiſm was adminiſtered upon converſion, that therefore it is the initiating, and entring ordinance into Church-communion: when by the word no ſuch thing is teſtifyed of it."[53] While not to be circumcised was an excommunicable offense in the old covenant, "there is none debarred or threatened to be cut off from the Church, if they be not firſt baptized."[54] Since Bunyan rejects the argument that baptism replaces circumcision, any argument based on the practice of circumcision (e.g., that circumcision preceded admittance to Passover) does not impact his thinking.

Positively, Bunyan holds that a person's reception into the fellowship of the church or the grounds for extending Christian fellowship to any particular person rests not on their participation in the rite of baptism but on "a diſcovery of their faith and holyneſs."[55] It is this life of faith and holiness that Bunyan refers to by the shorthand "viſible Saints."[56] A "viſible

---

our Chriſtianity; nor grounds or rule to communion with Saints: ſervants they are, and our myſtical Miniſters" (Bunyan, *Confession*, 65). They are not the grounds of communion but, rather, serve the body of Christ in its visible communion and unity. Therefore, when Bunyan speaks of "communion" here, he most likely comprehends participation in the Lord's supper within it.

52. In *Differences in Judgment*, Bunyan states the matter with some force, saying, "*Receive him to the Glory of God:* [To the Glory of God] is put in on purpoſe, to ſhew that diſhonour they bring to him, who deſpiſe to have Communion with ſuch, whom they know do maintain Communion with God" (Bunyan, *Differences in Judgment*, 46–47).

53. Bunyan, *Confession*, 70. Baptism is typically understood, by Baptists and non-Baptists, as the ordinance of initiation into the life of the church. Bunyan's is a minority position (see Kiffin, *Sober Discourse*, 88–89).

54. Bunyan, *Confession*, 73. He adduces as his proof of this assertion the baptisms which John performed as well as the baptism that Philip performed on the eunuch. None of these baptisms, says Bunyan, introduced those baptized into the membership of a church (73–74).

55. Bunyan, *Confession*, 70.

56. Bunyan uses this phrase repeatedly in his work as the standard by which church communion should be extended: "I dare have communion; Church communion with

Saint" is one who "hath already ſubjected to that which is better; even to the righteouſneſs of God, which is by Faith of Jeſus Chriſt; by which he ſtands juſt before God."[57] The proof of a genuine Christian is a life that bears it out: the confession of faith and the good works that follow from it are Bunyan's stated requirements.[58] Bunyan calls these "moral duties Goſpellized."[59]

In Bunyan's thought, then, baptism is not a church ordinance of entrance into the church and the life of faith. It is, rather, a personal act of obedience by which the individual's faith is helped. In considering why people are baptized, Bunyan answers "That their own Faith by that figure might be ſtrengthened in the death and refurrection of Chriſt. And that themſelves might ſee, that they have profeſſed themſelves dead, and buryed, and iriſen [sic] with him to newneſs of life."[60] Baptism, then, is a personal act of obedience to Christ, by which a person's faith may be strengthened, but in which nothing is conferred upon the person baptized, no guarantee is made as to their spiritual state, and no church state should be inferred. Bunyan states the matter plainly, saying, "Baptiſm makes thee no member of the Church, neither particular nor univerſall: neither doth it make thee a viſible Saint: It therefore gives thee neither right to, nor being of

---

thoſe that are viſible Saints by calling" (Bunyan, *Confession*, 65). Citing Rom 15, Bunyan writes, "I am bold to hold communion with viſible Saints as afore; becauſe God hath communion with them; whoſe example in the caſe, we are ſtreightly commanded to follow" (99 [89]). Not being a visible saint is his only rule of exclusion: "I onely exclude him that is not a viſible Saint" (49).

57. Bunyan, *Confession*, 94–95.

58. Bunyan, *Confession*, 78. He says, "By that word of God therefore, by which their Faith, experience, and converſation (being examined) is found Good; by that the Church ſhould receive them into fellowſhip with them."

59. Bunyan, *Confession*, 79.

60. Bunyan, *Confession*, 76–77. Elsewhere, Bunyan comments that baptism is "a ſign to the perſon Baptized, and an help to his own Faith" (Bunyan, *Confession*, 98 [88]).

memberſhip at all."[61] A failure to be baptized as a believer, says Bunyan, does not "unchriſtian" a person.[62]

What matters, according to Bunyan, is the living experience of Christ and acceptance by God in the life of a believer.[63] It is this that becomes a rule in Bunyan's catholic outlook. He says, "Faith, and Holineſs, are my profeſſed principles, with an endeavour, ſo far as in me lyeth, to be at peace with all men."[64] This is not to say that the outward circumstances are unimportant; rather, for Bunyan, they are of comparatively less importance.[65] Therefore, in his estimation, they should not be made a rule for church communion.

In this regard, Bunyan shows his indebtedness to Jessey, who, as shown above, held to similar principles of loving who God loves, accepting who God accepts, personalizing the ordinance, and grounding communion less in ritual and more in a common spiritual experience. The theological standard of communion is seen as Christ's acceptance of an individual, and the epistemological standard is visible sainthood, or a holy life. There is a move, then, toward experience as the bond of fellowship and communion that will prove key for Ryland's own catholicity.

61. Bunyan, *Confession*, 76; cf. Bunyan, *Differences in Judgment*, 14. Bunyan places a greater emphasis on Spirit baptism than he does water baptism. He calls Spirit baptism "the beſt of Baptiſms," citing it as the "the heart of Water-baptiſm" (98 [88]). The "one Baptiſm" of Eph 4:5 is not water baptism but Spirit baptism (96 [86]). He also calls being dead to sin and alive to God in Christ "the heart, power and doctrine of Baptiſm" (98 [88]). To be baptized by the Spirit, then, is to be given desire and power for a holy life. This, to Bunyan, is of greater importance than water baptism. With Spirit baptism as the heart of the matter, water baptism assumes a downgraded importance: it is "ſhaddowiſh" and "figurative" (64). Bunyan virtually strips baptism of any meaning beyond being an outward act that points toward an inward reality, though still of some spiritual help to the individual being baptized. The sacramental language found in his contemporary Benjamin Keach is absent in Bunyan (Keach, *Gold Refin'd*, 78–83; cf. Fowler, *More Than a Symbol*, 29–30). However, this need not be seen as uncatholic of him, as it was an aspect of his attempt to emphasize the common elements of the faith. It may be seen, then, as an expression of his catholicity.

62. Bunyan, *Confession*, 104 [94]; cf. Bunyan, *Differences in Judgment*, 46. This is an important assertion on Bunyan's part. In his thought, lack of believer's baptism is a "failure" but not a sin. In *Differences in Judgment*, he also calls it an "infirmity" (Bunyan, *Differences in Judgment*, 58). This is in contrast with his contemporary William Kiffin, who held that paedobaptists have committed a great violation of "Goſpel Order" and their practice is "as pernicious to Chriſtians as immorality" (Kiffin, *Sober Discourse*, 5). Having understood such people in that light, Kiffin's refusal of church communion to them stands to reason. Bunyan's understanding of their unbaptized state as a mere "failure," however, allows him to extend to them more charity than Kiffin could.

63. Bunyan, *Confession*, 94–95.

64. Bunyan, "To the Reader," *Confession*, [4].

65. Indeed, Bunyan says that a profession that has as its "greateſt excellency" a conformity to external circumstances is "not worth two mites" (Bunyan, *Confession*, 89 [79]).

Broadmead

The history of Broadmead goes back to 1640, when John Canne ordered it as a Christian church.[66] Like the Bedford church, there are early connections between Broadmead and the JLJ church in London. In November 1639, Henry Jessey was sent by his church to Wales to assist the churches there, one of which was the church in Llanvaches,[67] from which came Thomas Ewins, pastor of Broadmead from 1651–1670.[68] When Bristol was overtaken by Prince Rupert in 1643, the congregation was broken up and most of the people fled to London, where it is said that they joined with both the Jessey and Kiffin congregations before returning to Bristol.[69] For some time, Broadmead sent members desiring baptism to Henry Jessey in London, including two of the most prominent leaders of the church in the seventeenth century, the aforementioned Thomas Ewins and Robert Purnell.[70] In the ensuing decades, the Broadmead church would refer to the JLJ

---

66. Ivimey, *History of the Baptists*, 2:523. Canne is an interesting case in himself. In the Broadmead records, Terrill calls him a "Baptized man" (Underhill, *Records of a Church of Christ*, 18), indicating that he was himself a Baptist. Ivimey says as much: "Mr. Canne was a baptist, but did not make adult baptism a necessary prerequisite to church communion" (Ivimey, *History of the Baptists*, 2:523). However, Champlin Burrage called into question Canne's Baptist credentials by showing that Terrill's records of Broadmead prior to about 1654 suffer from either oversimplification or mistaken notions of the nature of the church in the earliest days (Burrage, "Was John Canne a Baptist?" 222–23). He dates Canne's visit to Bristol not to 1640, as Terrill says, but to 1648, and says that Terrill's insinuation that Canne was a Baptist is an "unconscious fabrication" (Burrage, "Was John Canne a Baptist?" 244; cf. Hayden, *Records of a Church of Christ*, 11–12). John F. Wilson reached similar conclusions to Burrage many years later (Wilson, "Another Look at John Canne," 34–48; cf. Hayden, "Broadmead, Bristol in the 17th Century," 352). To complicate matters further, William Axon, in the *Dictionary of National Biography*, asserts that Canne was not the founder of Broadmead but came only after they had begun meeting (Axon, "Canne, John," 863). The case is, to the present author, quite uncertain. Burrage may well go too far in calling Terrill's assertion a fabrication, even if unconscious; however, he does point out some deficiencies in current knowledge of the earliest days of Broadmead and the nature of Canne's theology. Further research is needed in this area.

67. Whiston, *Life and Death of Mr. Henry Jessey*, 9–10.

68. Ewins had also been a member of Jessey's church in London (Hayden, "Broadmead in the 17th Century," 351).

69. Hayden, "Broadmead in the 17th Century," 348; Ivimey, *History of the Baptists*, 2:528. While it may be that some joined with Kiffin in London, it seems unlikely that those who returned to Bristol to reconstitute the Broadmead congregation came chiefly from that church, as Kiffin and his church were at odds with the Broadmead practice of open communion, whereas the Jessey church supported such a practice. Later history supports this assertion, as the connections between Broadmead and the JLJ church continued and were strengthened in the ensuing years (more on this below).

70. In 1653, one year prior to the baptisms of Ewins and Purnell, Terrill mentions

church as their "beloved sister church," and there would be a continuous stream of communication and fellowship between the two churches.[71]

For the interests of this chapter, one person will be investigated as to his catholicity and his influence on Broadmead: Robert Purnell (1606–1666). Purnell is an overlooked yet vital part of the history of Broadmead. He was most likely a Bristol man involved in the carpet weaving business.[72] As mentioned above, he was baptized by Jessey along with Thomas Ewins,

---

another member, Timothy Cattle, becoming convinced of believer's baptism and being sent with a letter to Jessey, who baptized Cattle. After Cattle's baptism, Terrill says that "divers others of the church were baptized" (Underhill, *Records of a Church of Christ*, 42; cf. Child and Shipley, *Broadmead Origins*, 42). Hayden says that baptism did not become an issue until after 1650 (Hayden, *Records of a Church of Christ*, 47), so it is perhaps the baptism of Cattle which began the discussions regarding the ordinance. Purnell and Ewins were baptized in 1654, though Purnell had been convinced of believer's baptism for several years but had omitted actually receiving it (Underhill, *Records of a Church of Christ*, 51).

71. Underhill, *Records of a Church of Christ*, 198–99. Broadmead sent a letter to the London church in which they wrote of them as those "with whom we have had occasion of correspondence for many years past, and also from which we received help time after time; for which, next after the Lord, we return you thanks, for the Lord hath made you instrumental for our good, by your late pastor, that worthy and holy man, brother Jessey" (Underhill, *Records of a Church of Christ*, 198–99). These good relations would not last, for a breach between the churches occurred after the death of Ewins in 1670. It was due to the fact that both churches desired the same man, Thomas Hardcastle, to be their pastor. Broadmead called Hardcastle to be their pastor, which angered the JLJ church, since Hardcastle was, at the time, a member of the JLJ church and on a trial to become their next pastor. The letters between the two churches (Underhill, *Records of a Church of Christ*, 198–99, 203–5) show a strained, tense relationship, with no small amount of bitterness on the part of the London church and aloofness on the part of the Bristol congregation. However, the breach in the relationship does not reduce the influence and closeness of the two groups prior to 1670. Indeed, the very fact that Broadmead called a man from the Jessey church, whom the Jessey church was also seeking to call, shows a great similarity between the two churches.

72. Nott and Elizabeth, *Deposition Books of Bristol*, 13:37; cf. Hayden, *Records of a Church of Christ*, 19. Biographical information is, unfortunately, hard to come by and what has been published is not always of the most certain quality. Ivimey lists him as a London minister but later admits that "there is . . . no certainty that he was settled in London" (Ivimey, *History of the English Baptists*, 2:528, cf. 2:465). Ivimey's information about Purnell seems to have been limited to his *Little Cabinet Richly Stored* (Ivimey, *History of the English Baptists*, 2:465). Hayden says that he was a member of Broadmead for over thirty years (Hayden, *Records of a Church of Christ*, 19), but this is not possible, since Purnell died in 1666 and Broadmead was not founded until 1640. Bryan Ball calls Purnell a "founder-member" of Broadmead, but, unfortunately, he gives no documentation (Ball, *Great Expectation*, 91). According to Child and Shipley, Purnell was in Bristol and an active leader at the Broadmead church in the early 1650s, since it was in his home that Thomas Ewins was set apart as a pastor (Child and Shipley, *Broadmead Origins*, 62). While details are, unfortunately, lacking, the broad strokes of Purnell's life make it clear that he was a long-time and influential leader at the Broadmead church.

the pastor of Broadmead. While he was not a pastor of Broadmead, he was a part of the leadership of the church for many years, was called upon to preach in the absence of the pastor, and served as a stabilizing influence on the church during his tenure as deacon and later as elder. He also wrote several books which give insight into his theology in general and his catholicity in particular. More to the point of this work, the catholicity expressed in his written works is reflected heavily in the catholicity of Broadmead itself.[73]

Unlike John Canne, Robert Purnell was certainly a committed Baptist. His *A Little Cabinet Richly Stored with All Sorts of Heavenly Varieties, and Soul-Reviving Influences* is his most in-depth theological treatise; in it, he is not shy about his Baptist convictions. He gives several "precepts and examples . . . for the baptizing of a believer,"[74] and then issues a bold challenge to his reader: "Shew me the like for baptizing of children, and I will write a book of recantation, and acknowledge my error both to God and man : But I am fure thou canft not do it, without thou wilt make a new Scripture, or groffly pervert this."[75] This commitment and conviction, however, did not come at the expense of seeking unity and enjoying communion with all Christians. In fact, he took his fellow Baptists to task for their factionalism. In *A Little Cabinet*, he addresses the Baptists, "You that have taken up this Ordinance, beware of laying a greater ftrefs upon it, then [sic] ever God appointed you, *viz.* it was never appointed to break love, and Communion, and to quench the Spirit, and to juftle out fome other Ordinances, nor to fhut out the weak in the Faith, nor to put them upon doubtful difputations."[76] He goes on to ask several questions of the Baptists:

> know you not that all Saints are fellow-members, fellow-fouldiers, fellow-travellers, co-heirs, fellow-fufferers, and fellow-Citizens, having the fame father, being cloathed with the fame robe, ruled by the fame word, inclined to the fame work? will you fhut out thofe that God hath received, and ftop the mouth that God hath opened, and refufe communion with thofe that have fellowfhip

---

73. Hayden, "Broadmead in the 17th Century," 353. Broadmead was open communion until 1733, when a group of paedobaptists within Broadmead formed a separate congregation that became known as the "Little Church" (Anonymous, "Records of the Independent Church at Broadmead, 1757–1818," 2–5). This church met at Broadmead, and the pastor of the Baptist congregation at Broadmead was also the pastor of the Little Church.

74. Purnell, *Little Cabinet*, 258.

75. Purnell, *Little Cabinet*, 259.

76. Purnell, *Little Cabinet*, 261–62.

with the Father, and the Son, and that are faithful to what they know? are all blind that doth not fee by your eyes?[77]

Purnell held to a familiar version of the "communion of saints as saints." He explains, "Those saints that are affembled together according to a Gofpel inftitution, are a communion of Saints, arifing from a clear apprehenfion of their union with Chrift and his members."[78] Communion, therefore, rests not on baptism but on union with Christ. In *Little Cabinet*, he gives detailed instructions for the institution of a new church, writing:

> Let feven, eight, nine or ten, or more of thofe men that are moft found in the Faith, and moft unblamable in their lives and converfation, appoint one day to faft and pray together, and earneftly feek unto God for his direction herein, and toward the end of the day, let them one by one give an account of the work of grace upon their hearts, and of the hope that is in them, and then give your felves upon to the Lord, and one to another by the will of God, with no other Covenant then this, to endeavour as God fhall enlighten, and enable you to walk together in the appointments, Ordinances, and inftitutions of Chrift, the head of the Church, expreft, implied, and contained in the Scriptures of truth, which you take to be your rule.[79]

The qualifications for church membership that this new church should hold are that a person should be able to tell "about the time when, the place where, the manner how the Lord did firft appear to them in a powerful conviction, converfion, and regeneration, or fomething equivolent thereunto," as well as possess the ability to tell the "grounds and ends in defiring fellowfhip," which should be "that they might enjoy God in all his ordinances, and

---

77. Purnell, *Little Cabinet*, 262. In another work, he continues the same challenging rhetoric: "why then doe you imagine in your hearts, and fpeak evill of the *Independent*, becaufe he will not be rebaptized? Why do you fo judge the *Prefbyterian* for Baptizing children, to whom it doth not belong. They doe not fee by your eies, therefore they cannot walk by your rules: are they in darkneffe in this? fo once waft thou: Doeft thou outftrip them in this? it may be (nay I am fure) they do go beyond thee in other particulars of obedience: Doe they neglect the ordinance of Baptifme? that is their evill; but thou doeft reft upon it, and this is thy evill: do they fin in fleighting Baptifme, thou finneft in idolizing of it: Oh then, be fparing to cenfure, and judge thy Brother! . . . Again, you make Baptifme the ground of your communion, and fo diforder what God hath ordered; for the ground of communion fhould arife, firft, from that union you have with Chrift your head; and fecondly, from that near relation you have each to other, as being one in the fame fpirit" (Purnell, *Good Tydings for Sinners, Great Ioy for Saints*, 92–93).

78. Purnell, *Little Cabinet*, 199–200.

79. Purnell, *Little Cabinet*, 201–2. These men are to be "of years and sound judgement to difcern the Lords body" (269).

have a fellowſhip with thoſe that have fellowſhip with the Father and the Son."[80] Nothing whatsoever is mentioned by Purnell about baptism.[81] It is, rather, all about a shared personal spiritual experience. Admission to what Kiffin called "Church-fellowſhip" proceeds along the same lines, as Purnell states, "Now when a man comes to ſee that every one in whom the Lord Jeſus appeareth is a member together with him in the ſame body, whereof Chriſt is the head; then his heart longeſt to joyn himſelf in fellowſhip with ſuch, who have fellowſhip with the Father and the Son."[82] The question with which Purnell is concerned is not, "Has the person been baptized?" but, instead, "Has the person experienced a work of grace in their heart? Has God accepted them?"

In an earlier work, entitled *Good Tydings for Sinners, Great Ioy for Saints*, Purnell is even more pointed with regard to the ground of Christian union:

> The ground of this communion ſhall be ſpirituall union: and when this day is dawned, and the day-ſtar riſen in our hearts, *Ephraim* ſhall not envy *Judah*, nor *Judah* vex *Ephraim*; *Preſbyterians* ſhall not ſo bitterly cry out againſt *Independents*, nor *Independents* have ſuch hard thoughts of *Preſbyterians*. Yea, they ſhall be aſhamed to own one another by theſe fleſhly titles; but look upon and love one another as Chriſtians, members of the ſame body, heires of the ſame Promiſe, children of the ſame father: having all the ſame ſpirit, all clothed with the ſame robe, inclined to the ſame work; ruled by the ſame Word and Spirit. And ſo their love to each other ſhall ariſe from the Union in the

---

80. Purnell, *Little Cabinet*, 202.

81. To be fair, he does mention the "ordinances" here, which might be interpreted to mean that the person should have a Baptist understanding of them. However, while Purnell does hold that baptism and the Lord's supper are "confirming Ordinances" (Purnell, *Little Cabinet*, 255), he believes that they are both personal expressions of private faith: they "do not give us any right unto God and his Chriſt, and promiſes, but only ſeal up and confirm that right and intereſt which already we have in Gods Covenant of Grace" (257). More importantly, he holds that there are more than two ordinances which a Christian is to enjoy within the fellowship of the church (cf. Thompson, "Toward Baptist Ecclesiology," 109n112; "People of the Free God," 240n87). In fact, he names eleven "ordinances of the Gospel," including the assembling of Christians together; preaching, prophesying, and hearing the word preached; prayer and supplication; singing and praising God together; baptism; the Lord's supper or breaking of bread; collections for the poor; the reading of Scripture; private and public admonition; suspension (one step removed from excommunication); and excommunication (199). Therefore, that a person is to enjoy "the ordinances" means far more to Purnell than a right understanding of baptism. It is, essentially, a participation in the life of the church.

82. Purnell, *Little Cabinet*, 200.

Spirit. And againſt this Church-State, the gates of hell ſhall not prevaile.[83]

Against other "Church-States," one may assume that Purnell believes that the gates of hell shall surely prevail. It is as pointed a statement as to his belief with regard to catholicity and the communion of the church as he makes in his published work. His catholicity, then, is rooted in the Christian's shared experience of a "powerful conviction, converſion, and regeneration," which, being present, is sufficient to ground communion, even in the absence of agreement or participation in the rite of baptism.

Purnell's influence is seen throughout Broadmead history, most notably in the man whom they chose as their pastor after Purnell's death. Thomas Hardcastle followed the pastorate of Thomas Ewins and was known as a man of "great moderation and catholicism."[84] His statement on church fellowship, made in a preface to one of his works, shows his own brand of catholicity and the abiding influence of Purnell in Bristol:

> To conclude, this is no Point of Controverſie, but rather an effectual means to reconcile Differences; thoſe that cannot now joyn together in Prayer, will in a very little while if they be true Saints ſit together Praiſing God, Rejoicing in and Loving one another in a larger meaſure than ever they Loved their moſt Dear Relations or intimate Friends upon Earth. The ſhortneſs of time there is to differ in, the abſolute neceſſity, and incomparable Excellency and Sweetneſs of mutual Love here and full Communion hereafter, I deſire may ſway with me to watch over my own Heart, that I ſtand not at a diſtance in Spirit from any Saint of God upon the account either of apprehenſion or injury; as to the Former I do not know that I was ever under a Tentation to Love any one leſs for his True Conſcience though not of my ſize.[85]

Echoes of Purnell may be heard in Hardcastle's appeal: they are both seeking a fellowship comprised of "true Saints" or, in Purnell's language, those who have experienced "powerful conviction, converſion, and regeneration." For

---

83. Purnell, "To the Reader," *Good Tydings for Sinners, Great Ioy for Saints*, 2.

84. Calamy and Palmer, *Nonconformist's Memorial*, 3:426. Cf. Ivimey, *History of the Baptists*, 2:532. Hardcastle was a member of the Jessey church in London and was the subject of the controversy between the two churches. While Purnell would not have had a direct influence on Hardcastle, he would have influenced the church to look for a man like Hardcastle (a catholic Baptist).

85. Hardcastle, "Preface to the Reader," *Christian Geography and Arithmetick*, [9–10; there are no page numbers on the page; these are the actual pages on which the quotation is found]. This is quoted with minor modernizing alterations in Calamy and Palmer, *Nonconformist's Memorial*, 3:526–27, and Ivimey, *History of the Baptists*, 2:534.

both, fellowship rests on a shared spiritual experience rather than agreement and participation in a particular ritual of the church.

The catholic stream that has been shown in Henry Jessey and John Bunyan is demonstrably present also in Broadmead: the ground of communion is not rituals or shared broad theological convictions but is, rather, a shared experience of Christ. It is seen in one of the forefathers of the Particular Baptists, Jessey; in one of the most well-known Particular Baptists of the seventeenth century, John Bunyan; and in one of the most influential churches of the time, Broadmead. While it may yet be a minority position among Particular Baptists, the catholic spirit that is open to friendship, cooperation, fellowship, and even joint participation in the Lord's supper with those outside of its own tradition is a vital part of the history of the Particular Baptists. Broadmead itself is representative of what has come to be known as the Bristol Tradition.[86] The Bristol Tradition is a moderate Calvinistic expression of the Christian faith, centered on the evangelical doctrines of incarnation, atonement, and the revelation of God in the Bible. It gave birth to the Bristol Education Society, which, while focused on the Baptist denomination, sought not to make Baptist ministers but "able and evangelical ministers."[87] Ryland was shaped by the Bristol Tradition through his father, and he would later assume the primary leadership for it when he became the pastor of Broadmead and President of the Bristol Baptist Academy.

Confessions

Confessions are snapshots of the theological convictions of a group at a specific moment in time. For this reason, they are important for understanding the self-identity of the groups which produce them. In the case of the Particular Baptists, their confessions demonstrate, among other things, something of a latent catholic spirit that existed among them in the seventeenth century.[88]

---

86. For more information on the Bristol Tradition, see Cross, "To Communicate Simply You Must Understand Profoundly," 54–67; Cross, "Early Bristol Tradition as a Seedbed for Evangelical Reception among British Baptists, c.1720–c.1770," 50–77.

87. Anonymous, *Account of the Bristol Education Society*, 1.

88. This section on the confessions will use the term "catholic spirit" rather than catholicity. If catholicity is defined as including the Lord's supper in a visible manifestation of the unity of the church, then the confessions are not quite in that category. At least, they are not so in the same manner as those considered in the rest of this chapter or in Ryland. However, there is a "catholic spirit," a spiritual instinct to share fellowship with those who share in Christ, present in the confessions, as will be shown below. The catholic spirit of the early Baptists has been recognized in previous studies, though it

Two main Particular Baptist confessions emerged in the seventeenth century: the *First London Confession* of 1644 and the *Second London Confession* of 1677.[89] In setting out what they believed, the documents served both an apologetic and didactic purpose. With regard to the apologetic intention of the confessions, the title of the 1644 *Confession* gives some hint, as it is styled *A Confession of Faith of Those Churches Which Are Commonly (Though Falsly) Called Anabaptists*. To be charged with being an Anabaptist had theological and political implications, none of which the Particular Baptists wanted. Theologically, the Anabaptists were thought to deny some of the foundational tenets of the faith, including original sin, the supremacy of God's grace in salvation over against free will, and eternal salvation. With regard to politics, even in 1644, the events of the Münster uprising in 1534 were still in the collective memory of the English people; Anabaptists, thus, had a reputation for rejecting lawful authority and denying the place of the magistracy. The seven churches that made that confession sought to

---

has never been traced out at length. Though he uses the term "catholicity" rather than "catholic spirit," Renihan agrees, writing, "Genuine catholicity marked the lives of the Particular Baptists" (Renihan, "Practical Ecclesiology," x). He goes on to note that this "catholicity" was seen most especially in the acceptance of "the more rigorous groups which seceded from them at various points during the 1630s and 1640s" (Renihan, "Practical Ecclesiology," 27). In other words, the more conservative groups, though they seceded from the established Baptist churches, were not themselves "excommunicated" for their stricter theology and practice. Nor did the seceders "excommunicate" their less strict brethren, as shown above with Hanserd Knollys returning to the JLJ church to baptize Henry Jessey.

89. These two confessions are sometimes referred to by different dates, 1646 and 1689, respectively. The *First London Confession* was originally composed and signed by the seven Baptist churches in 1644. A later, revised edition was published in 1646. Important differences exist between the original 1644 and revised 1646 editions of the *Confession*, including the sections on baptism, the church, and scripture.

The *Second London Confession* was originally written in 1677, but it too was reissued in a second edition in 1689 after the passing of the Act of Toleration, with a third edition coming in 1699 that included a list of the signatories to the document. The reason for a whole new confession in 1677, rather than a further revision to the 1644 *Confession*, is stated in the preface to the 1677 *Confession* as stemming from the relative scarcity of the earlier confession and the fact that there were many others who had joined the Baptists in the intervening years ("To the Judicial and Impartial Reader," 1677 *Confession*, 2). For present purposes, unless referring to a unique aspect of a later edition, the original dates of composition will be used.

There were several other confessions drawn up by the Baptists in the seventeenth century, such as Thomas Helwys's *Declaration of Faith* (1611); the *Faith and Practice of Thirty Congregations* (1651); the *Somerset Confession of Faith* (1656); the *Standard Confession* (1660); and the *Orthodox Creed* (1678). For more information on these confessions, see William Lumpkin, *Baptist Confessions of Faith*. For varying reasons, none of these attained the reputation of the 1644 and 1677 *Confessions*.

distinguish themselves from the Anabaptists.⁹⁰ The preface to the 1644 *Confession* states their concerns, saying that they wish to respond to those who have "ſmote us and taken away our vaile" and who charged them with "holding Free-will, Falling away from grace, denying Original ſinne, diſclaiming of the Magiſtracy, denying to aſſiſt them either in perſons or purſe in any of their lawfull Commands, doing acts unſeemly in the diſpenſing the Ordinance of Baptiſme, not to be named amonſt Chriſtians."⁹¹

With regard to the didactic purpose of the confessions, this is seen most clearly in the 1677 *Confession*, the preface of which says:

> One thing that greatly prevailed with us to undertake this work, was (not only to give a full account of our ſelves, to thoſe Chriſtians that differ from us about the ſubject of baptiſm, but alſo) the profit that might from thence ariſe, unto thoſe that have any account of our labors, in their inſtruction, and eſtabliſhment in the great truths of the Goſpel; in the clear underſtanding, and ſteady belief of which, our comfortable walking with God, and fruitfulneſs before him, in all our ways, is moſt neerly concerned; and therefore we did conclude it neceſſary to expreſſe our ſelves the more fully and diſtinctly."⁹²

The purpose is to inform the wider world of their beliefs as well as teach and establish their own faith community in the "great truths of the Goſpel." At the risk of oversimplifying, if the 1644 *Confession* can be understood as a defensive document, the 1677 *Confession* may be seen as one in which the Baptists go on the offense. They hope not only to defend their name but also to help people to grow in the faith that they proclaimed.

The catholic spirit of the documents is expressed in different ways. The 1644 *Confession*, perhaps because of its shorter length, is distinguished by what it does not say. For example, the 1644 *Confession* does not explicitly state that non-baptized persons may partake of the Lord's supper, but neither does it make baptism a prerequisite to that ordinance. The section on baptism in the 1644 *Confession* reads, "That Baptiſme is an Ordinance of the new Teſtament, given by Chriſt, to be diſpenſed onely upon perſons profeſſing faith, or that are Diſciples, or taught, who upon a profeſſion of

---

90. The seven churches were Devonshire Square, Wapping, Great St. Helens, Crutched Friars, Bishopsgate Street, Coleman Street, and Glazier's Hall (Ivimey, *History*, 2:296).

91. "To All Christian Readers," 1644 *Confession*, 1–2. See also Kiffin [Kiffen], *Briefe Remonstrance*, 12, where Kiffin indicates that the term "Anabaptist" is not one of his choosing but is an epithet given him by his opponent.

92. "To the Judicious and Impartial Reader," 1677 *Confession*, 3.

faith, ought to be baptized."[93] In addition, the Appendix to the *Confession*, written in 1646 by Benjamin Cox, contained much stronger language excluding those not baptized as believers, but it was not incorporated into the *Confession* in the next revision of 1653, indicating some reticence on the part of the churches not to come across as too exclusionary.[94] Finally, the *Confession*'s understanding of the church, though including a "practical injoyment of the Ordinances,"[95] does not mention the proper mode or subjects of baptism, nor does it require baptism as a prerequisite to church communion.[96]

The 1677 *Confession*, as a longer document that enables the Baptists to express themselves "more fully and diftinctly," has much more to commend it in its catholic expression. The very method and shape of the confession speaks to this, for the framers of the confession intentionally modeled it on other statements, namely the *Westminster Confession of Faith* (1646–47) and the *Savoy Declaration* (1658).[97] While the *Confession* continues the 1644 *Confession*'s apologetic purposes in denying that the London Baptists are to be numbered along with Arminians, non-trinitarians, and non-federalists, the very structure and method of the *Confession* is, to paraphrase Renihan, a vigorous declaration of their desire to be counted among the English Reformed community.[98] Far from being the foundation of a "walled garden,"

---

93. 1644 *Confession*, XXXIX. The Lord's supper is not mentioned.

94. Of course, it should be admitted that, in 1646, the following phrase was added to statement on baptism: "and after to partake of the Lords fupper" (1646 *Confession*, XXXIX). The point still stands that the original *Confession* allowed for the potential of an open communion church to sign in good faith, and, even in the revision, the framers did not wish to use the more pointed appendix by Cox.

95. 1644 *Confession*, XXXIII.

96. For more information on the 1644 *Confession*, see McGlothlin, "Sources of the First Calvinistic Baptist Confession of Faith," 502–5; Nelson, "Reflecting on Baptist Origins," 33–46; Stassen, "Anabaptist Influence in the Origin of the Particular Baptists," 322–48; and White, "Doctrine of the Church," 575–82.

97. Samuel Waldron has shown that the 1677 *Confession* tends to follow the *Savoy Declaration* more closely than the *Westminster*, in those places in which the two differ (Waldron, *A Modern Exposition of the 1689 Baptist Confession of Faith*, 425–432; cf. Renihan, "Practical Ecclesiology," 35). The lines of influence, then, flow from *Westminster* to *Savoy* to the 1677 *Confession*, rather than from *Westminster* to *Savoy* and the 1677 *Confession* independently.

That it is evidence of a catholic spirit rather than a defensive maneuver meant to keep persecution to a minimum is seen in the reissue of the *Confession* in 1689 and 1699. While Baptist integration into society would take many years, official persecution was over by then. Reissuing the document would not have lessened persecution, but it would have shown the wider Reformed Christian world that the Baptists desired a place at their table.

98. Renihan, "Practical Ecclesiology," 37–38.

the 1677 *Confession* may more readily be seen as a catholic doorway into other traditions, albeit one limited to the Reformed community.[99]

That this was indeed intentional is stated clearly in the preface to the work. In it, the authors of the *Confession* reveal that they sought to "fix on ſuch a method as might be moſt comprehenſive of thoſe things we deſigned to explain our ſenſe, and belief of." They then say that they found no defect in "that fixed on by the aſſembly [Westminster], and after them by thoſe of the Congregational way [Savoy]." They go on to describe their reasoning for adopting the *Westminster Confession* and *Savoy Declaration* so closely, writing:

> We did readily conclude it beſt to retain the ſame *order* in our preſent confeſſion: and alſo, when we obſerved that thoſe laſt mentioned, did in their confeſſion (for reaſons which ſeemed of weight both to themſelves and others) chooſe not only to expreſs their mind in words concurrent with the former in ſenſe, concerning all thoſe articles wherein they were agreed, but alſo for the moſt part without any variation of the terms we did in like manner conclude it beſt to follow their example in making uſe of the very ſame words with them both, in theſe articles (which are very many) wherein our faith and doctrine are the ſame with theirs, and this we did, the more abundantly, to manifeſt our conſent with both, in all the fundamental articles of the Chriſtian Religion.[100]

The last phrase is key: by issuing what is, essentially, a Baptist version of *Westminster* and *Savoy*, the Particular Baptists wanted to convey their desire for inclusion in the broader Reformed world.

That is not all, however. The preface goes on to show a global and historical catholic spirit. It states that they want to show that they are in agreement:

> alſo with many others, whoſe orthodox confeſſions have been publiſhed to the world; on the behalf of the Proteſtants in divers Nations and Cities: and alſo to convince all, that we have no itch to clogge Religion with new words, but do readily acquieſce in that form of ſound words, which hath been, in conſent with the holy Scriptures, uſed by others before us; hereby declaring,

---

99. The same could be said of Jessey, Bunyan, and Broadmead, but the point still stands that these examples all sought to engage with and embrace a broader spectrum of Christians than those within the Particular Baptist tradition. They represent, therefore, a type of the catholicity later practiced by Ryland, though he expanded his sympathies further than any of the examples of this chapter. The difference between them is one of degree and not of kind.

100. "To the Judicious and Impartial Reader," 1677 *Confession*, 4.

before God, Angels, & Men, our hearty agreement with them, in that wholefome Proteftant Doctrine, which with fo clear evidence of Scriptures they have afferted: fome things indeed, are in fome places added, fome terms omitted, and fome few changed, but thefe alterations are of that nature, as that we need not doubt any charge, or fufpition of unfoundnefs in the faith, from any of our brethren upon the account of them.[101]

They self-consciously follow in the footsteps of those who went before them to show continuity with the British Reformed community, the global Protestant community, and the historic orthodox community.[102] Far from taking a stand to make themselves distinct, the framers of the 1677 *Confession* intentionally copied those who went before as a means of showing their solidarity with evangelical doctrine. While they wanted to defend themselves from false accusations, they also wanted, in all humility, to promote the peace and prosperity of the whole church. They write:

> There is one thing more which we fincerely profeffe, and earneftly defire credence in, *viz.*, That contention is moft remote from our defign in all that we have done in this matter: and we hope that the liberty of an ingenuous unfolding our principles, and opening our hearts unto our Brethren, with the Scripture grounds on which our faith and practice leanes, will by none of them be either denyed to us, or taken ill from us. Our whole defign is accomplifhed, if we may obtain that Juftice, as to be meafured in our principles, and practice, and the judgement of both by others, according to what we have now publifhed; which the Lord (whofe eyes are as a flame of fire) knoweth to be the doctrine, which with our hearts we moft firmly believe, and fincerely indeavor to conform our lives to. And oh that other contentions being laid afleep, the only care and contention of all upon whom the name of our bleffed Redeemer is called, might for the future be, to walk humbly with their God, in the exercife of all Love and Meeknefs toward each other, to perfect holynefs in the fear

---

101. "To the Judicious and Impartial Reader," 1677 *Confession*, 3–5.

102. See the discussion in Renihan, "Practical Ecclesiology," 37–38. Even in those areas in which they diverge from the path trod by the Presbyterians and Congregationalists, they are careful to explain that this divergence is not meant as an offense. Indeed, their hope seems to have been merely to do their brethren the courtesy of explaining their sentiments: "In thofe things wherein we differ from others, we have expreffed our felves with all candor and plainnefs, that none might entertain jealoufy of aught fecretly lodged in our breafts, that we would not the world fhould be acquainted with; yet we hope we have alfo obferved thofe rules of modefty, and humility, as will render our freedom in this refpect inoffenfive, even to thofe whofe fentiments are different from ours" ("To the Judicious and Impartial Reader," 1677 *Confession*, 5).

of the Lord, each one endeavoring to have his converſation ſuch as becometh the Goſpel; and alſo ſuitable to his place and capacity vigorouſly to promote in others the practice of true Religion and undefiled in the ſight of God and our Father. And that in this backſliding day, we might not ſpend our breath in fruitleſs complaints of the evils of others; but may every one begin at home, to reform in the firſt place our own hearts, and wayes; and then to quicken all that we may have influence upon, to the ſame work, that if the will of God were ſo, none might deceive themſelves by reſting in, and truſting to, a form of Godlineſs, without the power of it, and inward experience of the efficacy of thoſe truths that are profeſſed by them.[103]

The document thus presented is a document of peace.

Not only did the framers of the 1677 *Confession* seek a catholic outlook with regard to those outside of the Particular Baptist tradition, they also sought to foster a catholic spirit within it. While all the Particular Baptists could come to a general agreement as to the doctrines of original sin, election, and atonement, they could not do the same with regard to the proper recipients of the Lord's supper or the necessity of baptism prior to church membership. On both counts, the *Confession* is silent. The Appendix to the *Second London Confession* explains this silence:

> We are not inſenſible that as to the order of God's houſe, and entire communion therein there are ſome things wherein we (as well as others) are not at a full accord among our ſelves, as for inſtance; the known principle, and ſtate of the conſciences of diverſe of us, that have agreed in this Confeſſion is ſuch; that we cannot hold Church-communion, with any other than Baptized-believers, and Churches conſtituted of ſuch; yet ſome others of us have a greater liberty and freedom in our ſpirits that way; and therefore we have purpoſely omitted the mention of things of that nature, that we might concurre, in giving this evidence of our agreement, both among ourſelves, and with other good Chriſtians, in thoſe important articles of the Chriſtian Religion, mainly inſiſted on by us.[104]

For a document that is long on theological distinctives, the 1677 *Confession* is decidedly catholic in motivation and spirit. This is not to say that the framers would have agreed with Jessey, Bunyan, or Broadmead. Many

---

103. "To the Judicious and Impartial Reader," 1677 *Confession*, 6–8.

104. Anonymous, "Appendix," 137–38; cf. Renihan, "Practical Ecclesiology," 93. Renihan concurs that this silence was intentional, in order to "comprehend churches of both kinds" (Renihan, "Practical Ecclesiology," 93).

of them would not. Rather, it is to say that there was a catholic impulse that compelled them toward inclusion and concord.

Conclusion

This chapter demonstrated that Ryland's catholic pursuit of visible unity in Christ and in intimate fellowship expressed in life and service together, while not widespread in previous eras, was found in some important people and institutions, showing the context from which Ryland's catholicity arrived. For this chapter, it is important to note two things, however. First, the majority of Baptists, Particular or otherwise, held closed communion views in the seventeenth and eighteenth centuries.[105] The present work does not call that into question. It merely wants to add needed nuance. Second, just to reiterate, closed communion does not necessarily entail a non-catholic view of other traditions. However, open communionism is naturally related to a generally catholic view of others. For this reason, this chapter has focused on open communion Baptists as examples of catholicity prior to John Ryland.

With those caveats in place, the purpose of this chapter has been to show that, though they were in the minority, open communion Baptists were a noticeable minority in early Baptist history. While many Baptists responded to the animosity of the surrounding society by seeking more fervently after a "pure" church order, the minority whose catholic impulse drove them to seek and affirm fellowship with non-Baptists is noteworthy. From the early JLJ church, through to the influential John Bunyan, the regionally-significant Broadmead church, and the important 1644 and 1677 *Confessions*, there has been an openness to those who disagree and even oppose Baptist theology and practice. It is expressed in different ways and with varying emphases, but it is present and consistent. The catholic practice of John Ryland, therefore, was not unprecedented, as he stood in a narrow yet lengthy stream of catholicity.[106] Moreover, as will be shown in the next chapter, while Ryland followed in the footsteps of the Reformed catholicity of his forebears, he went beyond those bounds in seeking and accepting fellowship and partnership with Arminians, Anglicans, the Orthodox, and others.

105. Smith, "Preparation as a Discipline of Devotion in Eighteenth-Century England," 38.

106. Cf. Crocker, "Life and Legacy," 332, who states that the practice of Ryland was "a return, under new social contexts and in fresh manifestations, to the historic and modest catholicity present amongst the Protestant world, English Reformers and Dissenters in previous centuries before greater sectarianism and isolationism developed amongst many Baptists in the early seventeenth century and contributed to their decline."

4

Catholicity in Action

THE WORKING DEFINITION OF Ryland's catholicity, as stated in chapter 1, is that it is visible unity in Christ and in intimate fellowship that is expressed in life and service together for Christ. His catholicity exhibits an openness of welcome and cooperation, and it is a unity *expressed*, rather than merely stated. When he says that "we ought to take pleasure in the communion of faith,"[1] he means it not merely theoretically but practically. According to Ryland, Christian love "should extend to all who are of 'the true circumcision, who worship God in the Spirit, rejoice in Christ Jesus, and have no confidence in the flesh.'"[2] In the same work, he goes on immediately to call

---

1. Ryland, "Communion of Saints," *Pastoral Memorials*, 2:280. As shown in the first chapter, he makes it clear that he is pleading for the peculiar love between Christians rather than mere general love for all humanity.

2. Ryland, "Mutual Love a Mark of Christ's Disciples," *Pastoral Memorials*, 1:330. Note the demonstrative verbs in Ryland's exhortation: "It is not founded on expectation of temporal advantage, personal benefit, or party connexion; but on that relation to Christ, which is manifested by faith, works by love, and produces studious conformity to him. It extends to all such, as far as we are convinced they are of this description, whether they follow with us or not, or are of our society, denomination, or country; notwithstanding difference of sentiment on other subjects or even on the inferior parts of religion" (330). Ryland gives similar counsel to Carapiet Chater Aratoon (spelled Carapeit Chater Aratoon in the published letter) in India, advising him as to the relational dynamics between credobaptists and paedobaptists, "I believe these are very good young men, tho they differ from us as to Baptism, thinking that sprinkling is sufficient, instead of immersion, and supposing it right to baptize infants; yet this is almost the only thing in which they do not agree with us. We must act up to our own light, and try to keep the ordinances pure as they were first delivered. But we must love all who love our Lord Jesus Christ in sincerity, whether they follow with us or not. So I trust I do; and I do not question but you also are likeminded. At present we know but

for a demonstration of this love, writing of the "ways in which we should discover this love to the true disciples of Christ."[3] One of these ways demonstrates the action-oriented nature of Ryland's catholicity: "Show that you value their company. Let such be your chosen associates. All cannot, in this world, enjoy the society of many; but show you do not despise any, with whom you may reasonably expect to live for ever."[4]

For Ryland, the pursuit of catholicity means sharing in the spiritual life of other Christians and, as far as possible, striving toward a single goal together, which means that one should be able to discern it in concrete actions. His catholicity is clearly seen, therefore, in the activities it produced in his life. This chapter will examine several areas in which Ryland's catholicity is demonstrated in concrete actions in which he endeavors to "take pleasure in the communion of faith" with others. The chapter will, thus, look into his friendships with Christians from traditions other than his own, his ministerial cooperation with those outside his tradition, and his willingness to overlook significant differences in the name of Christian unity. Because it is the burden of this chapter to examine the broadness of Ryland's catholicity, it is necessary to present briefly the people with whom Ryland corresponded as well as their theological commitments when they differ from Ryland. This method was chosen so as to provide an orderly and expedient way of examining a large amount of information.

This chapter may also be seen as a test of the definition of catholicity found in the opening chapter. It will test whether the definition itself is correct, whether or not it is borne out in Ryland's practice, and whether there are limits to his catholicity.

Catholic Friendships

It is no new insight to recognize Ryland's broad friendships with and respect from those outside of his tradition. Such notices began with the funeral sermon given by Robert Hall Jr., in which he says of Ryland's strict Calvinist theology did not preclude him from "extend[ing] his affection to all who bore the image of Christ."[5] This is picked up soon after by Ryland's son, Jonathan Edwards Ryland, in the memoir he wrote for his father. The younger Ryland writes that "in reference to his fellow christians, he regarded the magnitude far more than the number of points of agreement; in

---

in part, and understand but in part" (Ryland, "Letter from Dr. John Ryland," 221–22).

3. Ryland, "Mutual Love a Mark of Christ's Disciples," *Pastoral Memorials*, 1:330.
4. Ryland, "Mutual Love a Mark of Christ's Disciples," *Pastoral Memorials*, 1:331.
5. Hall, "Sermon Occasioned by the Death of Ryland," *Works of Hall*, 1:217.

proportion as he saw the great essentials of religion pervading and moulding the character, his feelings of attachment were elicited and confirmed, whatever difference might exist on subordinate topics."[6] These sentiments, according to J. E. Ryland, were "gratified . . . by maintaining an extensive correspondence with ministers of various denominations,"[7] among whom he names "[Samuel] Hopkins, [Stephen] West, [Levi] Hart, and [Timothy] Dwight."[8] Later remembrances of Ryland include his catholic correspondence as a chief facet.[9]

Unfortunately, the catholicity of Ryland's correspondence remains often asserted and seldom studied. Even if Ryland's correspondents are named, little has been done to reveal the catholic content of the correspondence. Much work remains in this regard.[10] The section of this chapter that focuses on his correspondence will attempt both to supply that need and establish one of the central contentions of this work, which is that Ryland's catholicity may be discerned through his enjoyment of Christian fellowship with a broad theological and ecclesiastical base of correspondents, partners, and friends.

The way that this section will proceed is first by examining some of the commonalities between many of Ryland's correspondents. Many of those to whom Ryland wrote were adherents of the theology of the elder Jonathan

---

6. J. E. Ryland, "Memoir," *Pastoral Memorials*, 2:45. As will be shown in the following chapter, "character" is an important aspect of Ryland's catholicity, as it speaks to the role that experiential religion plays in his thought.

7. J. E. Ryland, "Memoir," *Pastoral Memorials*, 2:48.

8. J. E. Ryland, "Memoir," *Pastoral Memorials*, 2:49.

9. See the entries for Ryland in the following: Anonymous, "Ryland, John, D.D.," 1018; and Courtney, "Ryland, John," 50:56. The former entry is curious, however, as it states that in his correspondence with Americans Ryland frequently discussed "political and ecclesiastical principles" (Anonymous, "John Ryland, D.D.," 1018). Ryland's extant correspondence, with a couple of notable exceptions that will be discussed below, shows little discussion of either politics or ecclesiastical concerns, aside from giving his American friends data regarding the state of religion in England (see Ryland, "Letter to Samuel Miller," November 25, 1800; and Ryland, "Letter to Unknown Recipient," February 26, 1806) and briefly lamenting the tensions between the two countries (see Ryland, "Letter to Stephen West," March 31, 1814, 179; and Ryland, "Letter to Stephen West," March 27, 1815, 182). It is possible, of course, that the author had access to letters from Ryland that are no longer available. However, even acknowledging that much of Ryland's correspondence has been lost, it is somewhat unlikely that Ryland, who himself said that he does not like to participate in political matters (see Ryland, "Letter to William Wilberforce," March 26, 1821) and who did not make ecclesiastical principles his chief preoccupation, would frequently discuss those issues.

10. Michael A. G. Haykin has done helpful work in remedying this by providing an examination into some of the theological underpinnings of Ryland's catholic friendships (Haykin, "Sum of All Good," 343–48).

Edwards. It will be helpful, therefore, to investigate briefly Ryland's affinity for Edwards and Edwardsean theology. This section will then unfold on a person-by-person basis, providing brief biographical information about Ryland's correspondents and noting particularly their theological differences from Ryland. It will also note how Ryland addresses and interacts with them, showing how he sees each one, despite important differences, as a fellow Christian.

An unfortunate limitation is placed on this investigation by the loss of many of Ryland's letters.[11] It is known, for example, that Ryland wrote much to Andrew Fuller,[12] but few of those letters still survive. The same is true of Ryland's side of the correspondence with John Newton; Newton's letters survive, but Ryland's do not. There is, however, much that is left, including many letters written to fellow Baptists John Sutcliff, John Saffery, Andrew Fuller, and Joseph Tyso, as well as those addressed to non-Baptists like Jonathan Edwards Jr., Samuel Miller, Levi Hart, Stephen West, and William Wilberforce. Because the focus of this present work is on Ryland's interactions with those outside of his tradition, this section will concentrate on the latter group rather than the former.

Jonathan Edwards and Edwardseanism

Many of Ryland's correspondents were ardent followers of Jonathan Edwards (1703–1758), pastor of the Congregational church in New Haven.[13] Ryland was introduced to the works of Edwards by John Erskine, the Scottish minister.[14] Ryland became an unashamed Edwardsean and displayed

11. The causes of the losses are no doubt varied: over the years, fire, flood, forgetfulness, and neglect would have consumed many important letters. It is even possible that Ryland himself was a cause of the loss. He instructs his family to dispose of his diaries, hymns, and poems after his death (Ryland, "Autograph Reminiscences," 2), and it is reasonable to assume that he gave similar instructions with regard to personal letters. It is known that he gave such instructions to John Newton, for Newton writes to Ryland in 1774, "I burnt your letter this time as you desird" (John Newton, "Letter to John Ryland," January 22, 1774; cf. Grant Gordon, *Wise Counsel*, 47). Fortunately for later researchers, though not necessarily for Ryland, not everyone obeyed Ryland's instructions, as a letter to John Saffery remains that contains the injunction, "Of course you will keep this to yourself. You had better burn it" (Ryland, "Letter to John Saffery," May 29, 1815).

12. Ryland, *Work of Faith*, vi–vii.

13. For more information on Edwards, see Marsden, *Jonathan Edwards: A Life*; McDermott and McClymond, *Theology of Jonathan Edwards*; and Kling and Sweeney, *Jonathan Edwards at Home and Abroad*.

14. Erskine (1721–1803) was a minister of the Church of Scotland and is another example of Ryland's catholicity. Jonathan Yeager has done significant work in uncovering the relationship between the Rylands (J. C. Ryland and John Ryland Jr.) and

a profound appreciation of, knowledge of, and dependence on the works of Edwards. He named his second son "Jonathan Edwards Ryland" (1798–1866),[15] and he wrote on the inside cover of his copy of *The Life of the Late Reverend, Learned and Pious Mr. Jonathan Edwards* that Edwards was "the greatest, wisest, humblest and holyest of uninspired Men!"[16] One of ways in which Edwards exercised a formative theological influence on Ryland is seen in his understanding of the human will.[17] According to Edwards, there are two aspects of human ability: natural ability and moral ability. Distinguishing between these two is key for Edwards and, following him, Ryland. Edwards writes:

> We are faid to be *naturally* unable to do a thing, when we can't do it if we will, becaufe what is moft commonly called *Nature* don't allow of it, or becaufe of fome impeding Defect or Obftacle that is extrinfic to the Will; either in the Faculty of Underftanding, Conftitution of Body, or external Objects. *Moral* Inability confifts not in any of thefe things; but either in the Want of Inclination; or the ftrength of a contrary Inclination; or the want of fufficient Motives in View, to induce and excite the Act of the Will, or the Strength of apparent Motives to the contrary.[18]

Erskine, which largely centered around books and Edwardsean admiration. See Yeager, *Enlightened Evangelicalism*, 165–98; Yeager, *Jonathan Edwards and Transatlantic Print Culture*, 121–32; Yeager, "Letters of John Erskine to the Rylands," 183–95; and Yeager, "Microcosm of the Community of the Saints," 231–54.

15. He actually had two sons named Jonathan Edwards Ryland. The first was born December 9, 1795 and died after only a few days (Ryland, *England and Wales, Non-Conformist and Non-Parochial Registers, 1567-1970*, 29; cf. Ryland, "Text Book," December 6, 1795).

16. Edwards, *Life of the Late Reverend, Learned and Pious Mr. Jonathan Edwards*, copy held by Bristol Baptist College Archives. Ryland also writes to Joseph Kinghorn, "Were I forced to part with all mere human compositions but three, Edwards's 'Life of Brainerd,' his 'Treatise on Religious Affections,' and Bellamy's 'True Religion Delineated' . . . would be the last I should let go" (Ryland, "Letter to Joseph Kinghorn," undated, post-June 1790, 184). After the death of Andrew Fuller, Ryland feared that attacks would be increased on "American Divinity," for which Ryland was ready, saying, "Be it therefore known unto all men, that if I die soon, I shall not die repenting that I did not preach more of Sandeman or Cadworth's Gospel, but that I did not insist more [word missing] on those very things which I and my brethren have been reviled for believing" (Ryland, "Letter to John Saffery," May 29, 1815).

17. Ryland's agreement with Edwards stretches well beyond how he understood the will. Griffith shows that, even when Ryland does not quote Edwards directly, Ryland's thinking remains saturated with Edwards (Griffith, "Pure and Undefiled Religion," 90–91). However, it was Edwards's explanation of human ability and the will that led Ryland to answer the Modern Question in the affirmative (Ryland, *Serious Remarks*, 1:18–19; 2:18–27).

18. Edwards, *Freedom of Will*, 33–34. Edwards goes on to say that everything

Edwards's central idea is that there is nothing material lacking in human beings that keeps them from obeying God. To use an example, it is not as though God is bidding people to fly without giving them wings. Rather, it is that humans, though having wings, choose not to fly when bidden to do so.

Ryland read *Freedom of the Will* in 1775, and its categories of natural and moral abilities became his own. In his work *Serious Remarks on the Different Representations of Evangelical Doctrine by the Professed Friends of the Gospel*, Ryland produces a chart that shows his reliance on Edwards:[19]

Natural inability arises from some object without the will.	Moral inability consists in the opposition or disinclination of the will itself.
Natural inability is neither praise-worthy nor blame-worthy.	Moral inability is sometimes blameable, and sometimes commendable.
Natural inability is a sufficient excuse, for not doing any thing required.	Moral inability is no excuse at all, for any neglect of duty.

Ryland's understanding of human inability, derived from Edwards, also forms part of the core of his preaching ministry. In one sermon, he says that "the reason why men do not understand the language of Christ, is because their sinful disposition lays them under a moral inability to hearken to his words."[20] In another sermon, on Jer 13:23, Ryland writes that "Nat. Inab^y. [natural inability] equally excludes Virtue and Vice," providing as an example Mary's inability to rescue Jesus by rolling away the stone from His tomb.[21] Moral inability, on the other hand, "always implies Moral Good or Evil, & that in proportion to its Degree: if habitual & total, it implies [the] highest degree of moral Good, or Evil."[22] The inability of humanity to do good is moral, and, therefore, according to Ryland, human beings will be held accountable for their choices of good or evil. This was Edwardsean theology at its core.

---

naturally and physically necessary to perform an act of righteousness is present within even sinful human creatures: "There are Faculties of Mind, and Capacity of Nature, and every Thing else, sufficient" (38). However, the desire to do the thing is lacking: "Nothing is wanting but a Will" (38).

19. Reproduced from Ryland, *Serious Remarks*, 2:19.

20. Ryland, "Depravity the Cause of Spiritual Ignorance," *Pastoral Memorials*, 1:318.

21. Ryland, "Sermon Notes: Jeremiah 13:23," *Original Manuscript Sermons: Old Testament, Vol. II*. A word about Ryland's sermon notes will be helpful here. Ryland wrote his sermons in tiny script on small pieces of paper that could be wrapped around the pages of his Bible. Hundreds of these notes remain, most of which are held in the Bristol Baptist College Archives.

22. Ryland, "Sermon Notes: Jeremiah 13:23," *Original Manuscript Sermons: Old Testament, Vol. II*.

Ryland's indebtedness to Edwards was profound and unshakable. Preaching the funeral sermon for his friend Andrew Fuller, Ryland looks back on his life of commitment to Edwardseanism, and he is unmoved by criticisms that he promoted Edwards too much, saying, "but if I knew I should be with Sutcliff and Fuller to-morrow, instead of regretting that I had endeavoured to promote that religion delineated by Jonathan Edwards, in his Treatise on *Religious Affections*, and in his *Life of David Brainerd*, I would recommend his writings, and Dr. Bellamy's, with Dr. Whitaker's *Two Sermons on Reconciliation*, with the last effort I could make to guide a pen."[23]

Ryland's appreciation for the theology of Jonathan Edwards Sr. is illustrative of his catholicity, for, though Edwards was no Baptist, this proved no impediment to Ryland's valuing and promotion of Edwards. However, it was Ryland's appreciation of Edwards's followers that shows the depth of his catholicity with regard to the Edwardseans.

American Divinity

As can be seen by the quotation above regarding Bellamy and Whitaker, the same affection which Ryland had for Edwards extended also to those who held to Edwards's theology. These people came to be known as Edwardseans, and their theology was given the names American Divinity and New England Theology.[24] This movement was carried on by such men as

---

23. Ryland, *Indwelling and Righteousness of Christ*, 47. He also quotes Fuller's response to such criticism, given in the final letter that Fuller wrote to Ryland: "We have some, who have been giving out of late, that 'If Sutcliff and some others had preached more of Christ, and less of Jonathan Edwards, they would have been more useful.' If those who talk thus, preached Christ half as much as Jonathan Edwards did, and were half as useful as he was, their usefulness would be double what it is" (Andrew Fuller, "Letter to John Ryland," April 28, 1815, cited in Ryland, *Indwelling and Righteousness of Christ*, 34). This shows a little of Fuller's own catholicity. Like Ryland, he embraced American divinity, despite the fact that most of them were not Baptist. He also could speak well of Anglicans like John Newton, whom Fuller, like Ryland, called "Father Newton" (Fuller, "Final Consummation of All Things," 843). Unlike Ryland, however, Fuller did not hold to open communion, nor was he known for his broadmindedness. Indeed, when presented with the opportunity to partner with General Baptists in mission work, Fuller refused (Peggs, *History of the General Baptist Mission*, 148). For more on Fuller's catholicity, see Graham, "Union of Sentiments in Apostolical Doctrines," 105–22.

24. Ryland knew it by the name "American Divinity." He uses that term, or something like it, several times. See Ryland, "Letter to Stephen West," September 12, 1815, 185. It later became known as "New England theology." For more on New England theology, see Foster, *Genetic History of the New England Theology*; Sweeney and Guelzo, *New England Theology: From Jonathan Edwards to Edwards Amasa Park*; and Crisp and Sweeney, *After Jonathan Edwards: The Courses of the New England Theology*.

Jonathan Edwards Jr., Joseph Bellamy, Samuel Hopkins, and Stephen West, all of whom were correspondents of Ryland. The New England theologians were largely Calvinistic in their theological outlook, though with particular emphases that set them apart and, according to some, led them to diverge from Calvinistic orthodoxy.[25] Among the more notable contributions of the New England theologians was their construal of the doctrine of disinterested love. This doctrine taught, in its basic form, that true Christian love should reject self-interest.[26] Some of the American Edwardseans took this idea to an extreme, rejecting all self-regard as inconsistent with Christian love.[27] One of their conclusions stemming from this was the assertion that a person must be willing to be damned in order to be saved; that is, they must love God with a pure love that has no regard for self, even if that means damnation. The logic runs thus: since love has no regard for self, then whether one is damned or saved should have no bearing on one's love for God.[28] This was a controversial doctrine, and many wrote against it;[29] as will be shown below, even Ryland questions it in private correspondence with

---

25. See Helm, "Jonathan Edwards and the Parting of the Ways?" 42–60; Helm, "Different Kind of Calvinism?" 91–104; Helm, "Turretin and Edwards Once More," 286–96; Lucas, "He Cuts Up Edwardsism by the Roots," 200–214; Muller, "Jonathan Edwards and the Absence of Free Choice," 3–22; Muller, "Jonathan Edwards and Francis Turretin," 266–85.

26. Such an idea was not new to the Edwardseans. It is found, for example, in scripture passages like Phil 2:3–4 and in the devotional work of the French Protestant Pierre Jurieu, who writes, "Kill this Self-Intereſt, and this Self-Love which oppoſe the Reigning of my Love. This Self-Intereſt ought to be regulated, with reſpect to our Neighbour, and with reſpect to God. With reſpect to our Neighbour, for that our Love to our Neighbour may be pure, it ought to be difintereſted" (Jurieu, *Practice of Devotion*, 180). Jurieu continues, saying that it is to God "peculiarly we ought to Sacrifice all our Self-Intereſt" (180). It was no innovation, then, in substance but, rather, in extent of application.

27. Self-regard, or self-love, as Hopkins calls it, "is, in its whole nature, and in every degree of it, enmity against God. It is not subject to the law of God, nor indeed can be; and is the only affection that can oppose it. It cannot be reconciled to any of God's conduct, rightly understood; but is in its very nature rebellion against it" (Hopkins, *Nature of True Holiness*, 28–29). Spring says something similar: "all sin consists in self-love" (Spring, *Moral Disquisitions*, 15).

28. For more on the doctrine of disinterested love (or disinterested benevolence), see Hopkins, *Dialogue between a Calvinist and a Semi-Calvinist*, 141–67. On the differences between Hopkins's understanding of disinterested love and that of Edwards Sr., see Post, "Disinterested Benevolence," 356–68.

29. See Ely, *Contrast Between Calvinism and Hopkinsianism* 278–80. Ely's work places the words of Hopkins (and his fellow Edwardseans) in one table and the words of Calvin and Calvinists in the facing table, showing what he considers to be the stark differences between the two.

the American theologians.[30] It did not, however, prove to be an impediment to fellowship and partnership.

Jonathan Edwards Jr.

Jonathan Edwards Jr. was the son of the previously mentioned pastor and writer, Jonathan Edwards.[31] He was born in Northampton, Massachusetts Bay, on May 26, 1745 and was educated under his father as well as Samuel Hopkins and Joseph Bellamy. He was a tutor at Princeton (1767–1769), and pastor in New Haven (1769–1795) and Colebrook, Connecticut (1795–1799), before moving to Schenectady, New York, to serve as President of Union College (1799–1801). He died on August 1, 1801.

Edwards Jr. was a leading light of American Divinity. While in agreement with its unique emphases, he also added his own stamp to the movement in the form of his doctrine of the atonement. In three sermons given on the subject in 1785, Edwards Jr. expounds on his understanding of the atonement, writing:

> The atonement is the fubftitute for the punifhment threatened in the law; and was defigned to anfwer the fame ends of fupporting the authority of the law, the dignity of the divine moral government, and the confiftency of the divine conduct in legiflation and execution. By the atonement it appears that God is determined that his law fhall be fupported; that it fhall not be defpifed or tranfgreffed with impunity; and that it is an evil and a bitter thing to fin againft God.[32]

This understanding of atonement came to be known as the moral government theory and is seen at least as an innovation within the Edwardsean

---

30. Ryland writes to Samuel Hopkins, "What call have they to be willing to be damned, when God assures them Christ is able & willing to save them? and can be glorify'd more in their Salv[ation] than in their Damnation? It also seems strange that a Man sh[ould] from Love to God, be willing for ever to hate God, & blaspheme him" (Weaver and Haykin, "Significant Letter from John Ryland to Samuel Hopkins," 30). He also writes to Levi Hart on the possibility of a believer having no assurance of their salvation, saying, "Instead of leading a man to speculate on the probability of his future Regeneration, would it not be more to the point, and more agreeable to scripture to insist on the Invitations of the Gospel, and urge an immediate Applicat^n. to X^t.?" (Ryland, "Letter to Levi Hart," August 10, 1805).

31. For more on Jonathan Edwards Jr., see Ferm, *Jonathan Edwards, The Younger, 1745–1801*.

32. Edwards, *Necessity of the Atonement*, 14. For more on New England theologians, Edwards, and the atonement, see Park, "Introductory Essay," vii–lxxx, and Crisp, "Moral Government of God," 78–90.

tradition if not a departure from Calvinistic orthodoxy.[33] Edwards Jr., then, was not only outside of Ryland's ecclesiastical tradition, being a Congregationalist, he (and his friends in America) were pushing the boundaries of the broad Calvinistic heritage to which Ryland adhered.

Ryland was introduced to Edwards Jr. in a letter by John Erskine. Ryland and Edwards Jr. began corresponding in 1785[34] and continued to do so until the death of Edwards Jr. in 1801. Because of his great love and admiration for Jonathan Edwards Sr., Ryland was quite excited about the prospect of a friendship with the son. Ryland writes, "Your first letter was so unexpected, tho so extremely welcome, that it quite transported me. I sat down immediately, & wrote just as they crowded in a multitude of questions, some of wch. w^d. appear too minute to be sent so far. You w^d. however attribute it in good measure to my most sincere respect for your beloved Father, that evry thing relative to him and his family seem'd a matter of importance."[35] He then proceeds to ask personal questions about the Edwards family and shares intimate details of his own family situation, which was at that time full of mourning over the death of his first wife, Elizabeth. Ryland readily shares his feelings with Edwards Jr., beseeching him, after divulging his pain and struggles at the loss of his wife, "Do pray for me! I can pray but seldom with a degree of proper feeling, but if it will induce you to remember one who so much needs your prayrs, I can truly say, I do at many times mention you by name in private among others whom I pray and hope the Lord will blefs greatly."[36]

Not everything in the letter is of a personal nature, however, nor is it absent of confrontation or disagreement. Ryland is not afraid to object to some aspects of American Divinity, writing that "men on your side of the water" have excluded the idea that God is a creditor and human beings debtors and that the Americans have largely ignored those scriptures which speak to the idea.[37] Ryland demonstrates a detailed grasp of the various

33. Crisp, "Moral Government of God," 78–90.

34. Edwards wrote to Ryland first, and his introductory letter is dated May 28, 1785 (Edwards, "Letter to John Ryland," May 28, 1785). A note in Ryland's hand mentions that the letter was not received until nearly a year later on April 11, 1786.

35. Ryland, "Letter to Jonathan Edwards Jr.," June 29, 1787.

36. Ryland, "Letter to Jonathan Edwards Jr.," June 29, 1787. After inquiring of the children of Edwards Jr., Ryland writes, hopefully, "I wifh that there may be a Jonathan Edwards the 3^d for my poor motherlefs boy to correspond with." Ryland's wish did not come to pass, as Edwards Jr. named his only son "Jonathan Walter Edwards." It is not known if he and Jonathan Edwards Ryland ever corresponded.

37. Ryland, "Letter to Jonathan Edwards Jr.," June 29, 1787. This is related to Edwards's understanding of the moral government theory of the atonement, but Ryland sees it as opening the door to Arminianism; or, at least, he fears that Bellamy in this

writers of the American Divinity, remarking upon Joseph Bellamy's *True Religion Delineated*,[38] recent sermons by John Smalley,[39] and even the work of Edwards Jr. himself.[40] Ryland freely criticizes and raises clear objections to some of the work of Edwards Jr.'s peers, and he is cognizant of the fact that he may offend his new friend, saying, "You see dear Sir I write with great freedom & unreservedneſs, and if you think me wrong in what follows I am persuaded your Candor will excuse me."[41]

A second letter from Ryland to Edwards demonstrates in a different way the honest and agreeable debate that took place between the two men.[42] Ryland had received from Edwards a pamphlet on baptism written by a "Mr. Miller."[43] Ryland offers a detailed answer to the pamphlet, showing that he was not afraid of offending his friend through disagreement.[44] He goes on to implore Edwards to send either some of his father's writing or his own for publication in the new *Biblical Magazine*. He also shares a letter, which Ryland transcribed, from Felix Carey (1786–1822), the son of William Carey,

---

regard is harsher toward Antinomians than he is Arminians. In a section that he subsequently scratched out but which is still legible, Ryland writes, "Some say D^r. B. does not seem to have taken quite equal pains to rectify the Antinomians as the Arminians, they supposed the Arminians in America have been more respectable for Learning & some of them for a measure of piety than those who ran to the other extreme."

38. Ryland writes of objections that some have had in England to the doctrines espoused by Bellamy, such as the death of Christ being sufficient for more than the elect (see Bellamy, *True Religion Delineated*, 346–55).

39. Of these sermons, Ryland writes, "[T]here are somethings in M^r. Smalley's first sermon I can by no means fall in with, at least not without pretty long examination" (Ryland, "Letter to Jonathan Edwards Jr.," June 29, 1787). This demonstrates another important aspect of Ryland's catholic thought and practice: quite often, when he differs from his friends, he admits that he may well be wrong or could undergo a change of sentiment.

40. Ryland does not name the work to which he refers, but it is most likely *The Necessity of Atonement: And the Consistency Between that and Free Grace, in Forgiveness*. It is interesting that, when Ryland offers criticism of this work of Edwards, he does not critique Edwards's moral government theory of the atonement but, rather, focuses on Edwards's contention that the sufferings of Christ do not prove the equity of the law (Ryland, "Letter to Jonathan Edwards Jr.," June 29, 1787). It is interesting because Edwards's doctrine of the atonement was a considerable shift away from the traditional understanding of penal substitutionary atonement, similar to Smalley.

41. Ryland, "Letter to Jonathan Edwards Jr.," June 29, 1787.

42. Ryland, "Letter to Jonathan Edwards Jr.," August 28, 1801. Edwards Jr. died on August 1, 1801, so he never read this final letter from his friend.

43. This is most likely William Miller, who wrote a short book entitled *The Paedobaptist Mode of Administering the Baptismal Ordinance Defended*, which contains the arguments that Ryland answers in his letter.

44. Some aspects of Ryland's response to Edwards found their way into Ryland's book on baptism. See Ryland, *Candid Statement*, 8–9, Ryland, "Notes," v–viii.

respecting the developments of the mission in India. The letter shows an abiding friendship. Ryland refers to his friends in England, especially Andrew Fuller, who was in ill health at the time, as brothers to Edwards.[45]

Ryland's correspondence with Edwards Jr. is a premier example of the catholicity found in his correspondence. It is irenic and a way of sharing fellowship at a long distance, but Ryland was not afraid of disagreement. Disagreement, sometimes involving important theological issues, did nothing to breach their brotherhood.

Jonathan Walter Edwards

Jonathan Walter Edwards was born in New Haven, Connecticut, on January 5, 1772, the only son of Jonathan Edwards Jr. He was educated at Yale, where he graduated in 1789. After graduation, having distinguished himself as a classical scholar,[46] he served as tutor at Yale for two years.[47] Unlike many of Ryland's correspondents, J. W. Edwards was not a minister; his life would ultimately be dedicated to the practice of law. He served as an attorney in Hartford, Connecticut for many years, where "he had a brilliant career as a lawyer ... [and] was esteemed as an eloquent and able advocate, as well as a valuable citizen."[48] He also represented his district in the Connecticut State Legislature on six separate occasions. After many years of health difficulties, which impeded his progress in the law, he died on April 3, 1831 in Hartford.[49]

On the one hand, it would be easy, in light of Ryland's clear love of Jonathan Edwards Sr. and his extended family, to dismiss his correspondence with J. W. Edwards as another instance of him demonstrating that love and admiration, instead of an example of his catholicity.[50] To be sure, the letter

45. Ryland, "Letter to Jonathan Edwards Jr.," August 28, 1801.

46. He was a "Deans Scholar," though he was judged as second best of the class of Deans Scholars, behind Dan Bradley, who later served as a Congregational and then Episcopal minister (Sprague, "Jonathan Edwards, D.D.," 656).

47. Stiles, *Literary Diary of Ezra Stiles*, 478, 536. He became known for the oration he gave on the reception of his MA, in September 1792 (Stiles, *Literary Diary of Ezra Stiles*, 474), in which he "attacked the then existing law of this State, by which the eldest son was entitled to receive a double portion of the estate, upon the death of his father intestate" (Williams, "Edwards, Jonathan W.," 15:Appendix, 26). Such were his oratorical powers that a speech given by such a young man, who was not himself a lawyer, "excited much attention, and at the next session of the General Assembly, (October 1792) the obnoxious law was repealed" (Appendix, 26).

48. Dexter, *Biographical Sketches*, 4:636.

49. Williams, "Jonathan Walter Edwards," 15:Appendix, 27.

50. Indeed, Ryland says to J. W. Edwards, "As long as I live I shall be interested in their welfare [welfare of Edwards's family], as if they were my own near Relations. Such

from Ryland to J. W. Edwards evidences neither the depth of friendship seen in his letters with Jonathan Edwards Jr. nor the abundance of language of Christian fellowship in his letters with others like Stephen West. Moreover, Ryland demonstrates that he knows but little of J. W. Edwards himself, saying, "O my dear Sir I trust his [Jonathan Edwards Jr.] God is your God, and that your life & soul will be devoted to him."[51] However, other tropes in Ryland's correspondence are found in his exchange with J. W. Edwards. For example, they exchanged religious literature, a common occurrence in Ryland's correspondence, with Edwards sending a copy of R. Smith's *Discourse on the Death of Jonathan Edwards Jr.* as well as a volume of the *Connecticut Evangelical Magazine*. Ryland also enlists J. W. Edwards's help in disseminating the work of Edwards's grandfather in England, a regular phenomenon in Ryland's correspondence with Americans. Finally, it is obvious that Ryland sees J. W. Edwards as a part of the broader Edwardsean network in America, as he asks him to pass along greetings to Joseph Strong[52] and tells of a recent introduction via Timothy Dwight[53] to a Professor Hall.[54] This speaks in favor of his catholicity rather than against it, for Ryland is willing to enter into correspondence and even partnership with a man about whom he knows little more than some basic theological commitments.

It is important to realize that it is not as though Ryland was indiscriminate in his dealings with the Edwards family, as though he assumed that grace ran in the blood. In an unpublished musing on the free offer of the gospel found appended to a letter written by Andrew Gifford Sr. (1641–1721), Ryland writes about Pierpont Edwards (1750–1826), whom he says "still remains an infidel," using him as a negative example of one who deserves the gospel equally to an "unconverted Indian."[55] Ryland was, thus, not blind to the faults of the Edwards family. Moreover, J. W. Edwards showed every indication of being a committed Christian, even if Ryland did

---

interest do I naturally feel in consequences of the profit first derived from your Grandfather's writings, and the cord[l] friendship I experienced during a long correspond[ce] with your venerable Father" (Ryland, "Letter to Jonathan Walter Edwards," August 31, 1807).

51. Ryland, "Letter to Jonathan Walter Edwards," August 31, 1807.

52. Ryland, "Letter to Jonathan Walter Edwards," August 31, 1807: "I will thank you to give my best Respects to D^r. Strong, several of whose publications I have read with much pleasure."

53. Three years prior, Ryland had authored, with Andrew Fuller, a "recommendatory address" to Dwight's *The Nature and Danger of Infidel Philosophy*, 3rd ed.

54. Ryland, "Letter to Jonathan Walter Edwards," August 31, 1807. It is not known who "Professor Hall" was. It was, perhaps, Frederick Hall, who was professor of natural philosophy at Middlebury College.

55. Ryland, "On the Free Offer of the Gospel," undated. Ryland refers to him as Pierrepoint Edwards.

not know the specifics of his commitment as he did Edwards Jr. Two separate remembrances of him state his religion clearly. In the first, written while he still lived, it is said that he "appears an uniform and strenuous advocate for the cause of christianity, and a constant and serious attendant on the worship of God."[56] In the latter, written well after his death, Thomas Williams says of him, "As he advanced in life, the religion of the gospel seemed to take a stronger hold of his heart, and it imparted peace and hope to his closing hours."[57] He was a member of the First (Congregational) Church in Hartford, Connecticut, which he joined in August 1810 and from which he was dismissed September 1824,[58] along with his wife and ninety-five others, in order to form the North Church.[59]

Edward Dorr Griffin

Edward Dorr Griffin was born January 6, 1770 in East Haddam, Connecticut. He graduated from Yale College in 1790 and studied theology under Jonathan Edwards Jr.[60] His ministerial career began soon after the completion of his studies. His preaching was attended with tremendous response almost everywhere he went. Griffin was ordained by the Congregational Church in New Hartford, Connecticut, where "revival took place of such power and extent as to shake the town to its centre."[61] In 1801, Griffin was made co-pastor with Alexander M'Whorter of First Presbyterian Church

56. Anonymous, "Life and Character of Dr. Edwards," 1:109. This brief memoir, written anonymously, acknowledges its indebtedness to Ryland in a footnote. The memoir quotes repeatedly from letters Edwards had sent to Ryland, which Ryland had sent to the memoir's author.

57. Williams, "Edwards, Jonathan W.," 15:Appendix 27.

58. First Church in Hartford, *Historical Catalogue of the First Church in Hartford*, 62.

59. The North Church "was made up mostly of members of the First Church, who forsook their old nest in no ill-will and in no contention for principle, but simply and only because the edifice of that church could not accommodate all the people who wished to worship there" (Burton, "North Congregational Church," 1:389).

60. Nash, *Memoir of Griffin*, 11.

61. Nash, *Memoir of Griffin*, 18. Griffin himself described the scene: "This was the ftate of the people when, on a fabbath in the month of November, it was the fovereign pleafure of a moft merciful God very fenfibly to manifeft himfelf in the public affembly. Many abiding impreffions were made on minds feemingly the leaft fufceptible, and on feveral grown old in unbelief. From that memorable day the flame which had been kindling in fecret broke out" (Griffin, "Letter X: Revival of Religion in New-Hartford," 218). And again: "The fcenes which have been opened before us have brought into view what to many is convincing evidence that there is fuch a thing as experimental religion; and that mere outward morality is not the qualification which fits the foul for the enjoyment of God" (Griffin, "Letter XI: Revival of Religion in New-Hartford," 268).

in Newark, New Jersey.[62] His renown in the pulpit was such that he was awarded a DD from Union College in 1808 and was made Professor of Pulpit Eloquence at Andover Theological Seminary in 1809.[63] He would serve there for two years before becoming the first pastor of Park Street Church in Boston, Massachusetts. His time at Park Street would be short-lived, as he resigned that post in 1815. In 1821, he was asked to accept the presidency of Williams College, which he did and in which position he remained until a year before his death, his failing health necessitating a resignation. He died November 8, 1837.

Griffin was an Edwardsean,[64] though some of his theological emphases were more in line with Edwards's successors than Edwards himself. For example, he held to the moral government theory of the atonement as propounded by Edwards Jr.[65] Griffin writes that the "precise and only end" of the atonement was "the support of the law by showing God's determination to execute its penalty on transgressors."[66] Ryland's extant correspondence with Griffin is restricted to two pieces: a letter from Ryland to Griffin, and a copy of portions of Griffin's initial letter to Ryland copied by Ryland into a letter he (Ryland) wrote to John Sutcliff. In that letter, Ryland indicates that he knows little of Griffin, writing, "I have just rec^d. a long Letter from the Rev^d. Edw. D. Griffin of Newark, New Jersey, one of D^r. Edwd's Stud^{ts}. I suppose the same for whom he preached an Ordination Sermon."[67] This

---

62. Nash, *Memoir of Griffin*, 19. His ministry in Newark was also successful, with almost 400 joining the church during that period (23).

63. One memoir of Griffin pictures him in language that, while clearly exaggerating, communicates the impression that he had upon those who heard him: "Standing in the ecclesiastical assembly, like Saul among his brethren, he was head and shoulders above them all" (Waterbury, *Sketches of Eloquent Preachers*, 82). Despite this towering presence, he was an apparently humble man: "He was a very genial man. His warm, affectionate heart entered sympathizingly into the joys or griefs of others; and never was he more in his element than when, surrounded by his ministerial brethren, and discoursing with them on the interests of Zion, he became the radiant centre of the social circle. His colloquial powers were almost unrivalled, yet he had little of that egotism and lecturing style which characterize certain distinguished divines, and which, while it may display their talents, is sometimes tedious and repulsive" (83).

64. In Griffin's introductory letter to Ryland, Griffin writes, "I am decidedly attached to the discriminating doct^s. taught by the N. Eng^d. divines, and I hope I may add to that kind of Religion & preaching that which is denominated Evangelical" (quoted in Ryland, "Letter to John Sutcliff," January 26, 1807).

65. For more information on Griffin's contribution to the New England theology, see Cooley, "New England Theology and the Atonement," 153–62; and Kling, "Edwards in the Second Great Awakening," 130–41.

66. Griffin, *Humble Attempt*, 25.

67. Ryland, "Letter to John Sutcliff," January 26, 1807.

letter is important for understanding Ryland's practice of catholicity, as it shows that he did what he exhorted his hearers to do in being satisfied with the smallest likeness to Christ: "Take Complacency in the image of Chrift where ever it can be difcerned."[68] Griffin was largely unknown to Ryland, but he took solace in Griffin's own statements as to his theological commitments and had been encouraged by reading one of Griffin's sermons.[69] It is a small thing in a relatively short letter, but it tells much of the broad-minded benevolence in Ryland's practice of catholicity.

The letter to Griffin is also worth noting because of an explanation Ryland gives as to why he most likely will not continue correspondence with Griffin. Ryland writes, "My general concern for the Serv^{ts}. of our Lord Jesus Christ, and my peculiarly high regard for your excell^{t}. Tutor, and his venerable Father (ז״ל)[70] renD^{r}. your correspond^{ce}. very acceptable. But the duties of my station are so numerous that I can hardly avail myself of the good advice D^{r}. Edw^{s}. gave to his nephew D^{r}. Dwight in his Charge at his Ord^{n} page 20."[71] In this quote, Ryland declares his Christian love for all who serve the Lord Jesus Christ, and reveals his more particular concern for those of the Edwardsean stripe, but he says that he is unable to keep with the advice Jonathan Edwards Jr. gave to Timothy Dwight at Dwight's ordination, in which Edwards Jr. tells Dwight, "Over and above your preparations for the fabbath, take care to be conftantly increafing your ftock of knowledge, by reading, by reflection, by converfation, and by epiftolary correfpondence on the moft important fubjects, with men of thought and literature. This laft mentioned fource of improvement, though generally neglected, certainly promifes a great increafe of knowledge."[72] Edwards Jr.'s advice is, essentially, correspond with others on important matters and, thus, grow your knowledge and understanding. Ryland, however, says that the demands on his time are so great that, though he might like to do so, he cannot engage

---

68. Ryland, *Dependance of the Whole Law and Prophets*, 41. "Complacency" here refers to the pleasure of civility and friendliness (Johnson, "Complacency," in *A Dictionary of the English Language*, n.p.).

69. It seems as though Griffin had sent Ryland his sermon preached at the General Assembly of the Presbyterian Church on May 23, 1805, which was later published as *The Kingdom of Christ: A Missionary Sermon*. Ryland tells Griffin, "I am much obliged to you for your Mifsionary Sermon on the K^{m}. of Christ" (Ryland, "Letter to Edward Dorr Griffin," May 12, 1807). Ryland was not the only one who appreciated Griffin's missionary sermon. He was remembered for it many years after his death (Waterbury, *Sketches of Eloquent Preachers*, 85).

70. Ryland writes these letters in parentheses. They are an abbreviation of a Hebrew phrase used to honor the dead.

71. Ryland, "Letter to Edward Dorr Griffin," May 12, 1807.

72. Edwards, *Faithful Manifestation of the Truth*, 20–21.

in further exchanges. This is borne out in Ryland's extant correspondence. After this time, there are fewer and fewer letters to those outside of his Particular Baptist circles. His letters after this time often contain a reference to his many duties and include an apology for a short, hasty epistle. This does not speak against his catholicity. Rather, it shows its limits: even the best of intentions to reach across the aisle fail when time constrains a person to look after his nearest relations.

Levi Hart

Levi Hart was born April 10, 1738. He graduated from Yale College in 1760. During his time in college, he underwent a religious conversion.[73] After graduation, he studied theology under Joseph Bellamy,[74] with whom he developed and maintained an abiding friendship until the death of Bellamy in 1790.[75] Hart assumed the pastorate of the Congregational Church in Preston, Connecticut on November 4, 1762, in which position he remained until his death. He "had much to do in originating, sustaining, and directing the Connecticut Missionary Society."[76] He was a member of the Corporation for both Dartmouth College (1784–88) and Yale College (1791–1807), and he received a DD from the College of New Jersey. He died October 27, 1808.

Denominationally, Hart was a Congregationalist; theologically, he was an Edwardsean.[77] He helped to establish "a tradition of New Divinity control over postgraduate theological education which went virtually unchallenged in [Connecticut] until the formation of the Yale Divinity School in 1822."[78]

73. He was not an especially religious young man, but during his second year of college, he "was brought to consider his ways and turn his feet unto God's testimonies" (Sprague, "Levi Hart, D.D.," 590).

74. Sprague, "Levi Hart, D.D.," 590.

75. Hart married one of Bellamy's daughters. Sprague comments on their relationship: "Between Mr. Hart and his father-in-law, there was always the most unreserved and affectionate intercourse. For many years, scarcely a year passed that they did not exchange visits; and Dr. Bellamy rarely failed to pass one or more Sabbaths with Mr. Hart, and besides preaching for him, not unfrequently preached for some of his brethren in the neighbourhood" (Sprague, "Levi Hart, D.D.," 591).

76. Sprague, "Levi Hart, D.D.," 591: "His attendance at the annual meeting of its Trustees was uniform and punctual. But, long before that Society came into existence, he showed himself under the influence of the true missionary spirit."

77. Unfortunately, Hart did not publish much material, and little has been done in terms of academic research into his life and thought.

78. Conforti, "Samuel Hopkins and the New Divinity Movement," 309. Those who remembered his preaching remembered a man who "dwelt much upon the cardinal doctrines of the Gospel" (Sprague, "Levi Hart, D.D.," 591–92).

In this effort, he worked in concert with other New Divinity pastors, such as Joseph Bellamy, John Smalley, and Nathan Strong, as well as New Divinity men in Massachusetts like Nathaniel Emmons, Stephen West, and Ephraim Judson.[79] Hart was a vital part of the continuing growth of Edwardsean theology in New England.[80] He was close friends with and preached the funeral sermon of Samuel Hopkins.[81]

Ryland sees Hart as one of his "most valued correspondents,"[82] a statement that is borne out in the surviving letters from Ryland to Hart. Ryland shares with Hart intimate details of his friendships,[83] family life,[84] and the life of the academies in England.[85] In one letter, Ryland even wrote a mini-biography of himself, conveying information about his children, his work at the Academy, his friends, and his work promoting American

---

79. Conforti, "Samuel Hopkins and the New Divinity Movement," 309.

80. He rejoiced to hear of any report of ministers joining the "Edwardean Scheme against all opposers" (Conforti, "Samuel Hopkins and the New Divinity Movement," 122).

81. Hart, "Discourse . . . at the Funeral of the Rev. Samuel Hopkins," 217–40.

82. Ryland, "Letter to Levi Hart," 1805.

83. Ryland told Hart about Andrew Fuller's son and the trial he was to Fuller, John Sutcliff's late marriage, and Robert Hall's "insanity" (Ryland, "Letter to Levi Hart," August 10, 1805, 6).

84. Of his oldest son, John Tyler, he writes that he is "a decent Lad, but I fear has not internal acquaint^{ce}. with Religion" (Ryland, "Letter to Levi Hart," August 10, 1805, 4). Of his second son, Jonathan Edwards, he writes somewhat more: "I gave him the Name of two of the best of your Countrymen—may the Lord give him a double portion of their spirit, and I shall rejoice unspeakably. He is likely to prove a Scholar" (Ryland, "Letter to Levi Hart," August 10, 1805, 4). His only mention of his other children, all daughters, is somewhat shorter. He writes, "I have three young Daughters" (Ryland, "Letter to Levi Hart," August 10, 1805, 4).

85. He compared the method of the Bristol Baptist Academy with that of "Dodderidge's Academy," saying that it "was differently conducted from ours. Young men had more learning before they were admitted there but too often lefs Religion. For we admit none but Members of Churches, and scarcely ever without having had their Gifts previously tried by the Churches to wch. they belong. Among other Denominations it is more common to send Lads of hopeful parts to Academies, and bring them up for the ministry, in hope that they may be converted" (Ryland, "Letter to Levi Hart," August 10, 1805, 2). This speaks to Ryland's philosophy of ministerial education, which may be summed up in a sentiment that he repeatedly proclaimed: "we do not pretend to make Men Ministers, but to make young Ministers better Scholars" (Ryland, "Sermon Notes: Appeal for the Academy," June 1810, *Original Manuscript Sermons: Old Testament, Vol. II*). He repeats much the same idea two years later in an address to the Stepney Academy: "The London Education Society was not instituted with a design to *make men Ministers*, as some express themselves, who misconceive our object, if they do not wilfully misrepresent it, but to *make* young *Ministers* better *Scholars*" (Ryland, *Advice to Young Ministers*, 17).

Divinity.[86] He greets Hart as a brother, prays for the success of his ministry, and thanks him for his partnership in ministry.[87] However, this closeness and affection did not prevent honest disagreement between the two men. Ryland especially objects to the doctrine of disinterested benevolence mentioned earlier, an idea to which Hart held. Of this idea, Ryland writes, "I do think there is somewhat unscriptural here."[88] He later elucidates his point, "I firmly believe the necessity of div. Infl^{ce}. to bring any Soul to X^t. but this does not seem to me a Truth to be so prominently exhibited to Sinners, previous to the Representation of the Allsufficiency and willingness of Christ to save, as it is inculcated on Believers for their Instruct^n and Humiliation, that they may find they did not come to Christ of their own accord, but under divine drawings."[89] He would prefer that the willingness of Christ to save those who come to Him by faith be proclaimed prior to the explanation of the Calvinistic understanding of the necessity of God's grace in salvation. Ryland's concern, as ever, is pastoral.

That aspect of Ryland's catholicity in which he embraced people as fellow Christians, yet remained unafraid of detailing differences between them is seen clearly in the correspondence with Hart. Ryland writes, "I strongly incline to think that some of our American Brethren err, in their treatm^t. of Souls in such a state [of doubting their salvation]."[90] He then goes on to detail disagreements with Samuel Hopkins[91] and Jonathan Edwards Jr.[92] In

---

86. Ryland, "Letter to Levi Hart," August 10, 1805, 1–2. At the end of this letter, in which Ryland had shared so much personal information, he offered something like an apology for it: "I have filled the paper wth. things I did not design to mention when I began, but from the hint at the close of your letter I concluded it w^d. not be disagreeable, and thus I fell into a sort of chat about persons and things that we might have been likely to have mentioned on an interview" (7).

87. He closed one letter to Hart with these words: "We are much obliged to you and your Brethren for your kind Afsist^{ce}. and prayrs" (Ryland, "Letter to Levi Hart," January 18, 1808). It is not known what "kind assistance" Hart provided, but it is likely to do with mission work.

88. Ryland, "Letter to Levi Hart," August 10, 1805, 9. Ryland does not object to disinterested love in general but, rather, to the American construal of it mentioned above. Ryland wholeheartedly held to disinterested benevolence defined as a selfless love for and service toward others (Ryland, *Dependance of the Whole Law*, 4, 7).

89. Ryland, "Letter to Levi Hart," August 10, 1805, 10.

90. Ryland, "Letter to Levi Hart," August 10, 1805, 8.

91. Ryland writes to Hart, "I highly respect D^r. Hopkins, tho I feel rather confirmed in an apprehension that he goes on some points to an extreme. At least, I fear a tendency to dwell chiefly on the most difficult points of Divinity, and to make the most remotely imply'd truths, the first and most obvious to the view of New Converts" (Ryland, "Letter to Levi Hart," 1805).

92. The disagreement with Edwards Jr. was not theological in this instance, but had

another letter to Hart, Ryland acknowledges his and Hart's disagreement over baptism, and then sends a pamphlet on the meaning of the Greek word βαπτίζω.[93] Ryland's catholicity, then, was not of the quiet type, nor did it involve the ignoring of differences for the sake of peace. Ryland even welcomed a return in kind from Hart, saying, "I think you will excuse this, and will not be displeased if I send you a small pamphlet, rather practical than controversial, to which I have annexed several Quotations from Josephus, which seem to me worthy of notice as to the meaning of the Word βαπτίζω. I w[d]. thank you for any references of a contrary kind."[94] He welcomed disagreement, but, importantly, he did not allow disagreement to mean disbarment of fellowship. Indeed, in Ryland's practice of catholicity, disagreement was an essential part of true friendship.[95]

Samuel Hopkins

Samuel Hopkins is one of the more notable American names among Ryland's correspondents. Born September 17, 1721, Hopkins grew to be one of the leading theologians of the eighteenth century. After graduating from Yale in 1741, he studied with Jonathan Edwards Sr. and came to drink deeply from the well of Edwardseanism. He served as pastor of the North Parish of Sheffield from 1743–1769, from which he was eventually dismissed.[96] He continued his ministerial labors at the First Congregational Church in

---

to do with an incident that happened in Georgia with a man named John Johnson. The incident involved the decision as to who would take control of the Bethesda mission in Georgia. For more information on the incident, see Scott, "Final Effort to Fulfill George Whitefield's Bequest," 433–61. Edwards took the side of Johnson's opponents, while Ryland gave more credence to Johnson. Edwards intimates that one of the sources of tension was the increasing antipathy between the Americans and those from England (Edwards, "Letter to John Ryland," April 23, 1793).

93. Ryland, "Letter to Levi Hart," January 18, 1808.

94. Ryland, "Letter to Levi Hart," January 18, 1808.

95. This attitude is not confined to private correspondence, as Ryland welcomes correction and reproof in published work as well, writing, "If any man can prove that I have adopted any Corruption of Christianity, or that any part of my Creed is erroneous and unscriptural; as soon as I am convinced of it, I will abjure that part, and thank him for detecting my error. Or, if he will prove that I am incorrect in my statement of any doctrine, and will lead me into better views of truth, I will love him, and own myself obliged to him" (Ryland, *Necessity of the Trumpet's Giving a Certain Sound*, 45).

96. The occasion of his dismissal seems to have been a series of alienations between the church and Hopkins having to do with his theological views as well as cultural issues between him and the townspeople. Hopkins himself asked for his own dismissal (see Conforti, *Samuel Hopkins and the New Divinity Movement*, 83–88; Patten, *Reminiscences*, 53–54).

Newport, Rhode Island from 1770 until 1803. He received a DD from Yale in 1802. He died December 20, 1803.

Hopkins's theology proved to be very influential among the Edwardseans, so much so that the theology of Edwards's successors is sometimes called "Hopkinsianism."[97] Like the other American divines, Ryland appreciates Hopkins's theological works and treats him as a close brother, though he was not uncritical of him.[98] This candidness is captured in a letter written to Hopkins near the end of Hopkins's life, in which Ryland writes, "Tho I wish to call no man M^r. on Earth, I w^d. be highly obliged to seek after Truth as after hid Treasure, & I think your writings have assisted me in the search, tho I must follow slowly wherein I see few footsteps before you, & may never fully accord with all you have written."[99] In that one quote, we can see Ryland's love for and deference to Hopkins[100] but also his willingness to

---

97. Writing about the origin of the term "Hopkinsian," Hopkins says, "And since that time [the publication of a pamphlet that Hopkins believed was written by William Hart] all who embrace the caliniftic doctrines which were publifhed by Prefident Edwards, Doctor Bellamy, Doctor Weft of Stockbridge, and myfelf, have been called *Hopkintonians*, or *Hopkinfians*. Thus I am become the head of a denomination, who have fince greatly increafed, and in which thoufands are included, and a large number of minifters, who, I believe are the moft found, confiftent and thorough calvinifts" (Hopkins, *Sketches of the Life*, 97). In more recent years, Joseph Conforti has written several helpful works on Hopkins: *Samuel Hopkins and the New Divinity Movement*; "Joseph Bellamy and The New Divinity Movement," 126–38; "Rise of the New Divinity in Western New England, 1740–1800," 37–47, "Samuel Hopkins and the New Divinity," 572–89. Other works on Hopkins include: Post, *Christian Love and Self-Denial: An Historical and Normative Study of Jonathan Edwards, Samuel Hopkins, and American Theological Ethics*; and Jauhiainen, "Samuel Hopkins and Hopkinsianism," 107–17.

98. It is telling, however, that Ryland's criticisms of Hopkins and the American divines are all relayed privately in correspondence. They are offered in a spirit of collaboration rather than public critique. After the deaths of Sutcliff and Fuller, Ryland saw himself as the chief English defender against those who "cry out against American divinity" (Ryland, "Letter to Stephen West," September 12, 1815).

99. Ryland, "Letter to Samuel Hopkins," 1797.

100. In a dispute between Hopkins and Ryland's countryman and fellow Baptist Abraham Booth, Ryland played the part of mediator (at least to Hopkins), writing, "You must, my dear Sir, make some Allow^{ce}. for persons to whom many things in your System are altogether novel" (Ryland, "Letter to Samuel Hopkins," March 13, 1798). He also defended Booth with a somewhat back-handed defense: "He is a Man of Sterling Worth, & the most unblemish'd & exemplary Character. But sometimes when a good Man has long been used to contemplate on one side it is extremely difficult to get him to step round & survey it on the other" (Ryland, "Letter to Samuel Hopkins," 1797). However, he also says that he read Hopkins's initial remarks on Booth "with great pleasure" (Ryland, "Letter to Samuel Hopkins," 1797), and he distances himself from what he considered the extremes of Booth (e.g., he speaks of "the worst things Mr. Booth wrote" being welcomed in the *Gospel Magazine*, a high Calvinist periodical; Ryland, "Letter to Samuel Hopkins," March 13, 1798). Despite disagreements, Ryland remained

state his objections.[101] Ryland's chief objection to Hopkins is his emphasis on disinterested love. He questions Hopkins, "Now must they not disbelieve the Gospel, if they conclude there is no possibility of their being saved?"[102] Ryland's hesitance with regard to disinterested love had less to do with its biblical or theological basis and more to do with its pastoral usefulness: "That a sinner ought to own the perfect Equity of his Condemnat[ion], and to consider the very Sanction of the Law as an expression of divine Equity and Love of order, etc. I readily admit. But do we not puzzle people needlessly, to require them to be willing to be eternally tormented, & even eternally wicked, when Christ came on purpose to save them both from torment and sin?"[103] For his part, Hopkins answers Ryland's objections to his system. Indeed, his last letter to Ryland, sent only seventeen days before Hopkins died, is a lengthy letter detailing Hopkins's answers to Ryland's questions about the law, disinterested benevolence, and willingness to be damned.[104] However, like Ryland, Hopkins did not understand disagreement to mean disfellowship. He signed his letter, "Wish you may live many years, and do much good in the cause of Christ. Hope after that to meet you where Christ will abundantly reward his faithful servants. I remain your assured friend and fellow-servant in the gospel."[105] A consistent picture emerges of honesty, openness, and acceptance despite important differences.

Stephen West

Stephen West was born November 13, 1735 in Tolland, Connecticut. He graduated from Yale College in 1755 and went on to study theology under

---

very much on the side of Hopkins. He writes to him: "I pray God abundantly to succeed your Labors" (Ryland, "Letter to Samuel Hopkins," March 13, 1798).

101. He is clear about his intention to let him know of any objections to Hopkins's system: "Hereafter if any part shou'd admit of objections in my mind, I will take the Liberty of stating them" (Ryland, "Letter to Samuel Hopkins," 1797).

102. Weaver and Haykin, "Significant Letter from Ryland to Hopkins," 30.

103. Weaver and Haykin, "Significant Letter from Ryland to Hopkins," 30. Ryland was concerned with the simple, central truths of the Christian faith, rather than the more abstract notions drawn from scripture: "I have feared also a temptation to dwell upon a few truths, and some of them the most difficult truths of Religion, to the neglect of other parts of Revelation" (Weaver and Haykin, "Significant Letter from Ryland to Hopkins," 31). He feared that Hopkins dwelt too much on those difficult aspects, which could be to the ruin of otherwise faithful people.

104. Hopkins, "Letter to Dr. Ryland," September 1803, in *Works of Hopkins*, 2:752–58.

105. Hopkins, "Letter to Dr. Ryland," September 1803, in *Works of Hopkins*, 2:758.

Timothy Woodbridge.[106] In November 1758, he became Jonathan Edwards's successor at the Indian Mission in Stockbridge, Connecticut, and he was called to the church in Stockbridge on June 15, 1759.[107] West also served as President of the Congregational Missionary Society.[108] He died on May 15, 1819 in Stockbridge.

Initially an Arminian, he became friends with Samuel Hopkins,[109] who convinced him not only of the tenets of Calvinism but of Hopkins's own modification of Edwardsean Calvinism. Through Hopkins, West became acquainted with Joseph Bellamy, Jonathan Edwards Jr., and others who followed the theological trajectory of the elder Edwards.[110] West has been called "the most radical flank of the Edwardseans,"[111] and it is true that he went further than others in some regards. The Reformed heritage of the Edwardseans led them to a high view of God's sovereignty, such that they all held to the Westminster statement that "God from all eternity did, by the moſt wiſe and holy Counſell of his own will, freely and unchangeably ordain whatſoever comes to paſſe."[112] Stephen West pursued this to the conclusion that God ordained evil itself.[113] This goes beyond Hopkins, for example, who says that "all moral evil is deſigned by God to anſwer a good end, and is overruled for the greateſt good."[114] West, on the other hand, holds that "*moral evil* was a *neceſſary means* of the greateſt good."[115] For Hopkins, God *overrules* evil to bring about good, but for West evil is a necessary means of bringing about good. That is, God ordains the evil, so that he might bring about the good.

Ryland's introduction to West came through a letter, now lost, that West wrote to Ryland in 1814.[116] Ryland wrote at least five letters to West,

---

106. Sprague, "Stephen West, D.D.," 1:548.

107. Sprague, "Stephen West, D.D.," 1:548.

108. Anonymous, "Minutes of the Congregational Missionary Society," 482–84.

109. Sprague, "Stephen West, D.D.," 1:548–49.

110. Sprague, "Stephen West, D.D.," 1:550.

111. Guelzo, *Edwards on the Will*, 140.

112. Westminster Assembly, *Confession of Faith and the Larger and Shorter Catechisme*, 7.

113. See West, "Appendix," *An Essay on Moral Agency*, 4–7, 43–44.

114. Hopkins, *System of Doctrines*, 1:145.

115. West, *Essay on Moral Agency*, 178.

116. Edwards Jr. had sent Ryland West's *The Scripture Doctrine of the Atonement* in 1787 (Ryland, "Letter to Stephen West," March 31, 1814, 179), so Ryland was aware of West and his work well before beginning their correspondence. Also, Ryland indicates that West is the first American correspondent since Edwards Jr. with whom he has sought an extended epistolary relationship: "Since the death of my dear correspondent,

and they are among the most revealing of all his correspondence as it relates to his catholicity. Not only do these letters contain the usual acceptance of the recipient as a Christian brother,[117] as well as Ryland's objections to some aspects of American Divinity,[118] they also contain unique accounts of Ryland's practice of and beliefs about catholicity. He writes, "But I never could find my love to my Paedobaptist brethren impeded by thinking differently on that subject. Indeed, I think some subjects of diversity of judgment which do not change a man's usual denomination are far more important than others which do. But all who love our Lord Jesus, and in whom I can trace his image, I am sure ought to be dear to me."[119] As will be shown in the following chapter, this will prove key to Ryland's theology of catholicity.

In his letters to West, Ryland also offers details of his catholic practice. For example, in the March 31, 1814 letter, Ryland says that the Church of England had lately held a meeting for the Church Missionary Society. He tells West, "We shut up our evening meetings, and attended the services, which were very pleasant. Almost every one spoke kindly of other missions."[120] Ryland also tells West of the cordial friendships he had with the ministers of Bristol, writing, "All the evangelical dissenters are united pretty cordially. In the monthly lecture the Baptists, Independents, and tabernacle are united, and in the monthly prayer-meeting the Wesleyans and Lady Huntington's people join also. We generally breakfast together (the ministers of all these congregations) once a fortnight, at each other's houses in rotation."[121] Ryland, thus, provides a valuable look into his own thinking

---

Dr. Edwards, I have scarcely had time to seek out another, and the unhappy disputes between the two countries have rendered it more difficult to find a mode of intercourse. I heard, also, a few times from Dr. Hart, Dr. Stillman, and Dr. Foster, and indeed from Dr. Hopkins; but they are all gone" (Ryland, "Letter to Stephen West," March 31, 1814, 179).

117. Ryland writes, "I am glad to have an opportunity of writing again to one whom I so highly respect, and I hope this letter will find that your work is not yet finished" (Ryland, "Letter to Stephen West," March 27, 1815, 182). He also wishes West "great success" in his "society for the education of pious youth."

118. Ryland, "Letter to Stephen West," March 27, 1815, 183. Ryland offers both approbation and specific criticism of Joseph Strong's work: "I have been lately reading afresh the second volume of Dr. Strong's Sermons. I assent to nearly everything be advances; yet, taken as a whole, I feel that I could scarcely answer two objections which many readers in this country would bring. He introduces but *little* scripture, and especially he gives a smaller proportional exhibition of the *love* and *grace* of Christ than the generality of our best preachers" (Ryland, "Letter to Stephen West," March 27, 1815, 182). This disagreement, which was not insignificant, did not prevent Ryland from appreciating the sermons (Ryland, "Letter to Stephen West," March 27, 1815, 183).

119. Ryland, "Letter to Stephen West," March 31, 1814, 180.

120. Ryland, "Letter to Stephen West," March 31, 1814, 180.

121. Ryland, "Letter to Stephen West," March 31, 1814, 180. Apparently, this did

about his practice of catholicity, revealed to one who sat on the most radical end of the Edwardsean system.

Samuel Miller

Samuel Miller was born October 31, 1769 near Dover, Delaware. He graduated from the University of Pennsylvania in 1789, upon which he commenced his theological studies with his father, Rev. John Miller. Miller's father died before the son could complete his studies, so Miller continued studying theology under Charles Nisbet, President of Dickinson College. He was ordained as a Presbyterian minister on June 5, 1793 and began serving the United Presbyterian Churches of New York. His alma mater conferred the DD on him in 1804, an "uncommon, if not unprecedented" honor.[122] In 1806, he was selected moderator of the Presbyterian General Assembly. In 1813, he was chosen as the Professor of Ecclesiastical History and Church Government at the Theological Seminary at Princeton, in which position he remained until the year before his death. He was instrumental in the founding of the seminary[123] as well as promoting the interests of the Presbyterian denomination.[124] So intertwined was Miller with Presbyterianism that James Carnahan, a close friend, says of him, "For half a century Dr. Miller occupied a very prominent place in the Presbyterian Church in this country, so that his biography in his public relations would be, to a great extent, the history of his denomination, for more than fifty years."[125] He was also committed to educational advancement, serving as a Trustee of both Columbia College and the College of New Jersey.[126] Miller also served as

---

not include the Anglicans, though not because of Ryland or others rejecting them. Ryland tells West, "I have a very agreeable intercourse with the evangelical Episcopalians, though they hardly dare to come to meeting, for fear of their superiors." In addition to showing Ryland's practice of catholicity, this quotation also demonstrates the breadth of the meaning of "evangelical" for Ryland. It has been argued that "*real Calvinism* was for him synonymous with 'evangelical truth'" (Crocker, "Life and Legacy," 251), but, to West, Ryland speaks of Baptists, Independents, Wesleyans, and Lady Huntington's connexion under the heading of "evangelical."

122. Sprague, "Samuel Miller, D.D.," 601.

123. For more on the founding of Princeton Theological Seminary and Miller's role in it, see Noll, "Founding of Princeton Seminary," 72–110; Stanton, "Princeton's Pastor," 143–57; Stanton, "Samuel Miller," 4–17; and Stephens, "Samuel Miller, 1769–1850," 33–47.

124. Sprague, "Samuel Miller, D.D.," 604: "Dr. Miller was an honest, vigilant and devoted friend of what he believed to be the true interests of the Presbyterian Church."

125. Carnahan, "Letter to William Buell Sprague," 607.

126. Carnahan, "Letter to William Buell Sprague," 609. Miller's commitment to

the founder and long-time president of the New York Bible Society. He died January 7, 1850.[127]

As stated above, Miller was a Presbyterian through and through. He was committed not only to the general Calvinistic theology of Presbyterianism but was a staunch advocate of the entire system of Presbyterian government.[128] In this Miller is somewhat unique among American correspondents of Ryland: he was not an Edwardsean. Indeed, in the Old School-New School split in the Presbyterian Church, "he was inflexibly with the Old School."[129]

Despite this, Ryland addresses Miller as he did his many other correspondents: as a fellow Christian. He offers prayer for "God to succeed all your Labors."[130] Much of Ryland's correspondence with Miller relates to the work of the ministry, whether ministry at home or on the mission field. Regarding ministerial labors at home, Ryland gave Miller an account of the "State of Relig^n. in England,"[131] in which he gave statistics on the various denominations in England. With regard to mission work, he recounts the activities of the BMS missionaries, including the death of William Grant.[132] Ryland also asks for Miller's help in finding lodging and help for BMS missionary John Chamberlain on his way to the mission field in Bengal.[133] This aspect of the letters is especially telling, as Ryland writes to the committed

---

his work leading educational institutions was steadfast and consistent. Carnahan, who knew him well, says that he "had seldom been absent from the meetings of the Board, and was always an active and influential member" (609).

127. For more information on Miller, see the biography written by his son, Samuel Miller, entitled *The Life of Samuel Miller*.

128. His published works include: *An Essay on the Warrant, Nature, and Duties of the Office of the Ruling Elder in the Presbyterian Church*; *Infant Baptism Scriptural and Reasonable: and Baptism by Sprinkling or Affusion, the Most Suitable and Edifying Mode*; and *Presbyterianism, the Truly Primitive and Apostolical Constitution of the Church of Christ*.

129. Sprague, "Samuel Miller, D.D.," 604.

130. Ryland, "Letter to Samuel Miller" undated.

131. Ryland, "Letter to Samuel Miller," November 25, 1800. Ryland's description of Protestantism in England is revealing, as much for his own understanding as it is for the actual state of things. According to him, the Presbyterians have decreased in number "in conseq^{ce}. of their gen^l. departure from the Gospel." On the Methodists, Ryland writes that they "admit into Society every one who professes a Desire to flee from the wrath to come, excluding only the grofsly immoral, but they have many hearers who are not in society with them." The Independents and Calvinistic Methodists "nearly coalesce." The preachers in Lady's Huntingdon's Connexion keep separate and are "infected with pseudocalvinism." The Scottish Baptists "are few, very rigid, and of the Sandemanian Cast." The Particular Baptists were increasing both in England and Wales.

132. Ryland, "Letter to Samuel Miller," 1799.

133. Ryland, "Letter to Samuel Miller," May 8, 1802.

Presbyterian Miller as a co-laborer and fellow worker, rather than an outsider. They were both working toward the same goal, though doing so in separate ways.[134] In pursuit of that goal, Ryland at least twice sent books for the Princeton library.[135]

Thomas Scott

Thomas Scott was a minister of the Church of England. He was born on February 4, 1747 and served at several churches in Ravenston, Olney, London, and Aston Sandford. While in London, he helped found the Church Missionary Society in 1799. He is most well-known for his commentary on the Bible. He died on April 16, 1821.

Like many of Ryland's correspondents, Scott's soteriology was of the Calvinist variety.[136] Unlike those listed above, however, Scott was an Anglican. Ryland did not allow their differing convictions to become a stumbling block to communion. Indeed, Ryland's relationship with Scott was one of his longest, the two having commenced their friendship in 1779 and continuing in it until Scott's death.[137] Ryland's relationship with Scott is worth noting for its intimacy and breadth.[138] This is evidenced in Scott's last letter to Ryland, written just two months before Scott died. The letter survives in a handwritten copy made by Ryland, indicating the meaning that Ryland attached to the letter and its author.[139] The letter contains references to Scott's interest in the work of the BMS; an account of Ryland's sister's death;[140] shared prayer concerns regarding a mutual, unnamed acquaintance; Scott's expectation of soon dying; his celebration of Ryland's ministerial labors; and personal greetings from those in Scott's house to those in Ryland's. It is a short letter, but it is illustrative of the intimate relationships that Ryland conducted with those outside of his tradition.

---

134. Indeed, Ryland offers his hopes for the prosperity of the Presbyterian Missionary Society (Ryland, "Letter to Samuel Miller," 1799).

135. In both instances, Ryland sent volumes of Thomas Scott's Bible commentary (Ryland, "Letter to Samuel Miller," undated; Ryland, "Letter to Samuel Miller," May 13, 1806).

136. Scott, *Force of Truth*, 107.

137. Ryland notes this as a postscript to a letter that he transcribed from John Scott, son of Thomas, written a day after Thomas Scott's decease (Ryland, "Postscript to John Scott Letter," 8).

138. John Scott, son of Thomas, described Ryland as Thomas Scott's "so old, & kind, & valued a friend" (Scott, "Letter to John Ryland," April 13, 1821, 3).

139. Thomas Scott, "Letter to John Ryland," February 15, 1821, 1.

140. This is Elizabeth Ryland Dent, who died on December 29, 1820.

William Wilberforce

With the exception of John Newton, William Wilberforce is, perhaps, Ryland's most well-known correspondent. Born on August 24, 1759, Wilberforce was elected Member of Parliament for Kingston upon Hull in 1780, just weeks after his twenty-first birthday. He served in Parliament forty-five years until ill health forced him to resign in February 1825. Wilberforce is known today for his campaign against the slave trade, which was abolished in the British Empire in 1834. Wilberforce's religion was of the evangelical Anglican variety. He helped to found the Church Missionary Society as well as the British and Foreign Bible Society.[141] He died on July 29, 1833.

Like Jonathan Walter Edwards, Wilberforce is rare among extant Ryland correspondence in not being a minister. Moreover, their correspondence shows Ryland entering into the political arena, a place he was typically loathe to enter.[142] Wilberforce had written to Ryland asking about the issue of Catholic emancipation.[143] Ryland's letter to Wilberforce demonstrates both the breadth of his catholicity (e.g., in writing to an Anglican politician about political issues) as well as its limits, seen in what he has to say about Roman Catholics. Ryland sees giving rights to Roman Catholics as an undesirable thing. Indeed, he understands the present state of affairs as favorable to himself and the nation, writing to Wilberforce, "On the <u>one hand</u>, I have been afraid of seeming to distrust my own sword, and to ask for the aid of the civil magistrate to defend the cause of Christ."[144] To change the laws against Roman Catholics, in Ryland's understanding, would be to injure the cause of Christ. He goes on, however, to state the other side of the case: "On the <u>other hand</u>, while I am willing that the worst enemies of the truth should be opposed only by the word of God, and be left to try all

---

141. For more information on Wilberforce, see Hague, *William Wilberforce: The Life of the Great Anti-Slave Trade Campaigner*; Pollock, *Wilberforce*; Stott, *Wilberforce: Family and Friends*; Rennie, "William Wilberforce," 1–18; and Spring, "Clapham Sect: Some Social and Political Aspects," 35–48.

142. He writes to Stephen West, "I have no taste to intermeddle with politics" (Ryland, "Letter to Stephen West," March 31, 1814, 179). To Wilberforce, he later confessed, "I have never busied myself much in political concerns, having other business sufficient to occupy my whole time" (Ryland, "Letter to William Wilberforce," March 26, 1821).

143. Catholic emancipation was the process of relieving legal pressure on Catholics that had been instituted through the Act of Uniformity (1662) and Test Acts (1673). It began in 1778 with the Papists Act and culminated in 1829 with the Roman Catholic Relief Act.

144. Ryland, "Letter to William Wilberforce," March 26, 1821. Ryland is not entirely consistent on this issue, as, several years earlier, he had written to John Williams, pastor of the Baptist church in New York City, of his hope that "our Government will interpose again in their [the Baptists] favor" (Ryland, "Letter to John Williams," August 28, 1807).

that they can do by means of argument ag^t. it."[145] The other side of the case for Ryland is not that he embraces Roman Catholics as fellow believers, nor was it even that all people deserve the same rights that he enjoyed. Rather, it was that he does not want the state to fight his battles for him. Roman Catholics were, to him, some of "the worst enemies of the truth,"[146] and he did not necessarily want the British Empire to overcome them for him. Ryland concludes the matter thus:

> I have tho't the case of the Catholics differ'd from that of other erroneous persons. A man may indeed be a Catholic, and disbelieve the power of the Pope to dispense wth the obligation of an oath: tho I should fear that out of 12 men, who now think themselves sincere in denying that power, 8 or 9 w^d. be likely to change their opinion in case of a <u>Crisis</u>, when they might essentially serve their Church, by adopting it. But another point weighs more with me, viz. A man cannot be a Roman Catholic, and yet be heartily disposed to allow Liberty of Conscience to others.[147]

Ryland exhibits both a personal and theological distrust of Roman Catholics. It should be noted, however, that politics was not his first concern. He speaks on it only in response to a query, and, after answering Wilberforce's political question, he moved quickly to religious concerns. He copied a portion of Stephen Sutton's journal for Wilberforce[148] and gave a brief summary of the Baptist mission work in Jamaica.

This letter is illuminating of the complexities of Ryland's catholicity as well as what did or did not influence his catholicity. As will be shown in the following section, he is willing, perhaps begrudgingly, to extend an olive branch of Christian charity to Roman Catholics. One might expect, then, that the issues of Catholic emancipation and toleration would solicit his sympathies. However, Ryland seems unmoved by the Roman Catholic plight

---

145. Ryland, "Letter to William Wilberforce," March 26, 1821.

146. In another place, Ryland says that Roman Catholicism is a "spurious Christianity" (Ryland, "An Inquiry Concerning the Events to Be Accomplished by the Three Angels, Mentioned, Rev. XIV.6–11," 413). In reading the context in which he wrote that, one may reasonably infer that the emphasis is on "spurious" rather than "Christianity." This article is also signed by Eleutherides, which is one of Ryland's known pseudonyms (see Crocker, "Life and Legacy," 367).

147. Ryland, "Letter to William Wilberforce," March 26, 1821.

148. Sutton was a missionary for the BMS and was stationed in Murshidabad (spelled in contemporary writings as "Moorshedabad" and "Moorshudubad"), where he formed a school and itinerated as a preacher (Cox, *History*, 1:335). Illness forced him to return to England in 1823 (Cox, *History*, 1:336–37).

and would only support their cause because he would not want the government to fight his battles for him. The formation and expression of his catholicity, therefore, while taking place in a context of increased toleration for Roman Catholics, does not seem to have been impacted by that movement.

Another letter from Ryland to Wilberforce is, like those of Ryland to West in some respects, instructive as to Ryland's own practice of ministerial catholicity. In a letter since lost, Ryland had apparently written to Wilberforce with respect to the promotion of Establishment missions in India through the appointment of bishops for the region.[149] Ryland had been quite vocal against such because of a fear of the appointment of either High Church bishops, "who would not all[ow] full Liberty of Conscience to other Denomin^s.," or "more worldly formalists, unacquainted with vital, evang^l. X^y. [Christianity] who would oppose those of their own persuasion who were most zeal^s. for the Gosp^l. of X^t."[150] He writes to Wilberforce to apologize if he offended him, as he meant no offense by denominating Establishment clergy in those ways. What is interesting for present purposes is Ryland's fear that Wilberforce would take him to be fighting for his own Particular Baptist party, which, he indicates, could not be further from the truth. He did not want to be seen as a party man.[151]

Roman Catholicism

Ryland's aversion to Roman Catholicism was mentioned above, but it deserves a section of its own, as his relationship to Roman Catholicism is complex, showing both the limits and potential of his catholicity. Ryland had a deep distrust of Roman Catholicism. His "Confession of Faith" is worth quoting at length here, as it demonstrates the depth of his opposition to the Roman Catholic Church:

> With my whole ♥ I detest & with my Lips I protest against the tyranical usurpations, corrupt doctrines, and false worship of the Pope of Rome whom I verily believe to be Antichrist. His pretended Supremacy and Infallibility I deny. His Doctrine

---

149. Ryland, "Letter to William Wilberforce," June 1, 1812.

150. Ryland, "Letter to William Wilberforce," June 1, 1812.

151. Ryland says the same thing to the Baptist Association meeting in Chard, though in an even broader manner than to Wilberforce: "Let us purfue this bleffed object with diligence and ardor, with refolute felf-denial, and difinterefted love and zeal. Never, may there be room to fufpect that our aim is to increafe our income, increafe our influence, increafe our reputation among men, or to increafe the intereft of a party" (Ryland, *Certain Increase*, 31).

respecting the insufficiency of scripture, debaring the free use of it, adding to it unwritten traditions; the doctrine of transubstantiation, human merit, purgatory, forbidding to marry, idolatrously worshipping Angels & Saints, Images & relicks, of auricular confession & of absolution, of pardons, praying for the dead, indulgences &c. &c. I abhor as doctrines of Devils, and sooner than be reconciled to these Abominations or to that Church which is the mother of them, I hope God w^d. enable me to hate my own life for Christs sake & yield my body to the flames, if she that in past ages has been drunken with the blood of the Saints shou'd ever be suffer'd (wch. may God forbid) to revive her dominion over this Land.[152]

It takes no lengthy exposition to understand Ryland's feelings on the matter. He is no friend to Roman Catholicism. With this opposition and depth of feeling in mind, then, let us examine Ryland's catholicity toward Roman Catholics.

In a work entitled "Queries to Praying Proffessors [sic] of Every Denomination Respecting Political and Imprecatory Prayer,"[153] Ryland offers a rare olive branch to Roman Catholics. He writes, "May we not hope that there are many praying men in England; and are we sure that there is not one man who has the spirit of pray'r in America, on the side of the Congrefs? Are we sure there is not one praying Man in Holland? Nor one praying man among the French Protestants? Nor one man who worſhips

152. Ryland, "Confession of Faith," 17–18.

153. There is some uncertainty as to Ryland's authorship of this work. It is found, in handwritten form, in the Angus Library archives in a small common place booklet. The work is written in Ryland Jr.'s hand, but it was submitted to the *London Evening Post* under the name "Pacificus," which was a known pseudonym of J. C. Ryland (see Pacificus, *Modest Plea for Free Communion at the Lord's Table*, typeset copy held by the Northamptonshire Central Library Archives). It is possible that Ryland Jr. merely copied the work of his father into the booklet in which it is found. However, there are three arguments in favor of Ryland Jr.'s authorship, or, at the very least, with Ryland's assent to its contents. First, it is bound with another work that is undoubtedly Ryland's (letters signed by him to an unknown correspondent in London). They were apparently written around the same time and carry the theme of correspondence with people and groups in London. Second, it is difficult to see why Ryland would copy a letter written by his father with which he did not agree and not give his own viewpoint in response to it. In other places, Ryland does not hesitate to add to his father's work (see J. C. Ryland and John Ryland Jr., "Autographic Notes," *passim*). Finally, "Pacificus" was a relatively common pseudonym in that period, being used by Alexander Hamilton, Joshua Reed Giddings, Frederick Scott Oliver, and more (Carty, *Dictionary of Literary Pseudonyms*, 165). That Ryland Jr. would choose it is unsurprising, especially considering the content of the letter, which has to do with peace. Indeed, the final word of the letter is "PEACE," written in a stylized way setting it apart from the rest of the contents.

God acceptably, even among the Papiſts in France or Spain?"[154] While this is a small concession, couched as a hypothetical question, it is revealing for Ryland's catholicity. As shown above, Ryland was no friend to Roman Catholics, but here, even if briefly, he allows that it might be possible that a Roman Catholic could worship God acceptably, which is, for him in his historical and ecclesiastical context, a considerable admission.

In another place, Ryland again leaves the door open just a bit for acceptance of Roman Catholics as fellow Christians. Ryland left behind many poems, and one stands out from the rest as particularly helpful in understanding his stance toward Roman Catholics. It is entitled "Vegetable Characteristics or The Parsonic Garden," and in it Ryland compares the British Protestant personalities to various vegetables found in his garden.[155] While he focuses on the Protestants, Ryland includes the following about Roman Catholics:

> At present is the Garden not complete
>
> Nor all its Quarters uniform as yet
>
> Some Beds Episcopal in Gothic Stile
>
> Are quaintly cut by many an awkward Aile
>
> Declining Rome th'unnat-ral Plan devis'd
>
> Yet here are many Plants most justly prized.[156]

This is helpful in understanding the breadth of Ryland's catholicity in a couple of ways. First, the very fact that he includes Roman Catholics in his garden is significant in light of his views expressed elsewhere. Second, he includes them, and then goes on to say that even here there are plants that are "most justly prized." He does not elaborate, but it is another intriguing admission from someone so vehemently opposed to Roman Catholicism.

These are small but meaningful concessions on Ryland's part, and it perhaps reflects the influence of John Newton, who will be discussed later. Newton writes to Ryland that "if a Papist gave me good evidence that he loved my Saviour, I would beg leave of men, and ask grace of the Lord, that I might love such Papists likewise, with a pure heart fervently."[157]

---

154. Pacificus [John Ryland Jr.], "Queries to Praying Proffessors," undated, 2.
155. Ryland, "Vegetable Characteristics or The Parsonic Garden," *Poems*, 1:84–89.
156. Ryland, "Vegetable Characteristics or The Parsonic Garden," *Poems*, 1:85.
157. Gordon, *Wise Counsel*, 345.

Emperor Alexander I of Russia

Among the most unexpected of Ryland correspondents is Alexander Pavlovich Romanov, better known as Emperor Alexander I of Russia. Before continuing, the true provenance of the letter under consideration must be considered. The letter to the Emperor, while written in Ryland's distinctive handwriting, does not contain his signature but is signed by "Your Majesty's most humble Serv.t"[158] This leaves open the possibility that Ryland merely copied a letter written by someone else. The letter itself is designated as being from "the Secretary to the Baptist Missionary Society," which, because Alexander died in 1825, narrows the possibilities to four people: Andrew Fuller, James Hinton, John Dyer, or John Ryland. The letter makes reference to "Rev. Patterson," which is most likely the missionary John Paterson, who moved to St. Petersburg in 1812. In 1822, Paterson became involved with the Russian Bible Society and was supported by Alexander I. The internal evidence of the letter indicates that it was written after 1822, as its author writes that he was "deeply impressed with the pleasing account of your Majesty's Zeal for the propagation of the Sacred Scriptures." If this is so, then Andrew Fuller could not have written it, as he died in 1815, and neither could James Hinton, who resigned as secretary in 1817. That leaves only Ryland and Dyer. While Ryland left much of the work of the secretary position to Dyer, especially in later years, he still took part in the promotion of the Society.[159] Moreover, Dyer lived in and the society was headquartered in London during this period, making it less likely that Ryland would have a chance to copy a letter from Dyer. While it cannot be stated with absolute certainty, the most likely scenario is that Ryland wrote the letter to the emperor himself and made a copy before sending it.[160]

---

158. Ryland, "Letter to the Emperor of Russia."

159. As late as October 1824, seven months before he died and just three months before he preached his last sermon, Ryland traveled to Gloucester to raise funds for the society (Ryland, "Text Book," October 17, 1824).

160. One other bit of evidence in favor of Ryland's authorship of the letter is that he made a correction to it. The last sentence originally offered a prayer that the emperor would be "a highly-honoured instrument in preparing the Way for the universal reign of the prince of Peace, who is the Husband of the whole Church, and shall be called the God of the whole Earth." Ryland scratches that out, correcting it to read that he desires that the emperor would be "a highly-honoured instrument in preparing the Way for the universal reign of the prince of Peace, according to the prediction of the prophet Isaiah, the Husband and Redeemer of the Church shall be called the God of the whole Earth" (Ryland, "Letter to Emperor Alexander I," undated [post-1821]). Again, the likelihood is greater that Ryland would correct his own writing rather than that of another.

Alexander I was born December 23, 1777 and reigned from March 23, 1801 until his death on December 1, 1825.[161] He was not only a member but head of the Russian Orthodox Church. He took an interest in the scriptures and was supportive of the work of John Paterson in promoting the Bible in Russian.[162] It is this interest that brought the letter from Ryland. He writes of his pleasure at the Emperor's desire to propagate the scriptures and of his "pious efforts to promote pure and undefiled Religion" among the Russian people.[163] As with others he considered partners in the gospel, he shares missionary intelligence with the emperor.[164] The conclusion of the letter is especially catholic in its sympathies. He expresses his:

> sincere Veneration for your Majesty's character, and earnest prayrs that the everblessed God may long continue to shower down on yourself, your Imperial family, and your happy subjects, the richest of his blessings; and direct and prosper all your measures for the glory of his Holy Name, that you may be a highly-honoured instrument in preparing the Way for the universal reign of the prince of Peace, till according the prediction of the prophet Isaiah, the Husband and Redeemer of the Church shall be called the God of the whole Earth.[165]

Even if allowances be made for courtly language, this is still a remarkably catholic sentiment from Ryland. Russian Orthodox doctrine, at least in terms of its soteriology, is much closer to the Roman Catholicism he rejected than it was to Protestantism, still less to the Particular Baptist denomination. To be sure, Ryland does not plainly say that he believes that the Russian Emperor is a Christian. However, the language used is that of inclusion: Alexander has a "Zeal for the propagation of the Sacred Scriptures," he promotes "pure and undefiled Religion" among his subjects, and, according to Ryland, Alexander was endeavoring to glorify God in his life. These are not the words that Ryland used for unbelievers.

---

161. For more information on Alexander I, see Flynn, *University Reform of Tsar Alexander I*; Rey, *Alexander I: The Tsar Who Defeated Napoleon*; and Walker, "Enlightenment and Religion in Russian Education in the Reign of Tsar Alexander I," 343–60.

162. For more information on John Paterson, see Paterson, *Book for Every Land*; and Batalden, *Russian Bible Wars*, 36–48.

163. Ryland, "Letter to Emperor Alexander I," undated (post-1821).

164. Ryland, "Letter to Emperor Alexander I," undated (post-1821).

165. Ryland, "Letter to Emperor Alexander I," undated (post-1821).

John Foster

Ryland's relationship with John Foster is perhaps unexpected in a chapter focused on Ryland's catholic relationships with those outside of his tradition, seeing as Foster was himself a Baptist. However, Foster's theological commitments, especially with regard to judgment and everlasting punishment, diverge significantly from Ryland's and show how inclusive Ryland could be in his sentiments. In a letter to a young minister, who had asked Foster about the doctrine of future punishment, Foster writes about his doubts as to the doctrine of eternal conscious torment, saying bluntly, "Nevertheless, I acknowledge myself *not* convinced of the orthodox doctrine."[166] He goes on to explain that his issue with the doctrine was rooted in his understanding of the benevolence of God, saying:

> But endless punishment! hopeless misery, through a duration to which the enormous terms above imagined, will be absolutely nothing! I acknowledge my inability (I would say it reverently) to admit this belief, together with a belief in the divine goodness—the belief that "God is love," that his tender mercies are over all his works. Goodness, benevolence, charity, as ascribed in supreme perfection to him, cannot mean a quality foreign to all human conceptions of goodness; it must be something analogous in principle to what himself has defined and required as goodness in his moral creatures, that, in adoring the divine goodness, we may not be worshipping an "unknown God."[167]

Foster does not offer a positive doctrine of future punishment; he only offers his doubts about and critique of the orthodox position. He seems somewhat inclined to what is today called annihilationism and even holds out hope for universal redemption, though he stops short of advocating either:

> Some intelligent and devout inquirers unable to admit the terrific doctrine, and yet pressed by the strength of the scripture *language*, have had recourse to a *literal* interpretation of the

---

166. Foster, "Letter to a Young Minister," September 24, 1841, *Life and Correspondence*, 1846 edition, 2:263. Later editions of Foster's *Life and Correspondence* name Edward White, pastor of St. Paul's Chapel, Hawley Road, as the recipient (Foster, "Letter to Rev. Edward White," *Life and Correspondence*, 1861 edition, 232). White would have been twenty-two years old when Foster wrote to him, so that the name "young minister" would have, thus, been appropriate. Subsequent references to Foster's *Life and Correspondence* will be to the earlier edition.

167. Foster, "Letter to a Young Minister," September 24, 1841, *Life and Correspondence*, 2:264.

threatened destruction, the eternal death, as signifying *annihilation of existence, after* a more or less protracted penal infliction. Even this would be a prodigious relief: but it is an admission that the terms in question *do* mean something final in an absolute sense. I have not directed much thought to this point; the grand object of interest being a negation of the perpetuity of misery. I have not been anxious for any satisfaction beyond *that*; though certainly one would wish to indulge the hope, founded on the divine attribute of infinite benevolence, that there will be a period somewhere in the endless futurity, when all God's sinning creatures will be restored by him to rectitude and happiness.[168]

This is in contrast to Ryland, who believed that those who died apart from Christ experienced eternal conscious torment. In a sermon that was first preached in 1775 but not published until after his death, Ryland calls on his hearers, most of whom he took to be believers, to think about the destiny from which God rescued them: "Yet you also may find it profitable to pay a mental visit to those dark domains which you shall never enter in reality; to descend in idea into that place of banishment, and contemplate the everlasting burnings from which you were rescued by his almighty power."[169] The punishment in view is "everlasting burnings," and Ryland rebukes those who would call "eternal misery a fiction."[170] The heinousness of sin, according to Ryland, deserves "not only all the miseries of this life, and death itself, but also the pains of hell for ever."[171] Ryland still held these views at his ordination in 1781, in which he writes in his confession of faith, "I am fully

---

168. Foster, "Letter to a Young Minister," September 24, 1841, *Life and Correspondence*, 2:268. Earlier in life, Foster had even more divergent convictions, writing in a letter to Joseph Hughes, "That denomination of people in which I have been conversant, have stronger causes of exception than the colour of a waistcoat—my *opinions* have suffered some alteration. I have discarded, for instance, the doctrine of eternal punishments; I can avow no opinion on the peculiar points of Calvinism, for I have none, nor see the possibility of forming a satisfactory one. I am no Socinian; but I am in doubt between the orthodox and Arian doctrines, not without some inclination to the latter" (Foster, "Letter to Joseph Hughes," October 17, 1796, *Life and Correspondence*, 1:27). He goes on to relate recent correspondence in which he sought an Arian congregation in which he might preach. However, in just a few years, Foster would come to hold roughly Calvinistic views on most things: "My opinions are in substance decisively Calvinistic. I am firmly convinced, for instance, of the doctrines of original sin, predestination, imputed righteousness, the necessity of the Holy Spirit's operation to convert the mind, final perseverance, &c., &c." (Foster, "Letter to the Rev. Dr. Fawcett," January 15, 1800, *Life and Correspondence*, 1:84).

169. Ryland, "Salutations of Hell," 37.

170. Ryland, "Salutations of Hell," 42.

171. Ryland, "Salutations of Hell," 38.

assured ... of the most righteous tho awful Punishment of the Wicked Body and Soul in an eternal World of Misery"[172] Ryland did not change his understanding of the eternal state of unbelievers, preaching as late as 1822 that man "can even look beyond death, to a future state of rewards and punishments. He can forebode endless misery, or anticipate eternal happiness."[173]

Despite divergent views on a subject that Ryland considered of great importance, Ryland allowed Foster to preach at Broadmead regularly.[174] These lectures were delivered on the last Thursday of the month, for ten months out of the year, from 1822 through 1825. Lest anyone think Ryland was forced into allowing Foster use of his pulpit, Ryland writes approvingly of the lectures to John Dyer.[175] Moreover, Ryland and Foster were intimate friends until the end of Ryland's life. Indeed, Foster was at Ryland's bedside during his final illness.[176] Bristol Baptist College has in their archives a moving account of Ryland's last days, some of which were spent with Foster.[177] Written in Foster's hand, the accounts are dated May 20, May 21, and May 22, and Ryland died on May 25, 1825. Their last conversation in which Ryland was able to respond vocally, was May 20, 1825. Foster tells him, "You have need of patience." Ryland says that he is not able to pray aloud except with difficulty. Foster reassures him that "<u>He</u> whom you speak to, can hear <u>that</u>." Ryland complains that he can do nothing and has no strength. Foster again reassures him: "No, but he who has <u>all</u> strength will take care of you." The

---

172. Ryland, "Confession of Faith," 22. His reasoning that leads to his belief in eternal conscious torment is that "every Sin deserves a punishment someway or other <u>infinitely severe</u> to bear a Proportion to the real demerit of the crime" (Ryland, "Confession of Faith," 11).

173. Ryland, "Expansive Tendency of True Religion," *Pastoral Memorials*, 2:93. According to his sermon notes for this sermon (Ryland, "Sermon Notes: 2 Corinthians 6:13," *Original Manuscript Sermons: Old Testament, Vol. II*) and his "Text Book," this sermon was preached on May 5, 1822 at Broadmead. Such sentiments are found throughout Ryland's life and work. In other sermons, he addresses directly the belief in the annihilation of the unbeliever that Foster entertains, saying, "'The wages of sin is death,' even death eternal: not annihilation, but torment" (Ryland, "Why Will Ye Die?" *Pastoral Memorials*, 1:190). He says that for annihilation to be true, the scripture must be false: "Do you wish the Bible was not true? And why? That you may enjoy the pleasures of sin, and obtain the prize of annihilation!" (Ryland, "On Searching the Scriptures," *Pastoral Memorials*, 1:301).

174. J. E. Ryland, "Preface," in Foster, *Lectures Delivered at Broadmead Chapel*, iii.

175. Ryland, "Letter to John Dyer," 1824.

176. Foster, "Record by John Foster of His Last Conversation with Dr. John Ryland, Dated 20 May 1825."

177. Foster, "Record by John Foster of His Last Conversation with Dr. John Ryland, Dated 20 May 1825."

subsequent visits of May 21 and 22 seem to have consisted of Foster reading passages of scripture to Ryland, with Ryland saying nothing in return.

Correspondence with Women

Ryland's correspondence with women is important for understanding his catholicity, as it demonstrates that his Christian affection was not limited to males, which limitation, had that been his practice, would not have been difficult to maintain and defend in his day. While the extant material is not as voluminous as one might like, nor is it necessarily out of the ordinary of what one would expect from a pastor, what remains is instructive.

There are two letters to women who were grieving the loss of a loved one. The first is to a Miss Head, who had recently lost her sister. Ryland consoles and counsels her in her bereavement, telling her that he hopes that she is "enabled to realize the happinefs of her who is gone before you."[178] The second letter is to Sarah Pearce, the widow of Ryland's friend Samuel Pearce, who died October 10, 1799. Writing nearly a year after Pearce's death, Ryland corresponds with Sarah as a pastor and co-laborer. As a pastor, Ryland counsels Sarah, "I hope you do find the Lord able to support unD^r. all your trials. I felt much for your last, in the removal of the D^r. little babe, who bore the name of his father. But they are happy together, and when you join their company you fhall see that each was sent for home on the right day, and that your heavenly F^r. made no mistake."[179] As a co-laborer, Ryland keeps Sarah up to date on the progress of Samuel's memoirs, for which she had loaned Ryland many of Samuel's papers. In both letters, to Miss Head and Sarah Pearce, Ryland speaks to the women as equals.

There also exists a letter from Ryland to Maria Hope, who organized ladies' auxiliary branches for the Bible Society in Liverpool.[180] It is most instructive for Ryland's catholic spirit with regard to women. He updates Hope on the progress of his biography of Andrew Fuller, for which she had

---

178. Ryland, "Letter to Miss Head," undated. He also suggests some literature, two letters from John Berridge to David Edwards, that he believes Miss Head would find helpful in her grief.

179. Ryland, "Letter to Sarah Pearce," September 11, 1800.

180. Ryland, "Letter to Maria Hope," undated. The letter was written after Fuller's death on May 7, 1815 and before the publication of Ryland's memoir of Fuller the following year. Maria Hope has, unfortunately, been largely overlooked by historians. She was the sister of Samuel Hope, a wealthy banker who was an ardent supporter of the BMS (Haykin, "Review of *The Life and Thought of Andrew Fuller*," 149). Together, they were instrumental supporters of the work of the Baptist Missionary Society.

given an account of Fuller's first religious impressions.[181] He shares with her missionary intelligence relating to Lee Compere, who had recently been sent by the BMS to Jamaica. Ryland also solicits Hope's assistance with a delicate situation in Jamaica relating to the planters on the island who opposed the work of the BMS. In addition, Hope had asked Ryland if he would serve as the President of a society which Hope had set up in Liverpool, to which Ryland demurs, on account of his many labors elsewhere. Overall, Ryland writes to Hope in much the same way he writes to other, male correspondents: as an equal and a co-laborer in a common work. While it would not only be anachronistic but be going well beyond the evidence to suggest that Ryland was anything like a modern-day egalitarian, his correspondence with women demonstrates a depth to his catholicity that went beyond social as well as theological barriers.

Ministerial Cooperation

Ryland's commitment to the missionary cause is well known.[182] The focus on Ryland's missionary activity is typically upon his work in founding and supporting the Baptist Missionary Society. While that is surely where Ryland spent the bulk of his time and energy, there is evidence that the BMS was not the sole beneficiary of Ryland's missionary commitment.[183]

There is, first, Ryland's role as catalyst in the founding of the London Missionary Society. In August 1794, Ryland received the first communication from William Carey in India. In his excitement, Ryland found David Bogue and James Steven, two Independent ministers who just happened to be in Bristol at the time, and invited them to hear the letter read.[184] Carey's letter, and Ryland's excited sharing of it, stirred Bogue to desire an independent missionary society. He drafted a letter and submitted it to the *Evangelical Magazine*, which printed it in September 1794.[185] The letter spurred the Independents to a missionary zeal similar to that of the Baptists, and the London Missionary Society was formed the next year. Other than the initial

181. Hope is likely the "friend at Liverpool" who provided Ryland with letters relating to Fuller's religious experience (see Ryland, *Work of Faith*, 16; Haykin, "Review of *The Life and Thought of Andrew Fuller*," 149).

182. Stanley, *History*, 27–34; and Cox, *History of the BMS*, 1:7–9, 288–90.

183. Even in his work with the BMS, his catholicity is seen. He writes of Quaker cooperation with the BMS in a letter to John Sutcliff (Ryland, "Letter to John Sutcliff," September 23, 1802).

184. Ellis, *History of the London Missionary Society*, 87.

185. Bogue, "To the Evangelical Diffenters who practife Infant Baptifm," 378–80. Bogue signs the letter as "An Evangelical Dissenter."

impetus, Ryland did not participate in the founding of the Society proper, but he did later help in the founding of an auxiliary society for the LMS in Bristol. A contemporary newspaper account recorded the founding of the auxiliary society and places Ryland in the initial meetings.[186] Several years later, Ryland addressed a fundraising meeting of the auxiliary society, alongside many Independents as well as the Wesleyan missionary Samuel Leigh.[187]

Ryland's involvement with non-Baptist missions did not end there. Contemporary accounts place Ryland at the sixth anniversary meeting of the Wesleyan Methodist Missionary Society in Bristol.[188] While Ryland merely "rendered . . . assistance" at the meeting, he would later serve as the chairman of a meeting of the Wesleyan Auxiliary Society for the Northampton district when they held their fourth anniversary meeting at the Methodist chapel in Northampton, in which he worked alongside other Methodists such as Joshua Taylor, Richard Watson, and George Cubitt.[189] This activity is most surprising, considering Ryland's negative feelings toward Wesley and Wesleyans.[190]

His distaste for Arminianism was clear from his earliest published works. In one of these, published in 1771 when Ryland was only eighteen years old, he writes, "As to manner, I have not aimed to please critics; as to

---

186. The founding of the auxiliary society was full of what Robert Hall Jr. calls "pomp and pride" (Hall Jr., "Letter to John Ryland," May 1, 1815). There were several addresses and sermons given by prominent ministers. The newspaper account places Ryland in the midst of it all: "In the course of the proceedings, various appropriate addresses were delivered, particular by the Rev. Messrs. Bogue, Waugh, Lowell, Thorpe, Priestley, Bishop, Hill, Berry, Dr. Ryland, &c.; as also by Andrew Pope and Richard Ash, Esqrs. and various others" ("Bristol Missionary Society," *Bristol Mirror*, October 17, 1812). Ryland's "Text Book" does not contain any mention of a sermon delivered on the dates mentioned in the newspaper article. However, the article does not mention a "sermon" given by Ryland on the occasion but, rather, an address. It may be, then, that Ryland did not consider what he said to be a sermon and, thus, did not include it in his book of sermons.

187. *Bristol Mirror*, September 30, 1820. Again, the "Text Book" does not contain any mention of a sermon on the dates mentioned, but it may be that Ryland did not consider what he said (called in the article a "peculiarly appropriate speech") to have been a sermon.

188. *Bristol Mirror*, May 12, 1821. What Ryland's assistance was is unknown. He does not mention the meeting in his "Text Book."

189. *Northampton Mercury*, June 21, 1823. This meeting is corroborated by the "Text Book," in which he records having preached at College Lane in Northampton in the evening of June 15 and at Milton (near Northampton) on June 18, placing him in the area of the society meeting (Ryland, "Text Book," June 15, 1823 and June 18, 1823).

190. Ryland made little distinction between Wesley, Wesleyans, and Arminians. Indeed, he uses the labels interchangeably. See Ryland, "On the Alledged Impiety of Calvinism," 285.

matter, I have aimed to displease *Arminians*."[191] He later writes a brief article to "be of some service" to the Arminians, but it is clear that his "service" is meant to bring them over to his way of thinking rather than anything else.[192] To the Baptist church at Bedford, in his funeral sermon for his friend Joshua Symonds, Ryland counsels the church to look for a faithful pastor, describing him as a "man of the fame ftamp with all you have had yet, who fhall keep at equal diftance from real Arminianifm and falfe Calvinifm."[193] In his diary entry for June 8, 1785, Ryland writes about hearing Wesley preach, "Many things were good; all remarkably candid, but lax and injudicious; disapproved greatly of his representation of faith as consisting in assurance of personal interest in Christ, and love as all arising merely from a knowledge of God's love to us, though perhaps in heaven God might be loved for his own perfections. 'Offer it now to thy mistress, will she accept thee?'"[194] Ryland persisted in his clear rejection of and warning against Wesleyan theology until the end of his life. In the last essay he wrote for publication, he defends Calvinistic principles and offers criticism for those of Wesley and his followers. He does so on largely theological grounds, attacking specifically the Wesleyan emphasis on religious impressions, the doctrine of falling from grace, and the idea of general redemption.[195] Despite these theological objections to Wesleyanism, Ryland could nevertheless offer his assistance to the missionary efforts of those with whom he vociferously disagreed.

In the end, Ryland confesses that he accepts Arminians as fellow Christians. In a story told in the third person, he writes of a minister who had gathered with other ministers "who were of different denominations, and who held different opinions, not only respecting the most scriptural form of church government, but also concerning some articles of evangelical

---

191. Ryland, *Serious Essays*, xxi. This book, and that particular sentence, was important in the development of Ryland's catholicity. It will be examined in greater detail in chapter 6.

192. Ryland, "Hint Respecting Efficacious Grace," 315–17. This article was written under the pen name "Eleutherides," but on Ryland's copy of this volume of the *Evangelical Magazine* (held at the Bristol Baptist College Archives), he wrote the page numbers of articles he had written, and this article was one of them.

193. Ryland, *Christ, the Great Source of the Believer's Consolation*, 34.

194. Ryland, "Extracts from the Diary," 2. In an early letter to John Sutcliff, Ryland describes the "Doctrin and Policy" of the Arminians as "inimical to the Dissenters and I think contrary to the Word of God" (Ryland, "Letter to John Sutcliff," August 26, 1774).

195. Ryland, "On the Alledged Impiety of Calvinism," 285. Ryland does offer a bit of sophistry in his essay. He quotes a bad example of extreme Arminianism, but then says that "for such a man we would by no means make pious Arminians accountable" (285). He offers nothing more, so it is rather clear that Ryland produced the quote in order to cast Arminians and Wesley in a bad light.

doctrine."[196] Of this particular minister, he says that he "considers himself as a steady Calvinist," then he clarified that this minister "neither builds his faith upon that eminent Reformer, nor is he unwilling to acknowledge many who are usually denominated Arminians, as brethren in Christ."[197] As the essay unfolds, Ryland makes it clear that he is the "steady Calvinist" minister.[198] That being so, it is a revealing statement, in which he not only acknowledges Arminians as brothers in Christ, but takes a stand in relating to them as such.

Ryland also preached at least four times at what he called "District Meetings."[199] These were meetings of Baptist ministers for the encouragement of village preaching, which was a chief means of evangelism in those days.[200] At one of these meetings, Ryland used the opportunity to communicate his catholic convictions. On April 25, 1809, at Bridgewater, Ryland preached from Phil 4:21. He begins, "Though I am a Protestant Difsenter, yet I have been think^g. pretty often of late of that which is usual called the Apostle's Creed, and of the importance of being a sound Believer in some of its Articles."[201] While Ryland makes sure to note the limitations of the Creed,[202] he nevertheless leans heavily on it for his point. Though before a

---

196. Ryland, "On the Power of Sinners to Repent," *Pastoral Memorials*, 2:329.

197. Ryland, "On the Power of Sinners to Repent," *Pastoral Memorials*, 2:329.

198. The rest of the article is written in the first person, for example. Moreover, a draft of the article, written in Ryland's handwriting, is kept at the Bristol Baptist College Archives.

199. References to these are found in his "Text Book." He preached at district meetings on April 19, 1809 (Keynsham), April 25, 1809 (Bridgewater), April 28, 1813 (Paulton), and April 4, 1820 (Keynsham). The *Baptist Magazine* contains references to these meetings on these dates. See Anonymous, "Public Meetings," *Baptist Magazine* 1, 245–46; Anonymous, "Public Meetings," *Baptist Magazine* 5, 262; and Edminson, "Association. Wilts and Somerset," 207.

Note: a previous version of this section identified the district meetings as meetings of Methodist ministers. This has been corrected.

200. Booth, "Mr. Booth on Village Preaching," 282–85.

201. Ryland, "Sermon Notes: Philippians 4:21," *Original Manuscript Sermons: Old Testament, Vol. II*.

202. He seems to fear giving too much credence to the Roman Catholic Church and their use of the Creed. In his sermon notes, he says, "The Ch. of Rome has made too much of that Form of sound words, in setting it upon a level with the SS [Sacred Scriptures]. Some of the Popish Divines have not only affirmd more than can be proved, that it was made by the Apostles themselves, but have idly pretended that each contributed a separate Clause to compose it. It may be rated too high in some Protestant Churches, & Individ^s. have shown their Ignor^{ce}. in considering it as a prayr. As a very ancient & scriptural compendium of X^n. Doctrine it is respectable. Tho not a perfect Summary of divine Truth, for it does not touch, except by Implication on the Fallen state of Man while we cannot imagine a persons Salv. w^d. be endangered who did not know the N.

group of likeminded Baptists, Ryland implores them, as they seek to evangelize the villages in the country, to focus less on denominational distinctives and more on the centrality of Christ, "For my part, I sincerely wish that whether we repeat that Creed by Rote or not, we may have this truth impressed on our ♥s, that there is a holy, universal Ch. to wch. every S^t. in X^t. Jesus [Saint in Christ Jesus] belongs; & that all true X^s. are Brethren, who have one common Interest, & sh^d. have a peculiar Regard for each other." Ryland's theology of catholicity will be taken up in the next chapter, so it will suffice to say at this point that he understood relation to Jesus Christ as that which unites believers.[203] This relationship to Jesus was powerful enough to overcome even the most deeply rooted of theological differences, such that, as shown above, a committed Calvinistic Baptist could partner with and even promote the interests of Arminian Methodists.[204]

Ryland displays his mission-minded catholicity in a letter to John Sutcliff. The letter itself is an interesting specimen. It was originally a letter from Jacob Grigg to Sutcliff, in which Grigg, writing as a BMS missionary in Sierra Leone, provides Sutcliff with some of the latest mission field intelligence. The letter was apparently delivered to Ryland by mistake.[205] Ryland

---

[Name] of the Rom. Govern^r. who sentenced our Lord to [crucifixion]." Note: for the word "crucifixion," Ryland drew a cross, then wrote, immediately following, "cifixion."

203. This seems to have been a theme that was important to Ryland at these meetings. At a later meeting, on April 28, 1813 in Paulton, Ryland preached from Joel 2:27, in which he covers similar ground. He speaks of the "Inhabitation of God in his Church" (Ryland, "Sermon Notes: Joel 2:27," *Original Manuscript Sermons: Old Testament, Vol. 1*). Though he admits that God's "omnipres^t. Essence can b. no where excluded," Ryland holds that the text "points out his peculiar presence with his People." God's people, says Ryland, are a people "Not distinguished by blood, complection or country, nor by any merely external Denomination. But scattered thro various Countries, Tribes and Professions, yet distinguished from all other People on earth." He then goes on to show the various ways in which the people of God are peculiar: they are devoted to the Lord; they are in covenant with him; they bear his image; and they are formed by God for himself. It is a spiritual fellowship that binds Christians, not the badge of denomination or theological commitments.

204. It is important to note that Ryland is willing to partner with Wesleyan Methodists who were, undoubtedly, Arminian in their soteriology. In an early letter, Ryland writes to Sutcliff that it is "the wisdom as well as the duty of the dissenters to be friendly with the orthodox Methodists" (Ryland, "Letter to John Sutcliff," August 26, 1774). Crocker contends that "orthodox" here means "Calvinist" (Crocker, "Life and Legacy," 340). While it is probable that, at the early stage at which the letter was written (e.g., in 1774, when Ryland was only twenty-one years old), Ryland meant "Calvinist," it is equally clear that he expanded his understanding of "orthodox" in later years, as he was more than friendly with both Arminian and Calvinistic Methodists. His commitment to Calvinism did not change, but the broadness of his catholicity did, as did the harshness of his temperament toward those who disagree.

205. Ryland says, apologetically, "This Letter was bro't to me last Night by Governor

added to the letter and sent it on to Sutcliff. Ryland's contribution is written between the lines of Grigg's letter. In Grigg's letter, he had mentioned a man named Garvin, who wanted to join the BMS as a missionary.[206] Ryland writes to Sutcliff about Garvin:

> I hope you will consult Bro^r. Horne about the Weslean preacher mentioned herein. I shou'd be sorry to neglect any Conscientious Man who thinks our practice right and shou'd also [be] sorry to be eager to make a convert to a party or to let any other denomination of Christians justly suspect us of unfairness. I refer to the M^r. Garvin mentioned in the last page of this Letter. He has written to me himself, but says nothing about Sentiments. I sh^d. not refuse [him] for not being a compleat Calvinist, tho I think myself a very staunch one, much lefs sh^d. I refuse him for not calling himself by that name. But I sh^d. wish to know a little more whereabouts he is as to Sentiments, and whether he w^d. warmly oppose anything I think important Truth.[207]

Ryland, thus, distinguishes between "important Truth" that would disqualify a person from his recommendation and Calvinism. One may hold to "important Truth" yet reject Calvinism.

Ryland also rejoiced to see non-Calvinists succeed on the mission field. In a sermon on Ps 126:4, given at the monthly prayer meeting in Bristol, Ryland speaks of the progress of God's work around the world, singling out Moravians as well as Methodists:

> Faith and patience must be tried. The Moravians labor'd 13 y^{rs}. in Greenland before they met wth. succefs, but since then they have been useful to many souls. They have had a large harvest in the West Indi^s., where the Methodists also have done much good. They have had succefs among the American Ind^s. as the Anglo Americans have had in time past, and now are some hopeful appearances. The Morav^s. have a considerable harvest among the Hottentotts & Esquimaux, and have glean'd some Souls in Surnam. Dr. Vanderkamp and others, have a hopeful prospect in the South of Africa.[208]

Dawes, it was not sealed, therefore I read it" (Ryland, "Letter to John Sutcliff," June 1796).

206. This is John Garvin, a Methodist schoolmaster sent by the Sierra Leone Company. For more information on Garvin, see Dresser, *Slavery Obscured*, 174; Whyte, *Zachary Macaulay 1768–1838*, 73–78; Fyfe, *History of Sierra Leone*, 1:69–70.

207. Ryland, "Letter to John Sutcliff," June 1796.

208. Ryland, "Sermon Notes: Psalm 126:4," October 4, 1802, *Discourses on the Book of Psalms*.

His concern is not solely that the BMS succeeds; it is, rather, that there is a general fruitfulness of every missionary.

Ryland's catholicity is also seen in his willingness to preach in non-Particular Baptist churches, which he did throughout his preaching career. Beginning on July 2, 1772,[209] Ryland preached hundreds of times in churches outside of his denomination, including many Independent churches,[210] several Presbyterian churches,[211] and Anglican churches. These are not surprising, considering Ryland's previously demonstrated theological allegiances and published statements. However, Ryland also lent his ministerial ability to the General Baptists,[212] the Methodists, and the Seventh-Day Baptists.[213] It is important to remember that Ryland occupied those pulpits not as a debater, nor in an attempt to win them over to "his side." He understood himself to be there as a minister of the gospel, and he endeavored to speak on those things with which his audience would agree. In a letter to the editors of the *Baptist Magazine*, Ryland reveals how he conducted himself when in other pulpits. He writes about an address which he gave at a missionary prayer meeting in London, at the Baptist church on Eagle Street. In that address, he made mention of his belief in God's foreordination of all that comes to pass. Someone had written to Ryland afterwards complaining of Ryland's belief. Ryland defends himself, saying that he believed that he was only stating something with which everyone in the audience would agree. He writes that he would have spoken differently if he was in a different church: "I have no doubt, indeed, of the piety of some who

---

209. On that date, Ryland preached in London at the Independent Meeting on Bridwell Alley pastored by John Rogers (Ryland, "Text Book," July 2, 1772).

210. Ryland preached very often at the Independent church that met at Castle Green in Bristol. His "Text Book" contains seventy-five references to his preaching there, not counting the times that the "Monthly Lecture" met there.

211. Ryland preached many times at the Bridge Street church in Bristol. In the "Text Book," he references eighty-two times that he preached in that pulpit, again, not counting the times that the "Monthly Lecture" met there.

212. Ryland once preached in Whitechapel at the church of Dan Taylor, the General Baptist founder of the New Connexion (Ryland, "Text Book," December 30, 1810). Ryland is much more open to the General Baptists of the Taylor Connexion than he is the "Old Generals," as he saw Taylor and the New General Baptists as more evangelical in their thinking and preaching (Ryland, "Letter to Samuel Miller," November 25, 1800).

213. In his "Text Book," Ryland says that he preached at the General Baptist church in Oakham on July 19, 1772; in Moulton on November 12, 1772, October 21, 1773, and March 21, 1779; in Spratton on September 15, 1774; at John Brittain's church in London on June 30, 1776; and in Burton on July 2, 1783. He preached at the Methodist meeting in Redruth on June 6, 1803. He also preached at the Seventh-Day Baptist church in Stapleton on July 20, 1776, where he notes that there were "about 30 people almost all mad or asleep."

entertain prejudices against it; and had I been in their pulpit, I should not have obtruded my opinion on them, but have confined myself to topics of still greater importance, on which we agree."[214]

This is borne out in the notes of sermons which Ryland preached at non-Baptist churches. Indicative of his practice is the sermon preached at the Methodist meeting in Kelstone on June 10, 1803. Ryland preached from Ps 145:11, and his main point was that "Saints love to speak of the peculiar Glory of the K^m. of God, as restor'd in the ♥s of men, thro' the Mediation of his dear Son."[215] Nothing in the sermon would have been understood as a Particular Baptist distinctive, nor would it have incited evangelical Methodist opposition. Ryland also preached at the united monthly prayer meeting, at which ministers from all the dissenting churches met together. These sermons also display a catholic spirit in the sense that they emphasize what united the ministers rather than what divided them.

While Ryland's catholicity was broad, it is worth noting a few examples of its limitations. Though he at one time was friendly with John Webster Morris,[216] he later referred to him as "that Vile Sinner Morris" and feared that Morris would do insult to Andrew Fuller's memory by publishing an unauthorized biography.[217] He also spoke with decided prejudice against Thomas Coke, a leader among the Methodists, saying, "I heard D^r. Coke sev^l. yr^s. ago, say in the Ebenezer, 'He did not know who had been most useful in J^a. [Jamaica] the B^{ts}. or the Methodists,' when I inferred that I might know for if D^r. Coke c^d. have given his own denominat^n. the decided preference, I was sure he w^d."[218] He also allowed competitiveness to cloud his catholicity. While he rejoiced in the successes of the Moravians and Methodists, he could also lament that, after the death of James Coultart, a BMS missionary to Jamaica, the believers there will "be left a prey to ignorant

---

214. Ryland, "Letter to the Editors of the Baptist Magazine," published as "On the Divine Decrees," *Baptist Magazine* 14 (September 1822), 365–66.

215. Ryland, "Sermon Notes: Psalm 145:11," June 10, 1803, *Discourses on the Book of Psalms*.

216. Ryland, "Letter to Jonathan Edwards Jr.," August 28, 1801. Ryland writes of Morris's new *Biblical Magazine*, "I hope this Magazine will ans^r. some good end, and promote a better taste in divinity than either the Evangelical Magazine, or the New one printed at Bristol unD^r. the Title of the Theological."

217. Ryland, "Letter to John Saffery," May 22, 1815. That Ryland would use such a crude expression is, again, inconsistent with his beliefs expressed elsewhere. To Hart, Ryland expresses his dislike of "nicknames" (Ryland, "Letter to Levi Hart," 1805).

218. Ryland, "Letter to John Saffery," January 12, 1818. Ryland's dislike of Coke stretched over many years, as he makes similar remarks to Samuel Miller in 1800, denouncing Coke as having read "some very unguarded unsatisfactory acct^s. of their late succeſs in America" (Ryland, "Letter to Samuel Miller," November 25, 1800).

colored teachers, or fall into the hands of the Methodists. The latter are much alarmed, and ab[t]. to send out a No [Number] more mifsionaries thither, or rather have just sent some, & are sending more."[219] The same is seen in a letter to John Sutcliff, when Ryland writes, "I really fear we shall mifs some money thro the notion some people entertain that THE Society supports All the Mifsions."[220] Ryland, then, is not a perfect model of consistency. He is, however, a notable example of Christian love and charity toward those who "hold the head" along with him.

Missionary Work and Catholicity: The Unifying Nature of Working Together

The relationship between Ryland's catholicity and his involvement in missionary work is worth considering, as it points to the more general relationship of missions to interdenominational cooperation. In the burgeoning missionary movement, the world was opening up to the British Baptists. With their affirmative answer to the Modern Question, they believed that it was an incumbent duty to get the gospel to the whole world. They focused, therefore, on the proclamation of the gospel.[221] This had the effect of narrowing their theological focus when it came to partnership with others outside their tradition. Gone, or lessened, were questions of polity and the finer points of theological debate, replaced with a concern for the progress of the gospel to all people. This led to more cooperation within the denomination, which existed at a low level at times, and greater willingness to work with those outside the denomination as well.

An important conclusion drawn from this study of Ryland's catholicity is the unifying nature of co-laboring. In his published writings, Ryland had very little positive to say of Wesleyan Methodists or Arminians in general. Indeed, at times, he saw them as opponents to overcome rather than partners in a common work. However, when he began to see them as partners, Ryland softened toward them. This is not to say that he began to agree with them, for he surely did not. Despite this continued disagreement,

---

219. Ryland, "Letter to John Saffery," January 12, 1818.

220. Ryland, "Letter to Sutcliff," September 23, 1802. "THE Society" refers to the Church Missionary Society.

221. William Carey was the initial catalyst for missionary engagement, with his "Deathless Sermon" given at the association meeting in 1792 and his *Enquiry into the Obligations of Christians to Use Means for the Conversion of the Heathen* published the same year. He was joined by others, including Ryland, Fuller, and Sutcliff, in the formation of the BMS, an organization which Ryland served until his death (Cox, *History of the BMS*, 288–90; Stanley, *History of the BMS*, 4–33; Cross, *Useful Learning*, 357–59)

however, he partnered with them: he helped them raise money for their missionary society, he recommended Wesleyans to the mission field, and he took a moderate tone when he spoke in front of mixed (Calvinist-Arminian) audiences.[222]

Indeed, Ryland was at his most catholic when discussing the work of missions. At the 1794 meeting of the Western Baptist Association in Chard, Ryland preached on the increase of the kingdom of Christ, and he speaks there to the broadness of the missionary concern. He first urges a geographical broadness, saying:

> Nor let us confine our efforts, and much lefs our ardent prayers, to the increafe of true Godlinefs at home. Let us enlarge our views, and our plans for promoting the caufe of Chrift. A Negro Church of our own denomination is now planted on the coaft of Africa, and numbers who were formerly torn from thofe injured fhores, have been baptized into Chrift, in Jamaica, and North America. Let us remember in our prayers the free fettlers of Sierra Leone; and their Brethren in the American Ifles and Continent, who have been delivered from the yoke of Satan, tho' many of them are ftill held in flavery by Man. We truft, that before this time, our Miffionaries have reached the Eaft Indies, and are employed in rolling away the ftone, that the fable flocks of Hindoos may drink of the water of life. Let us be mindful of them before the throne; let us continue to fend them liberal fupplies. Let us be on the watch for frefh openings to fpread the Gofpel.[223]

Understandably, Ryland restricts his first exhortation to the Baptist denomination, as he is speaking before a gathering of Baptists. He speaks of their missionaries and of the work of the BMS in various places. However, Ryland is not content to confine his concern to the work of the Baptists. He goes on to say, "Let us look out for other Miffionaries, and beg of God to

---

222. To be fair, throughout his ministerial career, Ryland is found preaching in a variety of churches, including General Baptist churches as early as 1772. Caution is warranted in this regard for at least two reasons. First, what he preached in those churches is not known, as those sermons were never published, and the notes from them either never existed or have been lost. He could have preached broadly evangelical sermons in order to keep the peace, or he could have preached staunchly Calvinistic sermons. With regard to the former, it would be in keeping with his later catholic practice, though in favor of the latter is Ryland's early pugnaciousness toward Arminians. Second, more weight should be given to later actions, as they are the product of a mature minister with settled convictions and the ability to choose when and where he desires to preach, rather than taking every opportunity afforded him.

223. Ryland, *Certain Increase*, 30.

raife up fuch as fhall not count life dear to them, when compared with the falvation of immortal fouls. Let us enquire whither we may beft make another inroad on the kingdom of Satan? Our Moravian Brethren are fuccefsful among the Hottentots, fhall we make an attempt to evangelize the Cafres? Or fhall we fend a Miffion to any of the iflands of the Southern Ocean?"[224]

In Ryland's missionary catholicity, he understands that there are distinct missionary societies that send their own missionaries, but he believes that they are all taking part in one work. While the Moravians work among one group, the "Hottentots," perhaps the BMS could send a missionary to another, the "Cafres."[225] It was not a competition but a coordination of effort in the same work, with the same goals, for the same purpose. If the Moravians have reached this group, then the Baptists would go elsewhere; to do otherwise would be doubling up resources in one place.[226]

In Ryland, then, is seen the unifying nature of working together and seeing others as working toward a common goal. Ryland would never be comfortable with Arminian or Wesleyan theology, but he was comfortable with Arminian and Wesleyan missionaries. He could pray for their success, hope for their increase, and help to prosper their work. The young man who once "aimed to displease" Arminians became the pastor who chaired a meeting of the Wesleyan Methodist Missionary Society. The young pastor who warned against "Weslyte" doctrine and policy would recommend a Wesleyan Methodist as a missionary. Co-laboring in the missionary movement became a means of seeing those with whom he disagreed in a different light.[227]

---

224. Ryland, *Certain Increase*, 30–31.

225. There seems to be no relation between these two groups, other than they were either African or descendants of Africans. The Hottentots are the Khoikhoi people, a nomadic group in southern Africa, while the Cafres are descendants of African and Madagascan slaves.

226. Partnership between the BMS and Moravians was not unheard of. In a sermon raising support for the BMS, Ryland speaks of the work of Moses Baker in Jamaica. In the midst of his plea for a successor to Baker, Ryland says that the "Moravian Brethren lately bore testimony [to Baker] in the P. A. [Periodical Accounts] and an offer has been made of considerable aid for his support" (Ryland, "Sermon Notes: Sequel of Missionary Sermon on 1 Chronicles 29:5," *Original Manuscript Sermons: Old Testament, Vol. I*).

227. There is more to be studied in this regard. In particular, the connection between ecumenism and the missionary movement within the Baptist denomination would be a fruitful and much needed avenue of research (see Ward, "Baptists and the Transformation of the Church," 171–72).

Conclusion

This chapter has demonstrated that Ryland's catholicity is seen most clearly in two distinct but related areas: his broad friendships and his cooperation in ministry with those who were outside of his theological tradition. It has done so through a close reading of Ryland's correspondence as well as primary source materials. That this is a catholic impulse is seen in Ryland's own words to Stephen West, in which he roots his communication and cooperation with those outside of his theological and denominational tradition in that phrase in the Apostles' Creed: "I believe [in] the catholic church, the communion of saints."[228] His own understanding was that this was an expression of a catholic spirit. Though not without limits,[229] he was willing to overlook significant theological differences in order to demonstrate love toward others and work alongside them for the sake of their common interest in the gospel. An important contribution of this chapter is to show the breadth of Ryland's catholicity, which encompasses the Reformed world as well as the Arminian, the congregational as well as the Presbyterian and Anglican, the Baptist as well as the paedobaptist. Ryland is also at least willing to extend an olive branch toward Roman Catholics and the Orthodox. This also shows the differences between Ryland's catholicity and that of his seventeenth-century predecessors. Such development could happen, in part, because of the Toleration Act of 1689, which made possible the Christian pluralism into which Ryland was born. Indeed, a comparison of Ryland with his forebears illustrates David Thompson's point about the change that took place between the pre-Toleration and post-Toleration eras with regard to attitudes of Christians to other Christian groups. Thompson writes, "Until the mid-seventeenth century, most Christian groups regarded themselves as the only true church; this was what added a sense that the issue was a matter of life and death to the disagreements. Increasingly from that point, there was a readiness to recognise, albeit reluctantly, that others were Christian, too. Toleration meant the acceptance of Christian pluralism."[230]

---

228. Ryland, "Letter to Stephen West," March 31, 1814, 180–81.

229. Crocker names four "boundaries" of Ryland's catholicity: General Baptists, "unorthodox Methodists," Unitarians, and Roman Catholics (Crocker, "Life and Legacy," 352). As this chapter has demonstrated, the matter is far more complex than that: Ryland preached in General Baptist churches; "unorthodox Methodists" is not a phrase that Ryland used, and he would later work alongside Wesleyan Methodists in ministerial cooperation; Ryland formally rejected Unitarianism, but his relationship with Robert Hall Jr., to be examined in the next chapter, shows that he was willing, at least temporarily, to overlook non-Trinitarian views; and he was willing to countenance that a Roman Catholic could be among the redeemed.

230. Thompson, "Baptists in the Eighteenth Century," 261.

This chapter has also shown that the definition of catholicity offered in the opening chapter holds true in Ryland's practice, though with some limitations in application to Roman Catholics, Arminians, and others with whom Ryland had doctrinal or personal differences. The available evidence of Ryland's lived catholicity, as seen in his correspondence, ministerial partnerships, and close friendships, indicates that his practice was largely consistent with his understanding that believers should "take pleasure in the communion of faith, by the acknowledging of every good thing which is in our brethren toward Christ Jesus."[231]

---

231. Ryland, "Communion of Saints," *Pastoral Memorials*, 2:280.

5

Theological Foundations

THE PREVIOUS CHAPTER DEMONSTRATED John Ryland Jr.'s practice of catholicity. It remains, however, to examine the reasons for his catholic friendships and partnerships: what are the foundations of his catholic sentiments? This chapter and the next will approach the question from two different perspectives: the theological and the personal. This chapter will examine the theological foundation of Ryland's catholicity.

In attempting to outline any aspect of Ryland's theology, a certain limitation presents itself: Ryland's purpose as a writer. His published works are largely comprised of sermons.[1] The reason for this is simple yet worth stating: while he was the President of the Bristol Baptist Academy, Ryland's chief work was not for an academic community. He was, rather, a churchman. He was a pastor and denominational leader; the Academy of which he was President was founded and operated for the education of men for the ministry.[2] While Ryland believed in founding his practice on what he

---

1. Even his apologetic work defending believer's baptism began life as a sermon on John 1:25 (Ryland, "Preface," *Candid Statement*, v). The exceptions to this are his early poetic works (e.g., *Serious Essays on the Truths of the Glorious Gospel*; *Perseverance: A Poem*; and *Faithfulness of God in His Word Evinced*), and his biography of Andrew Fuller, *Work of Faith, Labour of Love, and the Patience of Hope*.

2. The founding documents of the Bristol Education Society, which supported the Academy, stressed the importance of an educated ministry: "The truth is, whatever prejudices may be formed in the minds of ſome men againſt learning, it is certain, that ſince the times of the apoſtles, who had thoſe miraculous helps which ſuperſeded every kind of learning, divine providence hath, in every age, put the greateſt honor upon it" (Anonymous, *Account of the Bristol Education Society*, viii–ix). Ryland took this aspect of the Academy seriously, as, when he arrived in Bristol, he restricted admission to the school chiefly to those who intended to continue in the ministry, though occasionally

understood to be biblical and rational principles, he did not systematize his beliefs in technical theological works.³ Therefore, though he did not write a treatise on his doctrine of the church or catholicity, his writings contain elements of his understanding that may be brought together into a coherent whole. Through a close reading of his works, this chapter will outline that whole.

Union with Christ and Catholicity

An examination of Ryland's published sermons, sermon notes, letters, and other writings reveal that his catholicity begins with his understanding of salvation, in particular his doctrine of union with Christ. Ryland often rests his practice on a simple belief: he accepts others because Jesus accepts them.⁴ Writing to Stephen West, Ryland says:

> As to smaller matters, concerning which even true Christians may differ, we must pray for divine guidance, endeavor to search the sacred scriptures impartially, and act up to our light: at the same time, guarding against laying an improper or disproportionate stress on such points; and avowing, both to our brethren and to the unconverted, that we consider the things on which all good men are agreed, as of far greater importance; and showing

---

admitting a student that he thought he could "have . . . fully unD^r. control" (Ryland, "Letter to Levi Hart," August 10, 1805).

3. With regard to the Bible, Ryland holds that the Scriptures "contain a standard of faith" (Ryland, "Ways of Death," *Pastoral Memorials*, 1:135) that functions as "a perfect rule, the infallible standard of faith and practice" (Ryland, "Scriptures Opposed to Impressions," *Pastoral Memorials*, 1:171). Additionally, the Bible alone is a sure revelation from God, that gives humanity an accurate portrait of "the true nature of things" (Ryland, "Characteristics of Divine Revelation," *Pastoral Memorials*, 1:169). As it pertains to reason, Christianity, according to Ryland, is reasonable and capable of rational explanation: "Reason determines that we may depend on these ['the bodily senses, the memory, the testimony of others, tradition, and historical records'] as sources of knowledge, and then admits a variety of truths on each of these grounds. And surely revelation may be as good a source of information as either of the former, and still better and more worthy of dependance; unless reason could prove revelation impossible, or that which professes to be so, false. Reason is suited to the discovery of truth, and truth must be favorable to virtue; and therefore, we may be sure right reason is favorable to true religion" (Ryland, "Use of Reason in Matters of Religion," *Pastoral Memorials*, 2:21).

4. In this way, Ryland sits comfortably in the stream of Baptist catholicity outlined in chapter 3, though with his own emphases. Of course, there remains the question of orthodoxy: what if a person does not have orthodox beliefs? Are they still acceptable? As will be shown below, Ryland's answer is in the affirmative, at least in some cases.

practically that we do so, and that we love all who love Christ in sincerity, whether they follow with us or not.[5]

While he never veered from his own Calvinistic Baptist theology, Ryland nevertheless does not allow denominational distinctives or even differing theological commitments to be a bar to fellowship and love. Ryland explains this catholic commitment in a sermon preached both in Northampton (1785) and Bristol (1809).[6] Here, Ryland exhorts the people to a special kind of love for Christian brethren:

> Our Lord is not here speaking of that sincere benevolence, which should extend to all mankind, including our personal enemies, and those who may be at present enemies to God. This he strongly inculcates elsewhere. The law of God requires it, the gospel promotes it, and true saints possess it. But the text relates to a higher kind of love, which we must admit is more confined in its objects. It includes complacency, and is restricted to those who are the true disciples and brethren of Christ.[7]

As outlined in chapter 1, Ryland distinguishes between what might be called mere politeness and Christian catholicity. He understands politeness to be the responsibility of all people to all others, including enemies.[8]

Christian catholicity, however, springs from a "higher kind of love" that is "more confined in its objects" to those who are "brethren of Christ." This special love of believers for other believers "is grounded upon their relation to Christ, and their resemblance of him."[9] The extent of a Christian's love

---

5. Ryland, "Christian Circumspection," *Pastoral Memorials*, 2:35–36. Ryland repeats this emphasis in an address published as *Eight Characteristics of the Messiah*, in which he says, "We become closely united in one body, with all who love our blessed Redeemer" (Ryland, *Eight Characteristics of the Messiah*, 11).

6. The sermon was published in the first volume of *Pastoral Memorials* without a date. However, Ryland's handwritten sermon notes for the sermon contain the dates and locations mentioned above (Ryland, "Sermon Notes: John 13:35," *Original Manuscript Sermons: Old Testament, Vol. II*).

7. Ryland, "Mutual Love a Mark of Christ's Disciples," *Pastoral Memorials*, 1:329.

8. On politeness and English society, see the summary of recent works in Carr, "Polite and Enlightened London?" 623–34.

9. Ryland, "Mutual Love a Mark of Christ's Disciples," 1:329. He continues with an appeal to biblical precedent: "John, in his second Epistle, describes it, as belonging to all who have known the truth, and as having respect to the truth which dwells in the objects of it. Yet it does not spring from mere attachment to speculative opinions, or a blind adherence to external forms" (1:329). It is interesting that Ryland could call what some would denominate important doctrinal convictions as "mere attachment to speculative opinions" and denominational commitments as "blind adherence to external forms." As will be shown below, doctrine remained important to Ryland, and his

for and embrace of another is the extent of Christ's love for and embrace of that person. To Ryland, the very gospel demands a broad catholicity: "If we understand the *nature* of the gospel, we must love one another. The religion of Christ is the religion of love. In the gospel is the most wonderful display of divine love . . . Christ loved his church, and gave himself for it. Surely then, his love must constrain us to love those, who are evidently loved by him."[10] Differences of opinion are by no means to be ignored, but neither are they to be a reason for disunity: "On points wherein true Christians may differ from each other, search the Sacred Scriptures for yourself. Unite more closely with those that you really think nearest the standard; but let nothing prevent your showing a sincere affection to all who hold the head."[11] His basic theology of catholicity is, thus, easily seen: all who "hold the head" are worthy of sincere affection. Union with Christ, then, is a central element of his overall theology of catholicity.

In order to show that this was a settled conviction, rather than the product of convenience, it will be beneficial at this point to demonstrate that this sort of understanding of catholicity is consistent throughout Ryland's pastoral career. As early as 1773, Ryland speaks in a sermon of the constraining effects of the love of Christ, saying, "It constrains to love him again, love him supremely, give him preference to evry obj., to love his people, for his sake, pray for them, relieve them."[12] In 1790 and 1795, Ryland preached from Rom 12:4–5, and he exhorts his hearers to "universal benevolence," saying, "There is no sure Found^n. for universal Benvol. to our fell^w. Men, but the Love of God. And it is the Union of true Believ^s. wth. X^t. w^{ch}. [believers with Christ which] lays the Found^n. of their special Love to each other. They are connected wth. him as y^r. com^n. [their common] Head,

---

devotion to the Particular Baptist denomination cannot be doubted, which makes this statement all the more remarkable.

10. Ryland, "Mutual Love a Mark of Christ's Disciples," 1:330. Ryland continues, "It is not founded on expectation of temporal advantage, personal benefit, or party connexion; but on that relation to Christ, which is manifested by faith, works by love, and produces studious conformity to him. It extends to all such, as far as we are convinced they are of this description, whether they follow with us or not, or are of our society, denomination, or country; notwithstanding difference of sentiment on other subjects or even on the inferior parts of religion" (Ryland, "Mutual Love a Mark of Christ's Disciples," 1:330). In this particular sermon, Ryland is somewhat repetitious on this point. Since John Foster estimates that the material found in *Pastoral Memorials* is roughly a third of what Ryland preached (Foster, "Ryland's *Pastoral Memorials*," 544), it is reasonable to conclude that Ryland must have felt the theme important enough to dwell on for some time.

11. Ryland, "Mutual Love a Mark of Christ's Disciples," *Pastoral Memorials*, 1:330.

12. Ryland, "Sermon Notes: 2 Corinthians 5:14," *Original Manuscript Sermons: Old Testament, Vol. II.*

& are all under the Infl^{ce}. of his Spirit."[13] In a letter to the "Little Church" of Paedobaptists at Broadmead, written in 1792, Ryland assures them of his pastoral catholicity rooted in communion with Christ: "It appears to me *so much the nature of the new creature*, (if I may so express myself,) *for true believers to have intimate communion with each other*, that nothing but clear precept or precedent for debarring a mistaken brother from the Lord's table, could induce me to refuse those whom Christ had evidently received, and who could be admitted without any injury to my own exercise of the rights of conscience, or without endangering any privilege of my own."[14] In a sermon on Isa 11:10 preached twelve times between 1809 and 1822, Ryland contends:

> Especially in proportion as we enter into the Spirit of his Gospel, our Union wth. him will produce Attach^{mt}. to each other. The [cross] is the great rallying Point for the true Catholic Church. Do you worſhip God in the Spirit, rejoice in X^t. Jesus, & place no Confid^{ce}. in the flesh? this will more closely unite true Saints in one Communion, than any outw^d. Denomination. Whether you wear my uniform, or of my Regiment, you are really of my side.[15]

In 1811, in a sermon on Ps 133, he says, "We sh^d. cultivate a Union of Sp^t. with all that are truly united to Christ, let them differ from us as much as ever they can, and be one in ♥ wth. him. Not that we sh^d. violate Consc. or sacrifice the Truth in the smallest Matters; but let us speak the Truth in Love, and whereunto we have attain'd, let us walk by the same Rule, and mind the same thing."[16] This quotation actually captures much of Ryland's

---

13. Ryland, "Sermon Notes: Romans 12:4–5," *Original Manuscript Sermons: Old Testament, Vol. II*. He goes on, "They are *one Body in Him*, all ſharing in the same Advantages resulting f^m. their Connect^n. with him" (Ryland, "Sermon Notes: Romans 12:4–5").

14. Ryland, "Letter to the Paedobaptist Church at Broadmead," *Pastoral Memorials*, 2:20. The idea of receiving those whom the Lord has received is conceptually descended from the dictum of Henry Jessey: "That which the Lord limits, we muſt limit. And what he limits not, what are wee, that we ſhould limit?" (Jessey, *Storehouse of Provision*, 94; cf. 113).

15. Ryland, "Sermon Notes: Isaiah 11:10," *Original Manuscript Sermons: Old Testament, Vol. I*. A comparison of the sermon notes with the "Text Book" reveals that Ryland first preached the sermon at Broadmead, repeating it in Salisbury, Tetbury, Northampton (College Lane), Downend, Edinburgh (at Rev. Mr. Aikman's), Counterslip, Newbury (at Rev. Mr. Winter's), Cardiff (where he went by mistake thinking there would be a missionary meeting), Taunton (for a collection for the mission), London (Prescott Street), and St. Sidwell's in Exeter.

16. Ryland, "Sermon Notes: Psalm 133," *Discourses on the Book of Psalms*.

practice: there is the maintenance of distinctions, disagreement if necessary, and a commitment to persevere in fellowship.

Ryland also sought to inculcate this sort of catholicity in new ministers, charging James Hinton at his ordination in 1801:

> This apostolic Expression, *Our* sufficiency is of God, should lead us to cordial Union with our Fellow-laborers. Paul is not inclined to confine the encouragement, given him by our Lord, to himself; he would invite others to share it with him. The cause in which your heart, my Brother, is engaged is not your's, but God's. Let us unite with all who are hearty in it. Let not the spirit in us that lusteth unto envy ever be indulged, but be thoroughly mortified. Never let there be any appearance of unfriendly competition, among the Ministers of the everlasting Gospel; but let us be ready to lend each other mutual aid, and combine in the most affectionate cooperation.[17]

In 1821, preaching the funeral for the Anglican Thomas Scott, Ryland, says:

> The source of salvation, the medium of acceptance, and the nature of future happiness provided for the people of God, are far more clearly discovered. It is here especially represented as the privilege of all true believers, to have, through their connexion with the exalted Mediator, the most intimate communion with each other: so with the church militant, and the church triumphant: they are one body; and the bliss of the latter is already made known to the former, and in some degree shared by them.[18]

The church on earth should reflect the unity of the church in heaven, at least in some measure.

As late as 1824, less than a year before he died, Ryland preached to the monthly prayer meeting of evangelical ministers in Bristol from Isa 62:1, urging them that "All Christ^s. fh^d. unite in earneft, ferv^t., const^t. prayr, for θe Coming K^m. of X^t., its extension in the World, θe Convers^n. of Souls around θem; & more of θe illuminat^g. Infl^s. of θe Sp^t. for θeir brethren."[19]

Consistent throughout his ministerial career is the belief that union with other believers is founded on union with Christ, with the practical

---

17. Ryland, *Difficulties and Supports of a Gospel Minister*, 30.

18. Ryland, "Spirits of the Just," *Pastoral Memorials*, 2:257.

19. Ryland, "Sermon Notes: Isaiah 62:1," *Original Manuscript Sermons: Old Testament, Vol. II*: "All Christians should unite in earnest, fervent, constant prayer for the coming Kingdom of Christ, its extension in the world, the conversion of souls around them, and more of the illuminating influences of the Spirit for their brethren."

result that believers ought to share in the life of all who are united to Christ. His catholicity, then, may be rightly said to be christocentric. However, his understanding is more complex and nuanced than it may at first seem. Questions remain, the most important of which are: 1) how is it that people are united to Christ and whence does this union arise? 2) how does one know if another person is so united to Christ? The second question is one that Ryland is especially keen to answer and reveals some important aspects of his catholicity. In order to answer it, however, the first question must be examined.

The Spirit, Salvation, and Catholicity

Michael A. G. Haykin has argued that Ryland's catholicity is founded ultimately on his understanding of the Holy Spirit's work.[20] Haykin demonstrates that Ryland founded his ideas about Christian fellowship on love for Jesus and being "led by the Spirit," by which Haykin says that Ryland meant having a Spirit-renewed mind and being taught to "obey, follow, and imitate God as his dear children."[21] Haykin is surely correct in this assertion, as Ryland says that the work of the Spirit is, in part, to bind Christians to other Christians, which he does through the work of love. Explaining the meaning of Gal 5:22, Ryland says that the fruit of the Spirit is love, which means "love to God, and love to man."[22] In another place, he makes the connection between the Spirit and Christian unity more explicit, saying that Christians are to "love the excellent and beautiful fruits of the Spirit in others."[23] This section will build on Haykin's understanding of the Spirit's role in Ryland's catholicity by outlining the part the Spirit plays in Ryland's understanding of the order of salvation.

Belonging to the Particular Baptist denomination, it should come as no surprise that Ryland's doctrine of salvation is of the Calvinist variety.[24]

---

20. Haykin, "Sum of All Good," 332–53.

21. Ryland, *Indwelling and Righteousness of Christ*, 18; cf. Haykin, "Sum of All Good," 344.

22. Ryland, "Enmity of the Carnal Mind," *Pastoral Memorials*, 2:15; cf. Ryland, "Love of the Spirit," *Pastoral Memorials*, 2:40.

23. Ryland, "Love of the Spirit," *Pastoral Memorials*, 2:40.

24. Most of the churches of the Particular Baptist denomination were Calvinistic. There were, however, a few that did not hold to the theology of Calvinism but retained the name Particular Baptists. In a letter to an unknown person in America on February 26, 1806, Ryland gave the statistics on his denomination, which included "about 400 Churches in England and 90 in Wales" (Ryland, "Letter to Unknown Recipient," February 26, 1806). He described a minority of them, saying, "10 or 12 of these may lean

Indeed, the education that his father, John Collett Ryland, afforded him was filled with the works of high-Calvinist authors.[25] While Ryland would later reject some aspects of high Calvinism,[26] he nevertheless continued to appropriate some of its most basic soteriological conclusions. Ryland quoted with approval the definition of faith offered by John Brine, who denominated faith as *"an approbation of God's appointed way of salvation*, upon a conviction of our guilt, pollution and misery . . . and is an *entire dependance* on Christ, for pardon, peace, acceptance, grace, and eternal life. This is a *reception* of the blessed Jesus, as what God makes him to be unto his people; namely, *All and in all."*[27] This definition is reflected in Ryland's personal confession of faith offered at his ordination in 1781, in which he

---

toward Arminianism" (Ryland, "Letter to Unknown Recipient," February 26, 1806). Ryland, unfortunately, does not offer any further information on the Arminian-leaning Particular Baptist churches. It is possible that they represent an early *rapprochement* between General and Particular Baptists that eventually resulted in the amalgamation of the two groups in 1891 (see Briggs, "Evangelical Ecumenism," 102–3). They may also demonstrate the influence of Dan Taylor's New Connexion on Particular Baptist life, in which the evangelical theology of the New Connexion Baptists was seen as sufficient to welcome them into the denominational fold. There is some evidence for this in Ryland's letter, as he mentions that the "new Genl β^s" ("the new General Baptists," his name for the New Connexion) are "much more evangelical" (Ryland, "Letter to Unknown Recipient," February 26, 1806).

25. Ryland's father and the high Calvinism to which he held shaped Ryland Jr.'s theological worldview, including, as will be shown in the next chapter, his catholicity. Ryland Jr. wrote of his early learning, "The second year after I had been deeply impressed by divine truth, my father allowed me to have my time pretty much to myself; and, instead of closer attention to literary pursuits, I spent those twelve months chiefly in reading divinity. At so early a period, it is not wonderful that I should altogether fall in with the sentiments of some excellent divines whose writings my father held in the highest esteem, and whom I found to be strenuous advocates for the doctrines of grace, to which I felt an ardent attachment" (Ryland, *Serious Remarks*, 2:7). These divines were the high-Calvinist pastors John Brine and John Gill. Ryland maintained an attachment to the doctrines of grace, but he came to depart from some of the opinions of these "excellent divines." He later wished that he had had an education more steeped in Edwardsean theology and less in that of Gill and Brine. In his personal diary, he lays some of the blame at the feet of his father: "I believe I may fairly attribute some confusion in my ideas, when so very young, to the want of more distinct instruction on some heads. O that my father had then thoroughly studied Edwards on the Affections! it might have rendered his ministry more useful to me and others" (Ryland, "Extracts from the Diary," June 12, 1786, 3).

26. As noted in chapter 1, Ryland rejected the high-Calvinist answer to The Modern Question.

27. Brine, "Letter to Rev. John Ryland of Warwick," April 15, 1755; cf. Ryland, *Serious Remarks*, 2:14. In *Serious Remarks*, Ryland defends his affirmative answer to the Modern Question. He does so using an interesting deployment of rhetoric, for, though Brine took the negative side of The Modern Question, Ryland uses Brine's definition of faith to argue for the affirmative.

defined faith as "a cordial Approbation of Gods Method of Salvation receiving his Testimony concerning his Son as worthy of all Acceptation and . . . embracing him in all those offices and for those Ends in and for which he is revealed in the Gospel."[28] Ryland does not alter the basic shape of Brine's definition. For both, religious truth (e.g., "God's appointed way of salvation" or "Gods Method of Salvation") was a matter of God revealing the truth and faith apprehending it.

The "truth" that faith apprehends is the gospel message.[29] In a sermon preached on June 28, 1819 at College Lane, Ryland posits three aspects of the gospel that he presents as a "summary of evangelical truth."[30] First, he roots salvation in *"the Grace of God* alone *that bringeth salvation."*[31] He defines this grace as "free, undeserved favor,"[32] by which definition he is enabled to include his understanding of sin,[33] God's sovereignty,[34] the goodness of the law,[35] and the judgment of God against humanity. He writes that grace is "favor to the ill-deserving, yea to the hell-deserving.[36] Grace is that sover-

---

28. Ryland, "Confession of Faith," 16.

29. Ryland called it the "system of truth" (Ryland, *Practical Influence*, 6). Cf. Ryland, "On Steadfastness in Religion," *Pastoral Memorials*, 2:296.

30. Ryland, *Practical Influence*, 6.

31. Ryland, *Practical Influence*, 6.

32. Ryland, *Practical Influence*, 7. This is not an uncommon definition. Samuel Hopkins defines it similarly as "free, unobligated, undeſerved favour" (Hopkins, *Two Discourses*, 53). Even John Wesley defined grace with the same phrase (Wesley, "Salvation by Faith," 1:13), though it is unlikely that Ryland borrowed it from him. This suggests, however, that it was a widely-used phrase among evangelicals with different theological traditions.

33. Grace is "undeserved," which means that the recipients must have sinned and made themselves unworthy.

34. Grace is "free," given by God to whom he chooses, a key Calvinist contention.

35. Again, grace is "undeserved." The recipients of grace broke God's standards (e.g., his law), thus earning judgment. Ryland continues, contending for the justice of the law and, by extension, the necessity of grace, "Though in itself, strictly speaking, it is nothing else but good news, yet it presupposes the truth of heavy tidings, and implies the justice of awful and alarming charges. Redemption from the curse of the law could be needful for those only, who were justly exposed to that awful penalty. Our liability to condemnation was such as to level all distinctions; all mankind are represented as lying at God's discretion, unworthy of his mercy, and righteously exposed to his displeasure" (Ryland, *Practical Influence*, 7).

36. Ryland may have borrowed this phrase from George Whitefield, as it seems to have been a favorite phrase of Whitefield's. Whitefield wrote, "In heaven they will ſing the louder for being called by ſuch an ill and hell-deſerving creature as I am" (Whitefield, *Select Collection of Letters*, 3:60). In another place, he wrote of himself, "Then should I, even ill and hell-deserving I, be entirely conformed to the copy of my great Exemplar" (Whitefield, *Select Collection of Letters*, 3:70).

eign exercise of divine goodness,[37] which bestows the blessing on them that had merited the curse of God."[38] Divine grace is the fountain from which salvation flows: "Every individual among us needs salvation by grace; nor can one of us warrantably hope to obtain it, in any other way."[39] The ultimate cause of salvation, then, is the grace of God.[40]

Second, while grace is the ultimate cause of salvation, Ryland explains the work of Christ on the cross as the mediating cause of salvation. He writes, "We are, moreover, taught, that salvation is granted only through the *mediation and atonement of Jesus Christ*."[41] It is through the cross of Christ that God demonstrates his perfect justice and grace: "Having displayed his hatred of sin, in the sufferings of that just one; he will now shew his love to righteousness, in bestowing eternal life, on all that believe in the name of his dear Son, as a reward of that obedience unto death, by which the Savior hath magnified the law, and made it honorable."[42] Ryland is especially keen to preserve the justice and moral rectitude of God in the atonement and connect it to the work of grace on the cross. He writes that "unless a demonstration of God's abhorrence of sin had been made in the sufferings of the Surety, it might have been surmised, that there was no great evil in transgression; and sinners might have inferred, that God never considered his threatenings as fit to be executed."[43] Ryland is eager to show the good-

37. It is possible that this phrase is borrowed from one of Ryland's favorite authors, Joseph Bellamy, who said that Jesus makes way "for the honourable exerciſe of the divine goodneſs" toward sinners (Bellamy, *True Religion Delineated*, 335).

38. Ryland, *Practical Influence*, 7.

39. Ryland, *Practical Influence*, 8.

40. Ryland can say, categorically, "Thus it is of God alone, that we are in Christ Jesus" (Ryland, "Relation of Christ to Believers," *Pastoral Memorials*, 2:52). He adds, "He provided a Saviour, unasked and unimplored. He revealed him, who would otherwise have been unknown. He brought us to close with him, and acquiesce cordially in his method of salvation. And I may add, he keeps us from wandering from him again, and so drawing back unto perdition" (2:52).

41. Ryland, *Practical Influence*, 8. He adds, "Be it known therefore to you, that by this Savior the forgiveness of sins is published unto you; and by him every one that believeth is justified from all things, from which ye could not be justified by the law of Moses" (8–9).

42. Ryland, *Practical Influence*, 9. Again, one may find similar phrasing in Bellamy, who writes, "His infinite love to righteouſneſs and hatred of iniquity, is alſo diſplayed in his promiſing eternal life and bleſſedneſs to *Adam* and to all his race" (Bellamy, *True Religion Delineated*, 29).

43. Ryland, *Practical Influence*, 10. Later in the same work, he says that "there can be no more of grace manifested in our salvation, than there would have been of justice expressed in our condemnation" (Ryland, *Practical Influence*, 23). He says something similar in other places. In *Serious Remarks*, in what he calls an "almost self-evident axiom," he writes, "There can be no more of grace in our salvation, than there would

ness, justice, and continued applicability of God's law in order to magnify the work of Christ in securing salvation. In one place, he deploys a logical chain in upholding the law, writing, "If our salvation is of grace, our condemnation would have been just; if our condemnation was just, the law we had violated was good; and if the law is good, it is right and just and good for us to delight in obeying it."[44] According to Ryland, then, the law is good, God is just, human beings are sinful in breaking God's law, and so any hope of salvation must reside in someone else who can merit it for humanity. That is the meritorious work of Jesus on the cross and in the resurrection. While Ryland still holds to a form of substitutionary atonement,[45] he is especially keen to portray the atonement in terms of God's moral government. In a journal he kept entitled "Hints and Queries on Theological Subjects," Ryland writes of the necessity and design of the atonement, holding that, through the atonement, God meant "to magnify a perfectly just Law, which was too good to be abated, much lefs to be abrogated" and "to justify God from all suspicion of favoring Iniquity, and of being indifferent to the conduct of his rational Creatures."[46]

Ryland's understanding of salvation as something external to the individual is key: God's grace resides within himself, and the atonement happened on the cross and was a divine work without human intervention. It is a finished work that must then be applied to the life of the individual. This is why union with Christ is such an important doctrine for Ryland. He writes particularly of what he calls a "vital union" that must subsist between

---

have been of justice in our damnation" (Ryland, *Serious Remarks*, 8–9; cf. Ryland, *Earnest Charge*, 13). The phrase seems to have originated in the association letter for the Northamptonshire Baptist Association, written for the meeting in 1792, the same meeting at which William Carey preached his "Deathless Sermon." In any event, grace and justice are repeatedly shown to be tightly wound together in Ryland's thinking.

44. Ryland, *Practical Influence*, 24. Grace is no excuse for lawlessness: "If you would shew yourselves the genuine followers of Paul, who followed so closely after his blessed Lord; let it appear, my beloved friends, that you love the practical part of his epistles, as well as the doctrinal part. FREE GRACE, said an old puritan, DEMANDS FULL DUTY" (Ryland, *Practical Influence*, 32). Ryland does not identify the "old puritan," but it could be either Ralph Venning or Francis Warham, both of whom used the similar phrase "free grace calls for full duty" (Venning, *Milke and Honey*, 9; cf., Warham, *Free Grace Alone*, 101). It is also possible, and perhaps most likely, that Ryland remembered the phrase from John Rippon's funeral sermon for John Collett Ryland. In that sermon, Rippon says, "His heart and his life join with the Puritans, who, in better days, faid, that 'free grace requires full duty'" (Rippon, *Gentle Dismission*, 34).

45. Ryland, *Practical Influence*, 24: "In his vicarious sufferings God gave the strongest evidence of his hatred of sin; the evil of which was manifested, far more affectingly and impressively, by the infliction of the penalty on so great a Substitute, than it could have been shewn in the punishment of the original offenders."

46. Ryland, "Necessity of the Atonement," 1.

an individual and Christ: "Let me then befpeak your moſt ſerious attention to a brief defcription of that VITAL UNION with Chriſt, which doubtleſs is principally intended in our text; without which your *viſible* Union with him is vain, and your pretenſions to a *virtual* Union are preſumptuous and wicked. All real believers are *vitally* united to Chriſt, being made one with him by the participation of his Spirit. By faith they live in him, and abide in him."[47] In a funeral sermon preached five years later, he says, "Yes, verily, you muſt be truly united to him, before you can lay a valid claim to his benefits. Not only by a ſecret union, conſtituted by the divine decree, as the elect were choſen in him before the foundation of the world; but by a *vital* union, the evident effect of divine operation on the ſoul. Union between you and Chriſt muſt be mutual, before it can be pleadable. He muſt be in you, as well as you in him."[48] It is through union that the meritorious benefits secured by grace and through Christ's work become the possession of the individual believer, such that, for Ryland, union with Christ becomes the *sin qua non* of salvation.

The importance of the Holy Spirit is shown in the fact that this vital union happens via the agency of the Holy Spirit. This forms the third part of Ryland's summary of evangelical truth, for he writes: "That salvation is *applied to the heart, by the effectual influence of the Holy Spirit*, is another principle truth of the gospel."[49] The Holy Spirit effects the vital union that is so important in Ryland's understanding of salvation. It is a consistent theme throughout his writings, as he says elsewhere, "The Means of Conveyance by which these Blessings are communicated to Believers is discovered to them. All thro Xt^s. Mediation and apply'd by the Influence of ye H. Sp^t. [the Holy Spirit]"[50] While salvation is "made known in the Gospel," it is "made

---

47. Ryland, *Seasonable Hints*, 35. "Vital" here means more than "important." The meaning of "essential" or "chiefly necessary" is given as the last possible meaning of vital by Johnson, with the rest of his definitions having something to do with life (Johnson, "Vital," n.p.).

48. Ryland, *Christ the Great Source of Consolation*, 11.

49. Ryland, *Practical Influence*, 11; cf. Fuller [Agnostos], *Reality and Efficacy of Divine Grace*, 13. He also made a "short remark" on two additional doctrines, "both closely connected with our salvation by grace," which are the divinity of Christ and the doctrine of election (Ryland, *Practical Influence*, 12). Ryland explained that these are important but also can be seen as part of the other three aspects of the gospel he had already mentioned, as the divinity of Christ makes his work on the cross effectual, and the doctrine of election is part of God's gracious work in overcoming human sin (12–13).

50. Ryland, "Sermon Notes: 1 Corinthians 2:10," *Original Manuscript Sermons: Old Testament, Vol. II*. In that same work, Ryland defines the work of the Spirit as "a special Influence on the Mind of Individuals, whereby the ♥ is disposed cordially to admit revealed Truths, wch. the natural Man, while unrenew'd, will certainly reject."

known [to the individual] by the Holy Spirit."[51] The Spirit's work, then, is to take that which belongs to Christ and impart it to those who believe.

Ryland's reasoning runs thus: because human beings are so sinful, a powerful external work must be applied to them by an external agent. Even though all the work necessary for salvation and forgiveness was finished by Christ, human beings are so blind and morally impotent that they cannot see to take hold of it for themselves.[52] Therefore, the Spirit is necessary, and his role in the application of redemption by uniting a person to Christ is a major theme in Ryland's work. This is seen in his definition of the Spirit: "By the Spirit, is to be understood the Holy Spirit, the third person in the ever blessed Trinity; to whom, in the economy of redemption, the application of salvation is allotted; and who alone is the author of all that is truly holy, right, and good, in the disposition of a saved sinner."[53] Christ is portrayed as meriting all righteousness, holiness, and redemption, but it is the Spirit who gives what is Christ's to his people. Ryland remarks, "And let it be particularly noticed, that as nothing made the *work of Christ* necessary, but our want of personal righteousness, and the greatness of our guilt; so nothing renders the *work of the Spirit* necessary, but the want of native purity, and the greatness of our depravity. And both these considerations evince most powerfully, that salvation is entirely of *grace*."[54] In another sermon, he says, "Though sinners are invited indefinitely to apply to the Saviour, and whoever hears the gospel has a full warrant to come to him for salvation; yet pride and self-righteousness, the love of sin and of this present evil world, would destroy all our hopes of success, who are called to perform an embassy for Christ, if it were not for the effectual energy of the Holy Spirit."[55] For Ryland, the work of the Spirit is necessary because the sin of human beings is so great, for it is the "effectual energy of the Holy Spirit" which overcomes human sinfulness so that a person will take hold of the promises offered in the gospel. Indeed, the Spirit is pictured as the necessary surety of Christ's redemptive work (e.g., the one who insures that Christ's work actually accomplishes something):

---

51. Ryland, "Sermon Notes: Psalm 98:2," *Discourses on the Book of Psalms*.
52. Ryland, *Efficacy of Divine Grace*, 7.
53. Ryland, "Indwelling of the Spirit," *Pastoral Memorials*, 2:16. He said something similar in an evangelistic address to a Jewish congregation: "Thus the Messiah speaks peace to true believers of every nation. His Gospel discovers, and his Spirit applies to the heart, the reconciliation he made by his sufferings on the cross" (Ryland, *Eight Characteristics of the Messiah*, 10). In this instance, the Messiah speaks through the application of his work to the heart by the Spirit. The work of Christ and the work of the Spirit are, thus, unified.
54. Ryland, *Practical Influence*, 11.
55. Ryland, "Pleasantness of Religion," *Pastoral Memorials*, 1:124.

"Now all this is in confequence of the atonement and righteoufnefs of Chrift. It would otherwife have been inconfiftent with the dignity of the Holy Spirit to cleanfe and renew our fouls, and to take up his abode in our hearts. But Chrift deferved that the application of his redemption fhould be thus abfolutely fecured; that he fhould run no rifk of having fhed his blood in vain; but might certainly enfure eternal life to as many as were given him."[56] The means by which the Spirit does his work is through overcoming sinful impulses and impressing upon the heart the precepts, call, and desires of God: "The influence of the Holy Spirit is needed and promised, not to reveal new truths, but to impress the heart with those already revealed, and to induce us honestly to apply them to our own case; to obey the precepts; to accept the invitations; to rely on the promises."[57] So important is the Spirit to Ryland's soteriology that the whole of salvation is, at times, credited to the Holy Spirit alone: "Yet if ever we fucceed, and any foul obeys the call of the gospel, we would chearfully attribute the whole praife of this happy effect, to the HOLY SPIRIT of GOD, who alone can conquer the groundlefs enmity of a finner, and bring him to a union of heart with the bleffed Redeemer."[58] Without the Spirit's work, Christ would have died in vain.

56. Ryland, *Christ Manifested*, 42. Ryland goes so far as to say that, even if one person for whom Christ died fails to believe and be conformed to the image of Christ, God has failed in his mission of salvation. He writes forcefully, "If thefe fhould fail,—if one coming foul fhould be rejected,—if one believer fhould be plucked out of Chrift's hands and finally perifh,—who would be the greatest lofer—you or Christ? You, a poor finite creature, would in that cafe lofe your all indeed,—but He muft lofe his own moft precious blood, lofe the dear-bought purchafe of his agonizing groans, lofe that reward which made him willing, made him long, to be baptized in wrath, Luke xii. 50. lofe that which was to make him full amends for all his bloody fweat and accurfed death. And the eternal God muft forfeit his word, break his oath, lofe the glory of his wifdom and juftice, and grace and truth, muft tarnifh all his perfections, and (heaven forbid the blafphemy of unbelief) muft give Satan room to boaft that the great plan of redemption is fruftrated or rendered incomplete" (Ryland, *Christ Manifested*, 38–39). See also Ryland's emphasis on the necessity of the Spirit's work in the economy of redemption: "Remember that the Application of redemption is no lefs neceffary than its Impetration; and as our guilt could be removed by none, but a divine Redeemer, fo our depravity cannot be fubdued, but by a divine Sanctifier" (Ryland, *Earnest Charge*, 18–19).

57. Ryland, "Scriptures Opposed to Impressions," *Pastoral Memorials*, 1:174. In another place, Ryland writes, "So then, this manifestation of Christ to the soul, is not by the discovery of new truths concerning him, not before contained in his word; but by impressing the heart with a lively sense of the excellence of discoveries already made in the Sacred Scriptures, the foundation for which was laid by regenerating grace; and which inward sense of the Saviour's excellence and glory is revived, and increased from time to time, by the influence of the Holy Spirit on the soul" (Ryland, "Divine Manifestations," *Pastoral Memorials*, 1:334–35).

58. Ryland, *Indwelling and Righteousness of Christ*, 24–25.

It is important to remember that Ryland does not deny the personal responsibility of the individual. Because he answered the Modern Question in the affirmative, Ryland believed in the duty of an individual to believe the gospel message.[59] He writes of the "wonderful union between Christ & his people," which is a "mutual Inbeing of X^t. in them, & they in Him," as "entirely owing to divine Appoint^{mt}., Infl^{ce}., & Operat^n."[60] However, he goes on to state that "tho it originates with X^t. and not with us, yet it cannot be known, nor pleaded, nor the benefit of it be claimed, till it becomes mutual, & then it is a cordial, voluntary, spiritual Union. X^t. dwells in ♥ by Faith, impart^g. Light, Peace, Purity & Liberty to the Soul."[61] Union is not "vital" until it is mutual; that is, vital union occurs only with the consent of both parties. In another place, Ryland goes so far as to portray vital union as the effect of human choice, saying, "None can enjoy evidence that he belongs to the election of grace, till he freely makes choice of Chriſt, as his prophet, prieſt, and king."[62] The work must be mutual, or else it is of no benefit to the individual.

Union with Christ may be seen, therefore, as the instrumental cause of Ryland's catholicity, meaning that individuals are brought into union with one another through their union with Christ. However, the work of the Spirit may be understood as the effectual cause, as it is by the Spirit that a person is brought into union with Christ and, thus, with others. While the preceding outline does not show Ryland depart from Calvinism in any significant way, it is nevertheless important to show the theological context of his catholicity.

Epistemology of Catholicity

Union with Christ by the Spirit reflects only part of the foundation of Ryland's understanding of catholicity. Ryland's catholicity was eminently a matter of practice, so there remains the matter of how one knows another

---

59. Ryland's Calvinism was not so high as to preclude God responding to human initiative. While he would be careful to preserve the credit for a person's salvation for God alone, he believed that it was possible for the human will to impact the divine will. Indeed, he once prayed, saying, "And now, by our united prayers, we would call down the influences of the Holy Spirit" (Ryland, *Certain Increase*, 1). God was not merely an intractable will but could be moved by the efforts of people.

60. Ryland, "Sermon Notes: 1 Corinthians 1:30," *Original Manuscript Sermons: Old Testament, Vol. II.*

61. Ryland, "Sermon Notes: 1 Corinthians 1:30," *Original Manuscript Sermons: Old Testament, Vol. II.*

62. Ryland, *Salvation Finished*, 23.

person is united to Christ by the Spirit, or the epistemology of catholicity. Ryland's understanding of union with Christ and the work of the Spirit leads him to adopt a fundamentally experiential epistemology of catholicity. As noted, Ryland holds to two "unions," secret and vital. The secret union is "conftituted by the divine decree."[63] This is God's election of a person to salvation. The vital union, however, is "the evident effect of divine operation on the foul."[64] It is "evident," which means that it should be seen in the experience of a believer.

Ryland holds that "the end of the Holy Spirit, in the work of regeneration and sanctification" is nothing less than to form a new people of God made in the image of Christ.[65] The seal of the Spirit on the believer is "the impression of the divine image on the soul," which "really conform[s] us to God, in the temper of our minds."[66] This encompasses both the present and guaranteed future of the work of the Spirit. On the future aspect of the Spirit's work, Ryland asserts, "For the Spirit of Illumination is the Earneft of the Inheritance of the Saints in Light, the Sanctification of the Spirit is the Earneft of perfect Purity, and Joy in the Holy Spirit is the Earneft of our entering into the Joy of our Lord."[67] A Christian's future holiness and glorification rest on the work of the Spirit. It is his work in the believer that accomplishes the matter, just as it is his work in the sinner to bring them to faith. Ryland portrays this work as a steady progression, a consistent conformity to the image in which humanity was created and renewed, writing, "A conviction that there is much more to be seen and admired in Christ, than has yet been manifested to the soul; and consequently an earnest increasing desire, to know, love, and enjoy more, which prevents resting in present

---

63. Ryland, *Christ the Great Source of Consolation*, 11.

64. Ryland, *Christ the Great Source of Consolation*, 11.

65. Ryland, "Christian Ambition," *Pastoral Memorials*, 2:85; cf. *Certain Increase*, 30, "the end of our life is Christ." At times, Ryland speaks of the Spirit doing this work, and at other times he specifies that it is the Spirit under the direction of Christ that does it: "Christ is in his people by the abiding influence of his Holy Spirit; who having renewed them in the spirit of their minds, so powerfully regulates their disposition and conduct; as to conform them more and more to the likeness of their blessed Redeemer" (Ryland, *Indwelling and Righteousness of Christ*, 17). Either way, the goal remains the same: conformity to the image of Christ.

66. Ryland, "On Grieving the Holy Spirit," *Pastoral Memorials*, 2:157. Ryland seems to confound the impression of the divine image on the soul with union with God, for he goes on to say that, because believers bear this impression, an immediate witness of God to the soul is unnecessary, "for God cannot deny himself, nor the soul that is one in affection and disposition with him" (Ryland, "On Grieving the Holy Spirit," *Pastoral Memorials*, 2:157).

67. Ryland, *Dependance of the Whole Law and Prophets*, 37.

attainments, and induces the soul to resolve never to stop its pursuit, till it shall enjoy all it wants, and awake in the complete likeness of Christ."[68]

The conforming work of the Spirit is crucial for Ryland's epistemology of catholicity. A person is awakened to their need for Christ, believes in him, and lives a holy life, which is a typical way that a Calvinist would frame salvation. What is important for Ryland is the emphasis placed on the holy life of a believer, for it is in that holy life that the likeness of Christ is discerned, and it is likeness to Christ that leads him to embrace others as fellow Christians.[69] Therefore, Ryland's emphasis on and understanding of the work of the Spirit in making believers holy by uniting and conforming them to Christ leads him to lean heavily on a person's experience of grace in determining his practice of catholicity.

For Ryland, it was a person's experience of Christ and demonstration of that experience in their life that mattered. He speaks to this in his

---

68. Ryland, "Divine Manifestations," *Pastoral Memorials*, 1:335. Ryland put the matter poetically in an early work:

What is the office of the Spirit?
Chriſt did for all his choſen bleed,
Whereby from puniſhment they're freed;
By him to heav'n they have a right,
For which the Spirit makes them meet.
How doth the Spirit make the saints meet for glory?
'Tis by his power they're born anew,
Are chang'd and cleanſed thro' and through,
Grace he implants, doth grace increaſe,
And gives them holineſs and peace.

(Ryland, *Compendious View*, 14–15.)

69. While Ryland's theology is of the Calvinistic variety, it is worth noting that his approach to catholicity shares similarities with that of Wesley. Wesley's catholicity rests largely on experiential grounds as well, with Wesley summarizing the person of a catholic spirit as someone who, though joined to a particular congregation which shares their peculiar theological distinctives, "at the same time loves as friends, as brethren in the Lord, as members of Christ and children of God, as joint partakers now of the present kingdom of God, and fellow-heirs of his eternal kingdom, all of whatever opinion, or worship, or congregation, who believe in the Lord Jesus Christ; who love God and man; who, rejoicing to please and fearing to offend God, are careful to abstain from evil and zealous of good works. He is the man of a truly Catholic spirit, who bears all these continually upon his heart, who, having an unspeakable tenderness for their persons, and longing for their welfare, does not cease to commend them to God in prayer, as well as to plead their cause before men: who speaks comfortably to them, and labours by all his words, to strengthen their hands in God" (Wesley, "Catholic Spirit," 1:354). While Wesley does not use the same vocabulary as Ryland, Ryland's ideas of holding to Christ as the head, union with Christ shown through a holy life, and communion with all those who show such evidence are seen clearly in Wesley.

remembrance of his Anglican friends Thomas Scott and John Newton, about whom he writes:

> We pretend not to search the heart, and expect to find ourselves sometimes mistaken as to those, whom, in the judgment of charity, we took for such as were renewed in the spirit of their minds. But while we admit, that God alone infallibly knows them that are his, yet we feel ourselves bound to treat those as real Christians, who appear to bear the fruits of the Spirit. As to such men as Newton and Scott, with whom I was intimately acquainted for so many years, I can no more doubt of their eminent and practical piety, than of my own existence.[70]

Though there was some measure of doctrinal agreement between the three men, as well as disagreement, it was not their doctrine that drew the heart of Ryland but their "eminent and practical piety." To put it another way, it was the likeness of Christ which he discerned within them through the manner in which they lived their lives that led to such intimate friendship. Ryland put into practice what he exhorted people to do in a sermon dedicated to the topic of the communion of saints: "But let this be remembered by us all—that no man can be sound in the Apostles' Creed, whether he be in the habit of repeating it or not, who does not feel a warm attachment to the holy universal church, to which every saint in Christ Jesus belongs; or who does not highly value the communion of saints, and love to maintain fellowship with those on earth whom he verily expects to dwell with in heaven."[71]

Ryland's emphasis is clear: catholicity is founded on wearing the image of Christ. He sought evidence for this not in the formal confession of others but in their "godly sincerity" and their "cordial union with Christ." In other words, he sought the evidence in the apparent experience of others. Because this experience is the effect of the work of the Spirit, one may say that Ryland's catholicity is pneumatological. However, because the discovery of these effects is through the other person's life and experience, Ryland's catholicity is also deeply and fundamentally experiential.

This does not deny the importance of doctrinal matters to Ryland, for he maintained the necessity and goodness of orthodox doctrine and theological distinctions. In his farewell address to the church at College Lane, he warns them to "watch and remember . . . with reference to the *articles of*

---

70. Ryland, "Memoirs of Scott and Newton," *Pastoral Memorials*, 1:350.

71. Ryland, "Communion of Saints," *Pastoral Memorials*, 2:282. In a letter to Stephen West, Ryland makes the same point in much the same language (see Ryland, "Letter to Stephen West," March 31, 1814, 181).

your FAITH."[72] While Ryland never denies the importance of right doctrine, but when he speaks of union with other Christians, he regularly distinguishes between right doctrines and truly important doctrines. For example, he writes that "the greater articles of faith on which we agree, should have more influence to unite us, than any smaller points on which good men can disagree, should have to divide us."[73] Doctrines on which good men can disagree are "smaller points."[74] For Ryland, Christian fellowship does not necessarily rise or fall on right doctrine.

A distinction should also be made between Ryland's personal theological convictions and those beliefs that he believes bind people together in Christian fellowship. He holds to a Calvinistic Baptist theology, but he does not only hold fellowship with Calvinistic Baptists. Rather, in terms of doctrinal requirements, a basic agreement on the sinfulness of humanity, the incarnation and deity of Jesus, the Trinity, the atonement, and the necessity of faith are what Ryland typically looks for in others in order to have communion with them.[75] Even admitting this, Ryland's chief emphasis is not doctrinal but experiential,[76] for there were times that Ryland could overlook significant doctrinal differences, even aberrations, to embrace a person as a fellow believer.

The example of Ryland's friend Robert Hall Jr. will illustrate this point.[77] Hall was eleven years younger than Ryland and eventually his successor at

72. Ryland, *Earnest Charge*, 6. He exhorts them that a "careful peruſal of Paul's epiſtles" would show them the importance of right doctrine and proper knowledge (Ryland, *Earnest Charge*, 6).

73. Ryland, "Communion of Saints," 2:281.

74. Writing of his esteem for men in the Church of England, Ryland says, "Strange would it be, if an agreement with our Episcopalian brethren, in *six and thirty* articles, except two sentences, should not have more effect to unite us, than a disagreement on *three* articles and *two* clauses could have to divide us" (Ryland, "Preface," *Candid Statement*, viii–ix). Those three articles and two clauses, which were the cause not only of division but of much strife, imprisonment, and even death for Baptists in the seventeenth century, are seen by Ryland as too small to divide genuine believers in the late-eighteenth and early-nineteenth centuries.

75. See Ryland's *Necessity of the Trumpet*, where he outlines what he states are "a few of the most essential Articles of revealed Truth" (Ryland, *Necessity of the Trumpet*, 10). These articles include the sinfulness of humanity; the supremacy of Christ, especially in his incarnation and atonement; the call of the gospel to all sinners; the necessity of faith; and the work of the Spirit.

76. Cf. Crocker, "Life and Legacy," 331–32, where Crocker asserts that Ryland makes agreement with Calvinism an essential aspect of his catholicity but then states that regeneration was the "chief mark necessary for catholicity" (332n8).

77. Their friendship is demonstrated in the correspondence that they shared for many years (see Nuttall, "Letters from Robert Hall to John Ryland," 127–31), as well as the fact that Hall Jr. preached Ryland's funeral sermon.

Broadmead. Ryland had known and appreciated Hall Jr.'s father, Robert Hall Sr., and would have met Hall Jr. through that friendship.[78] In a letter to Levi Hart, Ryland describes Hall, writing that Hall had been "for some months laid aside by Insanity," that "his Zeal for the Divinity of X^t. and the Atonement has for some years greatly increased,"[79] and that he "long haesitated [sic] respecting the personality of the Holy Spirit," though Ryland believes that he was "getting right on that head."[80] This indicates that Ryland was aware of some defects in Hall's mental state as well as in his theological convictions, and even that, at the date of the letter, Hall was not quite "right" on the subject of the Holy Spirit. Despite this, Ryland affirms to Hart that he "had seen in his youth such strong evidence of his real Religion" that he had great hopes that Hall would not be "drawn off from the Gospel."[81] Ryland had seen this evidence "in his youth," meaning that Ryland could see evidence of Hall's "real Religion" despite Hall's bouts of insanity and theological unorthodoxy.[82] Ryland does not spell out what this "strong evidence" was in Hall's youth, but of the adult Hall he writes, "I know of no man of singular genius, that discovers lefs pride of Talent than R. Hall. He wonderfully increases in apparent

---

78. Robert Hall Sr. is the author of *Help to Zion's Travellers* and *The Doctrine of the Trinity Stated*, which exercised significant influence on Ryland, Fuller, and Sutcliff and the movement toward moderate and evangelical Calvinism (Cross, *Useful Learning*, 278). Ryland called Hall Sr. one of his chief counsellors and, sixteen years after Hall Sr.'s death, Ryland could say that he missed no man more (Ryland, "Preface," *Help to Zion's Travellers*, v).

79. Four years prior to Ryland's letter to Hart, Hall Jr. indicated in a letter to Ryland his commitment to orthodoxy, writing that he is "very loth to take any step that may appear like a countenancing the socinians in sentiments which I hope I shall never fail to consider to my dying day as the last corruption of Christianity" (Hall Jr., "Letter to John Ryland," May 25, 1801, cited in Nuttall, "Letters from Robert Hall to John Ryland," 127). It is not certain which sentiments he so vehemently rejected, but it would seem likely that it was the Socinian rejection of the divinity of Christ and, perhaps, their view of the atonement.

80. Ryland, "Letter to Levi Hart," August 10, 1805, 7.

81. Ryland, "Letter to Levi Hart," August 10, 1805, 7.

82. Letters from Hall to Ryland in the 1780s indicate that Ryland was having difficulty believing that Hall was not a Socinian. Hall denies the charge, saying, "I do not recollect a time when I was lefs inclined to that system than at present" (Hall Jr., "Letter to John Ryland Jr.," August 12, 1785). However, Hall also defends the Unitarian Joseph Priestley, saying that "with respect to Dr. P. from the candour & opennefs of his temper, from the piety & integrity of his life & his cordial attachment to truth wherever he meets with it, I am induced to believe that he pofsefses all those dispositions that are efsential to the enjoyment of heaven & that had he an additional light with respect to the sacrifice of Christ he would cordially embrace it" (Hall Jr., "Letter to John Ryland Jr.," August 12, 1785).

piety and Devotion also."⁸³ It is not Hall's theology that provides evidence of Christianity, but his life of humility and piety.⁸⁴

Ryland highly values this practical outcome as the evidence needed for Christian acceptance and fellowship. In this case, humility was enough to convince him that a man with questionable beliefs⁸⁵ will inevitably prove himself to be a true Christian. Indeed, humility was a central virtue in Ryland's epistemology of catholicity, for humility, according to Ryland, is not merely the possession of a meek spirit. It is, rather, the fruit of an experience of divine grace and the work of the Holy Spirit in uniting and conforming an individual to Christ. He writes, "The first original *source* of true humility is *a sight of the divine glory*."⁸⁶ Therefore, Ryland says, "True humility is an eminent part of that *right spirit* which is produced in regeneration: no man can be a Christian without it; and it is never to be found in the world but in real saints."⁸⁷ The identity of a true saint is thoroughly experiential, discovered through the possession of humility that stems from a sight of the divine glory. During his earlier life and even at the time Ryland described him to Levi Hart, Robert Hall Jr. was possessed of a theology that was, by Ryland's own account, somewhat less than orthodox. However, Ryland is assured that Hall Jr. was indeed a Christian based on the character of his life.⁸⁸ This demonstrates that the source of Ryland's confidence that a person

---

83. Ryland, "Letter to Levi Hart," August 10, 1805, 7.

84. Ryland apparently saw something that Hall himself failed to see, as Hall would later intimate that he was arrogant as a youth (see the discussion in Cross, *Useful Learning*, 376-77).

85. These beliefs would have been questionable to Ryland according to Ryland's own published works. For example, Ryland held to the necessity of Trinitarian theology (Ryland, "Doctrine of the Trinity," 1-4, 59-63) and the divinity and personality of the Holy Spirit (Ryland, "Love of the Spirit," *Pastoral Memorials*, 2:45). For more on Hall's early theology, see his letter to the Broadmead church, in which he affirms his belief in the divinity of Jesus, denies that he is a Calvinist, modifies the doctrine of election, and claims to be a materialist (Hall Jr., "Letter to Broadmead," December 9, 1790, *Works of Hall*, 3:19-20; cf. McNutt, "Ministry of Robert Hall, Jr.," 109-16).

86. Ryland, "Humility," 498. Highlighting the practical nature of truth, Ryland notes that "all the *doctrines* of God's *word* are calculated to humble us" (558). Along with joy and holiness, Ryland understands humility to be an eternal characteristic of the believer, one which grows with "the most rapid and uninterrupted progress... for ever" (Ryland, *Certain Increase*, 16).

87. Ryland, "Humility," 498. He later adds, "If you are not humble, you are not *orthodox at heart*" (499). In another place, writing of humility, Ryland asserts, "True greatness consists in union to God and his whole obedient kingdom; and the more self is denied, the more entire is that union" (Ryland, "Humility Essential to True Greatness," *Pastoral Memorials*, 1:267).

88. It should be pointed out that there exists a difference between Ryland's *personal* catholicity and that which was practiced by the institutions he led. For example,

is a Christian is not whether their confession is perfect or denominationally acceptable; it is, rather, whether the Spirit's work is evident in their lives. Again, this is not to say that Ryland thinks doctrine unimportant. There are those who are clearly outside the boundary of his catholicity, such as William Huntington and John Rowe.[89] However, Ryland does not set the limit of his catholic embrace at the boundary of Calvinism, Baptist convictions, or even what are commonly termed "secondary matters,"[90] but would embrace as brothers and sisters all whom he, in their actions and experience, perceived loved the Lord Jesus in sincerity. Therefore, the final and most definitive evidence Ryland requires for Christian fellowship is shared spiritual experience. As he puts it in one sermon, "The more fruit we bear, the easier will it be to prove our union with Christ."[91]

Ryland places great emphasis, then, on inner piety and its outworking in the life of an individual. He says:

> Inward religion, if it be genuine, will show itself, not only in our words, our profession, our attendance on public worship, and ordinances, but also in our deportment among men, by acts of righteousness, self-denial, meekness, and true benevolence;

---

the Baptist Academy restricted admission to those of a like mind, a change from the practice under the previous President, Caleb Evans (see Evans, *Sketch of the Several Denominations*, 87). Rather than seeing this as a discrepancy in Ryland's catholicity, it may rather be an example where he made a distinction between his personal practice and the role he played as a denominational leader. The Baptist Academy was meant to train Particular Baptist ministers, and so such is who was admitted under his presidency. We see a similar trait in Ryland in his pastorate at Broadmead. During Ryland's tenure, Broadmead was not an open communion church. Though Ryland held to open communion beliefs as their pastor, he did not require the church to follow them but, instead, led the institution according to the needs and desires of the institution.

89. Huntington was a controversial minister who attacked Ryland's preaching of the moral law, and Rowe was a Unitarian minister against whom Ryland wrote *The Partiality and Unscriptural Direction of Socinian Zeal*. Neither of these men were comprehended within Ryland's catholicity. Ryland himself admits that there are limits to his catholic friendships in a diary entry, "Mr. Horsey and Mr. Edwards, the two Independent ministers, spent the evening with me; we had a good deal of improving conversation. I know not how to extend my charity quite so far as they to people wide in their sentiments" (Ryland, "Extracts from the Diary," February 5, 1788, 4). Even in this quotation, however, evidence of Ryland's catholicity may be found, as "Mr. Horsey" is John Horsey, minister of the Castle Hill church in Northampton, and "Mr. Edwards" is Benjamin Edwards, minister of the King's Street church in Northampton. Both of these were Independent churches, and Horsey's orthodoxy with respect to the person and work of Christ was questioned by his contemporaries (Coleman, *Memorials of the Independent Churches of Northamptonshire*, 32). Nevertheless, Ryland could carry on friendships with and labor alongside such men.

90. *Pace* Crocker, "Life and Legacy," 331.

91. Ryland, "Christian Fruitfulness," *Pastoral Memorials*, 1:341.

delight in the communion of saints, readiness to sympathize with our Christian brethren; in taking complacency in the image of Christ, labouring to extend his cause, pitying the souls of men, adorning the doctrine of God our Saviour; and in doing good to the bodies of men, with a farther view to their spiritual benefit, that we may recommend religion to them, and bring them to a conviction of its reality and importance.[92]

His is an epistemology of experience: does he perceive the other person as having experienced the same work of the Spirit as he? That is all that he requires. If he can perceive it, then he will welcome the other person as a brother or sister.

This facet of his theology of catholicity would prove to be a doorway through which he entered into partnerships with those outside of his denomination and tradition. As shown in the previous chapter, by situating Christian fellowship within the sphere of shared spiritual experience, and including "laboring to extend his cause, pitying the souls, of men, adorning the doctrine of God our Saviour," Ryland is willing to partner with and promote such diverse people and groups as the Orthodox Emperor of Russia, General Baptists, Methodists, Anglicans, Presbyterians, and Congregationalists.

Conclusion

One aspect of the present research has to do with the sources of Ryland's catholicity. This chapter showed the theological sources of his desire for visible union in Christ with other believers outside of his own theological tradition. Because Ryland rooted his understanding of catholicity in relationship to Christ in "one common body,"[93] this investigation into the theological foundations of his catholicity began with his understanding of union with Christ: because a person is united to Christ by faith, Ryland believes that he has no authority to reject that person. Ryland's catholicity may first be understood as christocentric. However, because of his understanding of salvation as the work of the Spirit within an individual, granting them faith and ingrafting them into Christ, his catholicity also has a deeply pneumatological element to it. Finally, with a deed-oriented catholicity such as Ryland's, the epistemology of catholicity becomes important: how does one know that another person is united to Christ? For Ryland, the answer to that lay in the discovery of the work of the Spirit through the lived experience

---

92. Ryland, "Christian Fruitfulness," *Pastoral Memorials*, 1:340.
93. Ryland, "Letter to Stephen West," March 31, 1814, 181.

of the other individual. Can the presence of the Spirit be discerned through the life and experience of the other person? If so, then Ryland judged that that person, even if possessed of a theology that diverged significantly from his own, was united to Christ and, thus, worthy of his affection and communion. Ryland's theology of catholicity is, therefore, christocentric, pneumatological, and experiential, with Ryland taking a special interest in the evidences of union with Christ in the experience and life of the individual.

6

Personal Foundations

IN THE PREVIOUS CHAPTER, the theological foundations of John Ryland's catholicity were examined. In this chapter, the personal foundations of his catholic beliefs and practice will be investigated. If the previous chapter was about how Ryland justified his catholicity intellectually, this one will look into those from whom Ryland learned it. As it relates to his catholicity, there were two primary influences: his father, John Collett Ryland, and John Newton.[1] This chapter will examine the life and works of both men as well as Ryland's relationship with them in order to show how they helped to shape his ideas about catholicity.

John Collett Ryland

Born on October 12, 1723 at Bourton-on-the-Water, to Joseph and Freelove Collett Ryland, John Collett Ryland[2] was, by all contemporary accounts,

---

1. There were others who influenced Ryland more broadly. Perhaps the greatest among these was Robert Hall Sr., whom Ryland classified with John Newton as "counsellors of my youth" (Ryland Jr., *Indwelling and Righteousness of Christ*, 37; cf. Ryland Jr., "Memoirs of Scott and Newton," *Pastoral Memorials*, 2:346, where Ryland calls them his "wisest and most faithful counsellors, in all difficulties."). Hall Sr.'s influence on Ryland was both theological and personal. Theologically, Hall Sr. gave Ryland the theological framework for understanding the gospel as an offer to sinners, thus clearing the way for the affirmative answer to the Modern Question (Ryland Jr., *Serious Remarks*, 2:19). Personally, Hall Sr. was a counselor for Ryland in his darkest days after the death of his first wife, as seen in a tender letter from Hall Sr. to Ryland just a few weeks after her passing (Hall Sr., "Letter to John Ryland," March 8, 1787).

2. In this section, in order to avoid confusion, it will be necessary to differentiate the

an extraordinary, if eccentric, man.³ He was converted during a revival of religion in 1741 at the Baptist church at Bourton-on-the-Water under the pastoral ministry of Benjamin Beddome (1717–1795), who proved to be a mentor and friend to him.⁴ By the influence of Beddome, J. C. Ryland entered upon his training for the ministry at Bristol Baptist Academy in 1744, where he studied under the tutelage of Bernard Foskett and Hugh Evans.⁵ From Ryland Sr.'s diary entries from this time, it is clear that his time at school was one of dramatic spiritual turbulence.⁶ On February 11, 1743,

---

elder and younger John Ryland. The elder Ryland will be referred to as "J. C. Ryland" or "Ryland Sr.," while the younger will be called "Ryland Jr." Unfortunately, this makes for more cumbersome reading, but the resulting clarity is worth it. In addition, more biographical information will be given for Ryland Sr., since he is less well-known than Newton.

3. Newman, *Rylandiana*, vi. "Extraordinary" and "eccentric" were common appellatives for Ryland Sr. Olinthus Gregory described him as "a very extraordinary man, whose excellencies and eccentricities were strangely balanced" (quoted in Newman, *Rylandiana*, 192). Augustus Toplady, in a review of Ryland Sr.'s *Contemplations*, said of him, "One would imagine, on a perusal of this animated and noble dissertation, that its author was all soul, unincumbered with a single particle of flesh and blood" (Toplady, "Review of *A Contemplation on the Immortality*," 182). John Webster Morris, a junior colleague of J. C. Ryland in the Northamptonshire Baptist Association, said, "For zeal and fidelity he had few equals, and none could surpass the bold and daring nature of his eloquence. His eccentricities were numerous and remarkable, his piety unquestionable; to a stranger his manners were sufficiently terrific, though in reality no man possessed more genuine kindness, or more enlarged and disinterested benevolence" (Morris, *Biographical Recollections*, 30).

4. As mentor, Beddome "led him forward to the work of the miniſtry with the foſtering hand of a wiſe and kind parent" (Rippon, *Gentle Dismission*, 37–38). As to their friendship, Beddome called Ryland Sr. his "dearest friend," and the two kept in contact well after Ryland Sr. left Bourton-on-the-Water (Newman, *Rylandiana*, 137–39).

5. Ryland Sr.'s relationships with these two men were quite different from one another. He called Evans "my dear and honoured friend and father" (J. C. Ryland, "To the Gentlemen and Other Several Christians," xv). For Foskett, Ryland Sr. held less affection, recording many years after his time in Bristol, "Foskett should have spared no pains to educate our souls to grandeur, and to have enriched and impregnated them with great and generous ideas of God in his whole natural and moral character, relations, and actions, to us and the universe. This was thy business, thy duty, thy honour, O Foskett! and this thou didst totally neglect" (quoted in Newman, *Rylandiana*, 37). This sentiment toward Foskett's educational philosophy and abilities was not unique to Ryland Sr. John Rippon shared it, conceding that Foskett was not "the firſt of tutors," and that "his method of education was limited rather than liberal; ſevere rather than enchanting; employing the memory more than the genius, the reaſoning more than the ſofter power of the mind" (Rippon, *History of the Baptist Academy at Bristol*, 22).

6. The antipathy toward Foskett was nurtured during these dark days, as Ryland Sr. wrote in his diary, dated April 1, 1745, that Foskett "chid me exceedingly—and Spoke some Severe Words which make a lasting Impreſsion on my Soul—but if he knew my desires & endeavours—to approve my self sincere in the preſence of God—and the

he writes, "My heart is exceeding full of sin and darkness. I know not how to act. O God, if thou dost not help me out I am undone."[7] Almost a year later, he is in the same condition: "Oh, what a dead, sleepy life have I lived last year. Ignorance, darkness, atheism, unbelief, enmity, pride, sloth, selfishness, deadness and hardness of heart, worldly-mindedness, intemperance in eating and drinking, immoderate sleeping, uncharitableness, stupidity in secret prayer and self-examination, reading, meditation, &c., hypocrisy in all my conduct in the family and in the church, with ten thousand other evils of heart and affections, lip and life."[8] Despite these ongoing spiritual trials, Ryland Sr. proved to be an able student and a promising minister.[9] He was set apart for the ministry by the Baptist church at Bourton-on-the-Water on May 2, 1746, and twenty-three days later he began serving as the pastor of the Baptist church in Warwick.[10] He served in Warwick for thirteen years until 1759, when he moved to Northampton in acceptance of a call to shepherd College Lane Baptist Church. He was admitted to the church on February 17, 1760 and formally ordained as pastor on September 18, of the same year. He held this position for the next twenty-six years, leaving in 1786 for Enfield, where he died on July 24, 1792.[11]

Doubts I do—and have for a Long time Labour'd under—about some of the Fundamentals of all Natural & Reveal'd Religion—I believe he woud not be so Severe in his Reflections—upon me" (J. C. Ryland, "Diary: April 1745," 7).

7. Newman, *Rylandiana*, 28.

8. Newman, *Rylandiana*, 31–32. John Ryland Jr. would later write that his father's struggle encompassed a total of twelve years altogether (John Ryland Jr., "Rise and Progress of the Two Society's," n.p.; cf. Robinson, "Experience of John Ryland," 21). Rippon indicates that the struggle lasted much longer than twelve years, pointing out that some of these "many horrid temptations" lasted as late as 1788 (Rippon, *Gentle Dismission*, 47), which is after Ryland Sr. left Northampton for Enfield.

9. Culross, *Three Rylands*, 16.

10. Ryland Jr. noted in the margins of his copy of *An Account of the Life of the Late Reverend David Brainerd*, that May 25, 1746 was "the first Sabbath my dear Father spent at Warwick" (Ryland Jr., Marginalia, in Jonathan Edwards, *Account of the Life of the Late Reverend David Brainerd*, 420, copy held in the Bristol Baptist College Archives). He was not formally ordained by the church in Warwick until 1750 (Anonymous, "Warwick Church Book, 1714–1759," n.p.). His call was reviewed and renewed annually until then (Wright, "John Collett Ryland," 21).

11. The connection between Ryland Sr. and College Lane does not appear to have been severed even by his move to Enfield. In the church book for College Lane, Ryland Sr.'s death is recorded, and it states that he had "been a Member of this Church two and thirty years, and resident pastor six and twenty years" (Ryland Jr., "College Lane Church Book, 1781–1801," 138). That he would still be a considered a member is not surprising, as he did not join another church in London. However, the reference to him being the "resident pastor" for twenty-six years is intriguing and raises the question, "Did the church still consider him to be their pastor, just not in residence?"

J. C. Ryland proved to be a profound influence on his oldest son, John,[12] especially in the area of his catholicity.[13] The father's catholic influence is seen in three areas. First, J. C. Ryland was a Calvinistic Baptist in the tradition of John Gill and John Brine, both of whom he held in the highest regard.[14] With regard to Gill, Ryland Sr. said that all "difficulties in divinity," among which he named "the Divine attributes, Divine persons, Divine decrees, and the Divine transactions," had been "cleared up, as far as they possibly can be" by Gill in his *Body of Divinity*.[15] With regard to Brine, he gave the charge to J. C. Ryland at his ordination.[16] However, as might be expected of someone so often called eccentric, Ryland Sr. did not allow himself to fit in another person's mold.

Most notably for present purposes, J. C. Ryland had a much more catholic view of Christianity than did Gill. Gill wrote a treatise entitled *The Dissenter's Reasons for Separating from the Church of England*, in which he stated, "We diſlike the church of *England* becauſe of its *Conſtitution*, which is human, and not divine,"[17] and went on to say that the doctrine which was preached in the Church of England was "very corrupt, and not agreeable to

---

12. Champion, "Theology of John Ryland," 17. Ryland Sr. had five children: John; Herman Witsius; James; Elizabeth; and Rebecca. Herman Witsius eventually moved to Canada and worked in the Canadian government; he died in 1838. Elizabeth married Joseph Dent, a deacon at College Lane; she died in 1820. James spent time working in London and died in 1818 (Jay, *Autobiography*, 1:323). Rebecca died at age five (Ryland Jr., "Autograph Reminiscences," 32–33).

13. He was an influence in many other areas, of course. Ryland Jr., as a boy and young man, drank deeply from the well of his father's Calvinism. At fifteen years old, Ryland Jr. began to read the works of John Brine. Of his reading of Brine, he said in his private diary, "I trust with much profit on the whole, but not with some disadvantage; as it led me to fall into his opinions too indiscriminately" (Ryland Jr., "Autograph Reminiscences," 36–37).

14. Whenever he was in London, J. C. Ryland would attend services at Brine's church at Currier's Hall, Cripplegate (Rippon, *Gentle Dismission*, 51). He wanted to be buried in Bunhill Fields, in London, where Brine and Gill were both buried: "Of late it was Mr. Ryland's own deſire to be buried in Bunhill-fields, London, where, among many others whoſe memories were dear to him, are interred the *three great Johns*, as he uſed to call them. John Owen, John Gill, and John Brine." He did not get his wish, as, after his death, his body was brought to Northampton for burial in the family grave at College Lane Baptist Church (51).

15. Newman, *Rylandiana*, 44.

16. Rippon, *Gentle Dismission*, 42. Brine's address was published as *The Solemn Charge of a Christian Minister Considered*. In addition, a document entitled "Social Religion or the Agreement of a Gospel Church," authored by Brine, was inserted into the Warwick Church Book on January 20, 1758, while the church was under the care of J. C. Ryland (Anonymous, "Warwick Church Book, 1714–1759," 52).

17. Gill, *Dissenter's Reasons*, 3.

the word of God," concluding, therefore, that it "cannot be a true church of Chriſt."[18] Ryland Sr., on the other hand, was more than happy to embrace as Christian brothers men from the Anglican church, which is seen clearly in his friendships with James Hervey (1714–1758) and George Whitefield (1714–1770). Ryland Sr. met Hervey while serving as the pastor at Warwick. They began exchanging letters in 1752, and their friendship and correspondence continued until Hervey's death. During these years, Ryland Sr. would, with his family, spend his vacations with Hervey, and Hervey would come during his leisure time to visit with the Rylands.[19] Their relationship grew very close, with Ryland Sr. referring to Hervey in a letter as his "dearest and best of friends."[20] Many years after Hervey's death, Ryland Sr. produced a biography of his dear friend. In it, Ryland Sr. is unapologetic in his profuse love for his departed friend. In the preface, he answers the objections to hagiography, saying, "If any perſon ſhall cenſure me, as having ſaid too high or too kind things of his character, let them candidly conſider that I was obliged to write the truth . . . If God, from all eternity, decreed to illuſtrate his perfections in the uncommon natural genius, the peculiar and ſhining excellencies, with the moſt ſublime ſpirit of religion, in this ſingular perſon, who, and what, was I, that I ſhould withſtand God?"[21] His defense is, essentially, it is not a hagiography if it is true.

It is important to note the reason for Ryland Sr.'s connection to Hervey. Though the style of his remembrance of Hervey is hagiographical, it stems from his deep regard for Hervey's piety. He wrote, "James Hervey, in this

18. Gill, *Dissenter's Reasons*, 5. Gill would get very specific in his denunciation of the Church of England: "And though the 39 articles of the church of England are agreeable to the word of God, a few only excepted; yet of what avail are they, since they are seldom or ever preached, though sworn and subscribed to by all in public office? And even these are very defective in many things: There are no articles relating to the two covenants of grace and works; to creation and providence; to the fall of man, the nature of sin and punishment for it; to adoption, effectual vocation, sanctification, faith, repentance, and the final perseverance of the saints; nor to the law of God, Christian liberty, church-government and discipline, the communion of the saints, the resurrection of the dead, and the last judgment" (5).

19. Newman, *Rylandiana*, 7. It was during one of these visits that the well-known story of John Ryland Jr. reading Ps 23 in Hebrew to Hervey took place (Taylor, *History of College Street Baptist Church*, 30; Summers, "John Ryland, D.D.," 751; Park, "Letters of Dr. John Ryland to Dr. Stephen West," 178; and, more recently, Cross, *Useful Learning*, 353n449).

20. J. C. Ryland, "Letter to James Hervey," October 10, 1758. The letter is addressed to "My dearest and best of friends" and does not contain the name of Hervey in it. However, a letter written by Hervey to Ryland Sr. on September 30, 1758 shows that his letter is an answer to that of Hervey, point by point (Hervey, "Letter to John Collett Ryland" September 30, 1758, in J. C. Ryland, *Character of Hervey*, 2:60–61).

21. J. C. Ryland, "Preface," *Character of Hervey*, ii.

life, for twenty-fix years, ftood nearer to God's heart than millions of angels: he was more intenfely united to CHRIST, joined or glued to the LORD, and made one fpirit with him."[22] Later, he wrote, "His foul was inlaid with all manner of lovely *ornaments* and *beauties*. Every thing that could adorn a man of fcience; every grace that could adorn a Chriftian; every perfection that could beautify an angel, and the lineaments of every feature of the incarnate God, were to be found in this holy man."[23] It was not necessarily Hervey's theology that attracted and excited Ryland Sr; it was his holiness and the apparently abundant evidences of grace in his life. In a phrase, it was Hervey's evident experience of God that drew Ryland Sr. to Hervey. This experiential aspect of Ryland Sr.'s catholicity is also seen later in Ryland Jr.'s own catholic understanding.

As to Whitefield, the beginning of Ryland Sr.'s relationship with him is unknown. It is possible that they came to know one another through James Hervey, or vice versa.[24] He seems to have first heard Whitefield preach in 1744.[25] By 1760, however, when Ryland Sr. was newly-installed as the pastor at College Lane in Northampton, his relationship with Whitefield had deepened considerably. A letter written by James Slinn to Elizabeth Whitefield tells of a visit of George Whitefield to Northampton. Whitefield was faced with a rowdy crowd, but "he preached them silent."[26] The next day, Ryland Sr. appeared as a host and enforcer of discipline for Whitefield: "dear Mr. Riland took a great deal of pains, and was in the heat of the Battle, and came off conquor; reasoned, as 'Gentlemen, hear the word of God!' and *gave them broadsides in Lattin* (for it was in his cortyard)."[27] Whitefield and J. C. Ryland would also make time to see one another when they were in the same town together. When John Ryland Jr. revised and condensed his early diaries into a single volume, he kept the entry for September 8, 1767, in which he writes, "M[r]. Whitefield came to see my Father, and preached at

---

22. J. C. Ryland, *Character of Hervey*, 17.

23. J. C. Ryland, *Character of Hervey*, 58.

24. It is known that Hervey and Whitefield were friends. They exchanged letters (Hervey, "Letter to George Whitefield," 1741, in J. C. Ryland, *Character of Hervey*, 2:i–ii), and Whitefield would lodge with Hervey when he was in the same town (Hervey, "Letter to John Collett Ryland," August 1755, in J. C. Ryland, *Character of Hervey*, 2:35). It is reasonable that one could have provided an introduction to the other for Ryland Sr. However, this is speculation.

25. Hayden, "Evangelical Calvinism," 136.

26. Slinn, "Letter to Elizabeth Whitefield," September 24, 1760, in John Waddington, *Congregational History*, 449.

27. Slinn, "Letter to Elizabeth Whitefield," September 24, 1760, in John Waddington, *Congregational History*, 449.

Castle Hill."[28] He also kept the entry for June 27, 1769, in which he says he went to London with his father, and they visited Whitefield while there.[29]

Grant Gordon also recently discovered a letter from Whitefield to J. C. Ryland.[30] While the letter itself is largely unremarkable, it demonstrates two salient points for the purpose of this chapter. First, it shows that J. C. Ryland and Whitefield carried on a lasting, catholic friendship. The letter is dated 1759, and Ryland Jr.'s diary indicates that Whitefield and J. C. Ryland were still friendly ten years later, which was only a year before Whitefield's death. Whitefield's Anglicanism was no barrier to their friendship, nor were his evangelistic appeals to sinners, in which he most assuredly "offered" the gospel to unbelievers, something to which Ryland Sr. was opposed.[31] Second, the letter shows that this lengthy relationship was more than a surface-level acquaintance. Whitefield demonstrates knowledge of the workings of Ryland Sr.'s school,[32] exhibits a concern for mutual friends,[33] and hints that they carried on a more extensive correspondence than has been preserved.[34] Ryland Sr.'s relationship with Whitefield is helpful in understanding the catholicity he passed on to his son, as it demonstrates that not only did differences in traditional theological commitments (e.g., baptism and church government) not keep Ryland Sr. from having fellowship with other

---

28. Ryland Jr., "Autograph Reminiscences," 29.

29. Ryland Jr., "Autograph Reminiscences," 38.

30. Gordon, "Revealing Unpublished Letter," 65–75.

31. Ryland Sr. writes, in his definition of the gospel, "The word *offer* is not so proper as declaration, proposal, or gift" (Newman, *Rylandiana*, 50). Indeed, he thought his own son's answer to the Modern Question wholly wrong (J. C. Ryland, "Sermons: January 1791," n.p.; cf. Newman, *Rylandiana*, 78). Conversely, Whitefield says: "We are to offer Jeſus Chriſt univerſally to all" (Whitefield, "A Faithful Minister's Parting Blessing," 2). "Were thoſe who are in hell to have ſuch an offer of mercy as you have, how would their chains rattle!" (Whitefield, "Christ the Believer's Refuge," 37). "Thoſe who are come here this Night out of curioſity to hear what the Babbler ſays, thoſe who come to ſpend an idle Hour to find ſomething for an Evening-Converſation at a Coffee-Houſe, or if you have ſtopped in your Coaches as you paſſed by, remember you have had *Jeſus Chriſt* offered you; I offer *Jeſus Chriſt* to every one of you" (Whitefield, "Folly and Danger of Being Not Righteous Enough," 295).

32. Gordon, "Revealing Unpublished Letter," 66: "May the Glorious Emanuel visit Him & all under Your care with His great salvation!"

33. Gordon, "Revealing Unpublished Letter," 66: "Pray tell Him [a Captain Wilson] that He is duly remember'd & that I have no doubt that He will continue to be Xt's faithful soldier until life's end."

34. Whitefield references a letter he received from Ryland Sr., in which he made "proposals" that Whitefield promised to dutifully deliver "at all proper opportunities" (Gordon, "Revealing Unpublished Letter," 66). Ryland Sr.'s proposals to Whitefield are unknown.

Christians, but he also did not allow differences over current controversial issues (e.g., the free offer of the gospel) to be a bar to Christian communion.

The second aspect of Ryland Sr.'s life and thought that reveal the catholic environment that shaped Ryland Jr. is his ministering with, worshiping with, and promoting the interests of those outside of his ecclesiastical tradition. An example of this is provided in his pattern of ministry at the end of his life.[35] When Ryland Sr. moved to Enfield, though he accepted no call to the pastorate, he preached at several churches in the area,[36] among which were Independent chapels, Congregational churches, Baptist churches, and churches in Lady Huntingdon's Connexion. Indeed, when he was not engaged in preaching at local churches, Ryland Sr., along with all of his students, regularly attended the worship services of Lady Huntingdon's chapel.[37]

While perhaps not as prominent as his eccentricities, this aspect of Ryland Sr.'s life did not go unnoticed by his contemporaries. In his funeral sermon for Ryland Sr., Rippon said of him, "His love to the feveral denominations of good men was ardent. Baptifts, Independents, Methodifts, and Epifcopalians, *talk* of candour, but he *exercifed* it: if there ever was a man who cordially faid, *Grace be with all them who love our Lord Jefus Chrift in fincerity*, the man of whom we fpeak was he."[38]

Ryland Sr. reveals his understanding of catholicity in his definition of the concept of Christian charity, saying, "*Charity* is a warm and hearty bent and propensity of the soul towards a close and sweet union with all true Christians, who agree with us in the grand essentials of salvation; delighting to promote their best interests, and rejoicing in the thought, that we shall see them eternally happy with us in the kingdom of the Son of God."[39] One may see here similarities between father and son with regard to catholicity and union with Christ. While Ryland Jr. makes it more explicit in his writings, Ryland Sr. would agree in substance that union with Christ leads to

---

35. Ryland Jr. was an adult by this point, so this particular activity was likely not an influence on him. However, this is meant to show a pattern of engagement for Ryland Sr. with those outside of his tradition that is also seen in Ryland Jr.

36. Newman, *Rylandiana*, 18.

37. Newman, *Rylandiana*, 16.

38. Rippon, *Gentle Dismission*, 46–47. William Jay echoed this appraisal of Ryland Sr., saying, "He was intimate with Mr. Whitfield and Mr. Rowland Hill, and much attached to many other preachers less systematically orthodox than himself; and labored, as opportunity offered, with them. He was, indeed, a lover of all good men; and, while many talked of candor, he exercised it. Though he was a firm Baptist, he was no friend to bigotry or exclusiveness" (Jay, *Autobiography*, 1:331–32).

39. Newman, *Rylandiana*, 43. Conversely, he defined bigotry as "such a blind and furious attachment to any particular principle, or set of principles, as disposeth us to wish ill to those persons who differ from us in judgment" (42).

and provides the foundation for union with other believers, regardless of their theological commitments.

Ryland Sr. also promoted the work of the Congregationalist Jonathan Edwards, though his relationship to Edwards is complex and certainly not as positive as that of Ryland Jr. On the one hand, J. C. Ryland pushed back publicly against the emphases of those who followed Edwards, most notably the idea of disinterested benevolence, mentioned earlier.[40] With his characteristic passion, he wrote against the idea, saying:

> It is impoſſible that Chriſt ſhould require this at the hand of any man in the world; becauſe it is contrary to the original principle of ſelf-love, and the grand law of ſelf-preſervation, created and blended with the eſſence, powers, and paſſions of the immortal ſoul of man; because it is contrary to the new and divine nature which the Spirit of God has created in the ſoul of every true chriſtian; it is utterly repugnant to God's revealed will, which is our ſanctification and ſalvation.[41]

On the other hand, he repeatedly recommended Edwards' writings and even published a book of Edwards's sermons, in the preface of which he called Edwards "the greateſt divine that ever adorned the American world."[42] Ryland Sr.'s understanding of human ability was derived from Edwards as well.[43] He was an early appreciator of and gave his continued support to Edwards.[44] His disagreement with Edwards and others did not lead to disbarment of either fellowship or ministerial cooperation and promotion.

---

40. Ryland Jr. also had reservations about disinterested benevolence as the American theologians defined. The key difference between Ryland Sr. and Jr. in this regard is that Ryland Jr. kept his concerns confined to private correspondence.

41. J. C. Ryland, *Contemplations on the Divinity of Christ*, 3:227.

42. J. C. Ryland, "Preface," 3. He said of the sermon that he knew "of nothing so good and so wisely adapted to diffuse the knowledge of Christ" (4), and that he knew "not its equal in the whole world" (5).

43. E.g., Edwards' distinction between natural and moral ability, on which, see chapter 4. Ryland Sr. wrote, "Natural inability arises from some obstacle extrinsic from the will, and is not the proper subject of praise or blame. Moral inability consists in the opposition or want of inclination of will, and may be either commendable or blameable" (Newman, *Rylandiana*, 53). As noted previously, Ryland Jr. held to a similar distinction, though he came to different conclusions about its implications as to the offer of the gospel.

44. It is possible that, like his contemporary Abraham Booth, Ryland Sr. appreciated Edwards but was somewhat skeptical of the American divines who followed him. Booth could quote Edwards approvingly (Booth, *Reign of Grace*, 155–57), but his appreciation of Edwards did not extend to the Edwardsean theologians. Indeed, *Reign of Grace* was seen by Hopkins as an attack on American Divinity. Hopkins called Booth's work "a wholly selfish religion" (Hopkins, "Letter to Dr. Ryland," November 24, 1797,

The final aspect of J. C. Ryland's catholicity to be considered is his belief in and practice of mixed communion. As noted previously, catholicity is broader than mixed communionism; however, as also noted previously, those who held to those positions quite often did so for catholic reasons. J. C. Ryland was no different. He and Daniel Turner[45] collaborated on a pamphlet in which they laid out their belief in and arguments for open communion.[46] The tract gives some insight into Ryland Sr.'s catholicity, at least as it pertained to the Lord's supper. He[47] roots his open communionism in a thoroughly catholic understanding of Christianity: "Becaufe, we believe, that all thofe, who appear to have received the Grace of our *Lord Jefus Chrift*; to live by faith upon him as their *Saviour*, and confcientioufly obey him as their *Lord*, muft have an *equal right* to ALL the privileges of the Gofpel, by virtue of fuch relation to him."[48] He appeals to Rom 14 for biblical precedent for the practice, saying, "In a word, I earneftly wifh our ftricter Brethren would ferioufly read, and without prejudice confider, the xivth and xvth chapters of the Epiftle to the *Romans*, where they will find

in *Works of Hopkins*, 2:749). He later insinuated that Booth was an unknowing antinomian (Hopkins, "Letter to Dr. Ryland," October 17, 1799).

45. Daniel Turner and New Road Baptist Church, Oxford are more examples of the catholic spirit within Baptist life during this time. Turner was an open communionist, and New Road Baptist Church was an open communion church. For more information on Turner and New Road, see Rosie Chadwick's edited volume entitled *A Protestant Catholic Church of Christ: Essays on the History and Life of New Road Baptist Church, Oxford*. Paul Fiddes sheds light to Turner's ecclesiology in "Daniel Turner and a Theology of the Church Universal," 112–27.

46. The details of the collaboration between John Collett Ryland and Daniel Turner are unknown. Part of the reason for this is the use of pseudonyms. Turner wrote as Candidus, while J. C. Ryland wrote as Pacificus. That this is so was assumed from at least 1778; see Booth, *Apology for the Baptists*, 131–32. The Candidus tract is more well-known today; at least, there are more copies of it available. The only known copy of the Pacificus tract is in the Northamptonshire Central Library. For more information on the two works, see Oliver, "John Collett Ryland, Daniel Turner and Robert Robinson and the Communion Controversy, 1772–1781," 77; Graham, "John Collett Ryland, Daniel Turner, and *A Modest Plea*," 34–42. For broader coverage of the open communion debate in British Baptist life, see Peter Naylor's *Calvinism, Communion, and the Baptists* and Michael J. Walker's *Baptists at the Table*.

47. Even though he collaborated with Turner on the pamphlet, and the words could equally be ascribed to both, for present purposes, Ryland Sr. as Pacificus will be singled out as the author.

48. Pacificus, *Modest Plea*, 1. He continues his argument, saying, "Becaufe, it is *undeniably evident* that JESUS CHRIST HIMSELF does accept of Paedobaptift *Chriftians*, when they remember Him at his table;—does indulge them the enjoyment of his gracious prefence there—enables them, in the exercife of the fame common faith, to feed upon the faving virtues of his precious body and blood, and thereby builds them up in the power and comforts of the divine life *equally* with us" (1).

a great deal to the purpofe of what I have been pleading for."⁴⁹ There is a chain of reasoning that leads Ryland Sr. to his appeal to the Romans passage. The chain begins: "Becaufe, if we believe fuch *Pædobaptists* as before defcribed to be fincere Chriftians, as we are bound to do, then it is evident in fact, that the points in Baptifm, about which we differ, are not fo clearly ftated in the Bible (however clear to us) but that even fincere Chriftians may miftake them."⁵⁰ Having established that paedobaptists are truly Christians, despite their misunderstanding of baptism, the chain continues: "In a word, becaufe we look upon the infifting upon unfcriptural terms of communion, and there by compelling ferious Chriftians to live in the neglect of a plain and important duty, or to fet up feparate focieties, to be the very reverfe of that candid, peaceable, benevolent, and *uniting fpirit* which appears every where in the Gofpel of Chrift, greatly prejudicial to the honour and intereft of true religion, and not a little contributing to the caufe of infidelity."⁵¹ In essence, Ryland Sr. makes the familiar argument that, if paedobaptists are truly Christian, then to separate from them in the Lord's supper is a dividing of the body of Christ.

How J. C. Ryland came to his open communion ideas is unclear. His early mentor in the faith, Benjamin Beddome, held to a closed communion view.⁵² Ryland's tutor at the Academy, Hugh Evans, was an open communionist, so he learned of the belief no later than his time at school, which ended in 1746.⁵³ However, the church at Warwick was a closed communion

49. Pacificus, *Modest Plea*, 3.

50. Pacificus, *Modest Plea*, 1. Like John Bunyan, Ryland Sr. denominates belief in the validity of infant baptism as a "mistake," rather than a sin.

51. Pacificus, *Modest Plea*, 2.

52. At least, Beddome held to this view when he was Ryland Sr.'s pastor. In his *Scriptural Exposition of the Baptism Catechism*, he enquired about the proper subjects of the ordinance of the Lord's supper, giving the answer, "They who have been baptized upon a perfonal profeffion of their faith in Jefus Chrift and repentance from dead works" (Beddome, *Scriptural Exposition of the Baptism Catechism*, 169). There have been some assertions that, in later years and well after Ryland Sr. had been in his congregation, Beddome embraced open communionism (White, "Open and Closed Membership," 332; cf. Naylor, *Calvinism, Communion, and the Baptists*, 54). This is by no means certain, as the evidence suggests that it was Beddome's assistant, William Wilkins, who promoted open communionism at the church at Bourton-on-the-Water and that, after Wilkins left, the church did not adopt the practice (Brooks, *Pictures of the Past*, 93). However, even if it is the case that Beddome accepted open communion beliefs later in life, it would have no bearing on his early influence upon Ryland Sr.

53. Cotton Mather wrote, in a sentiment that would be reflected in Ryland Sr., "Be not fuch a donatift, as to dream, that the people of God are no where to be found but in one party, which you have your greateft efteem for. But, look for them, as to be found under various forms; and let your judgment, how it fares well or ill with the people of God in the world, fetch its meafures not from the good or bad circumftances of

church, a stance with which Ryland Sr. seems to have agreed at the first. The Articles of Faith of the Warwick Baptist Church include a section on baptism and the Lord's supper, in which a closed communion doctrine is clearly stated: "We believe that Baptism and the Lords supper are ordinances of Christ, to be continued until his Second Coming and that the former is abſolutly requisite to the latter, that is to say, that those only are to be admitted into the Communion of the C[h]urch, and to Participate of all ordinances in it who upon profeſsion of their Faith, have been baptized by immersion in the Name of the Father, and of the Son, and of the Holy Ghost."[54] College Lane Baptist Church, to which Ryland Sr. went in 1759, held to open communion. It would seem that, at some point between his coming to Warwick in 1746 and his departure for Northampton, he changed his views. Indeed, some have held that it was precisely because of his change in views, and that College Lane was more amenable to his new understanding, that Ryland Sr. left Warwick for Northampton.[55] This is uncertain, but it is noteworthy that his friendship with James Hervey and George Whitefield, both Anglicans, began during this period.

In each of these instances of catholicity in J. C. Ryland, one may see the personal influence of the father on the son. The catholicity which Ryland Jr. learned from his father was "caught" rather than "taught." There is no

---

one party only, but from the prevailing or the ſuppreſsing of true piety, and what has a tendency to that, wherever it is to be met withal" (Mather, *Manuductio ad Ministerium*, 134). J. C. Ryland republished this book, writing in its preface, "I have been intimately acquainted with this excellent little book, for thirty-ſix years paſt; I firſt met with it in the ſtudy of my dear and honoured friend and father, the Rev. Mr. Hugh Evans, of Briſtol, when I boarded at his houſe, in the years 1744, 1745, 1746. The book has been of exceeding great uſe to me ever ſince" (J. C. Ryland, "To the Gentlemen and Other Several Christians," xv).

54. Anonymous, "Warwick Church Book, 1714-1759," n.p. The "Articles of Faith" are dated January 1, 1749.

55. This is not borne out by any primary source evidence. It seems to have begun with Newman's assessment of the reason for Ryland Sr. leaving Warwick: "It is highly probable that his differing with his people respecting terms of communion was the chief cause of his leaving them" (Newman, *Rylandiana*, 11). John Taylor followed Newman in his history of College Lane, writing that the "cold" letter of dismissal from Warwick is evidence of their hesitance to send their pastor to a "schismatic" congregation (Taylor, *History of College Street Baptist Church*, 25). More recently, Peter Naylor repeats Newman's claim (Naylor, *Calvinism, Communion, and the Baptists*, 55), as does Christopher Crocker (Crocker, "Life and Legacy," 45–46). While this is possible, the reason for Ryland Sr.'s move to Northampton is simply not known. It has also been stated that his departure was bitter, and that the letter of dismissal from the church in Warwick was "very sterile" (Crocker, "Life and Legacy," 46) and even "cold" (Newman, *Rylandiana*, 10). To be sure, the letter is not filled with much in the way of pathos, but neither was the letter calling him to the church in the first place (Anonymous, "Warwick Church Book, 1714-1759," n.p.). It is possible that the church normally communicated in this matter-of-fact way.

evidence that J. C. Ryland sat his son down and taught him the tenets of his catholic spirit. However, Ryland Jr. writes to Levi Hart regarding his history of embracing mixed communion, affirming that he "was always bro't up in the practice of open communion."[56] Ryland Jr. was "bro't up" with open communion seen in the example of his father.[57] This is, of course, unsurprising: fathers often have profound influence on their sons. This would have been especially so in the case of the two Rylands. The school which Ryland Jr. attended as a boy was that of his father.[58] The church in which he grew up was pastored by his father. When J. C. Ryland would have his non-Baptist friends visit him in Warwick and Northampton, the son was not shunted off to remain out of sight until the guests left; rather, the son was made part of the fellowship and saw his father interact with men from other denominations and traditions.[59] In many important ways, the chief religious influence, along with his mother, on the life, thought, and character of Ryland Jr., at least in his formational early years, was his father. So satisfied was J. C. Ryland of his son's progress in the faith, and as an able promoter of his educational style, that Ryland Jr. began to be employed as a tutor in his father's school at no later than age nineteen.[60] Moreover, at age seventeen, Ryland Jr. began preaching at College Lane, being called out to serve as co-pastor ten years later, a position in which he continued until his father left Northampton for Enfield, at which time Ryland Jr. became the sole pastor.

None of this is to say that Ryland Jr. uncritically appropriated his father's theology, manner, and methods. He assuredly did not.[61] Rather, it is meant

56. Ryland Jr., "Letter to Levi Hart," January 18, 1808.

57. There are some important differences between them, of course. For example, J. C. Ryland is unlikely to have ever worked with Wesleyan Methodists as his son did.

58. That Ryland Jr. was a student in his father's school is known from in his "Autograph Reminiscences," in which he speaks of sitting next to fellow students in class (Ryland Jr., "Autograph Reminiscences," 16).

59. See Ryland Jr.'s report of overhearing the sobering talk between his father, the Baptist preacher Robert Hall Sr., and the Independent preacher John Edwards in Ryland Jr., "Rise and Progress of the Two Society's," n.p.; cf. Robinson, "Experience of John Ryland," 21. The portrait of Ryland Jr. in his "Autograph Reminiscences" is of a young man deeply involved, from age fifteen at the latest, in the work that his father was doing. It was at that age that Ryland Jr. took the initiative, without his father's knowledge but with his later approval, to invite a Mr. Lloyd to preach in Northampton (Ryland Jr., "Autograph Reminiscences," 35).

60. Ryland Jr. notes that, in 1772, he "constantly afsisted" his father in the school and church (Ryland Jr., "Autograph Reminiscences," 45).

61. Not only did Ryland Jr. depart from his father's high Calvinism, there is also the much more sensitive issue of the personal relationship between father and son. There are indications J. C. Ryland's relationship with his son was strained, at least in the father's later years, both because of theological issues and more personal ones.

to demonstrate that Ryland Jr. was brought up in an environment that was shaped by his father's understanding and practice of catholic Christianity.

John Newton

Along with William Wilberforce, John Newton was among Ryland Jr.'s more famous British correspondents. The events of Newton's life are relatively well-known but worth covering in brief. Born on July 24, 1725, he was, by his own admission, irreligious as a boy and young man.[62] Newton eventually became involved in the slave trade and captained a ship on three slaving trips to Africa. While working on the slave ship *Greyhound*, Newton began to undergo a religious conversion.[63] His new-found faith did not prevent him from participating in the slave trade, as he continued working on slave ships for six years after the beginning of his religious convictions.[64] After his retirement from the slave trade, Newton became a tide surveyor,[65] but he

---

Theologically, Ryland Sr. believed that his son was wrong in his answer to the Modern Question. In what appears to be a contemporaneous account, which is recorded in a book of Ryland Sr.'s sermons but not written in his hand, Ryland Sr. remarks that his son and his friends (among whom were Andrew Fuller and John Sutcliff) had busied themselves rolling about on an empty barrel that the devil had thrown out for them, rather than drinking the wine of the kingdom (J. C. Ryland, "Sermons: January 1791," n.p.; cf. Newman, Rylandiana, 78).

Personally, Ryland Jr. writes about the time when his father remarried, saying simply, "But after my mother's death, in 1779, he married a Mrs Stott, whose former husband was a quarter-master, and many unpleasant consequences followed, which are best left omitted" (Ryland Jr., "Autograph Reminiscences," 11). There is evidence of money issues for the father (see Champion, "Letters of Newton to Ryland," 159; Payne, *College Street Church*, 53), with the son having to use his own salary to keep his father from deeper debt. This could be part of the "unpleasant consequences" that Ryland Jr. mentions. Newton also mentions problems between Ryland Sr. and Jr. and counsels Ryland Jr. on how to navigate his way through them (Gordon, *Wise Counsel*, 228, 241–42, 255–56).

62. Newton mentions having "took up and laid afide religious profeffion three or four different times" before he was sixteen years old. He understood religion as "a means of efcaping hell," but he confesses that he loved sin too much to part with it (Newton, *Authentic Narrative*, 23).

63. Newton recounts the events of the dawning of his conversion in *Authentic Narrative*, 108–33. It is called the beginning of conversion because, as Newton himself says, he did not consider himself at that time to have been a believer "in the full fenfe of the word" (133). However, he clearly understands that time to be the beginning of his awareness of the Lord's presence in his life (113).

64. Newton's retirement from the slave trade was not due to any moral opposition but was, rather, due to ill health (Newton, *Authentic Narrative*, 192). Indeed, Newton saw the hand of providence in his illness, as the ship on which he was next to sail lost many of the crew, including the man who took Newton's place as captain (193–94).

65. Bull, *John Newton*, 74–76.

was soon to feel called to the ministry.[66] He was ordained to the Anglican ministry in 1764 and appointed to the Church of St Peter and St Paul in Olney, where he lived and served for fifteen years.[67] In 1779, he accepted the position of rector at St Mary Woolnoth in London, in which position he remained until his death. He eventually came to repudiate his participation in the trafficking of human beings and campaigned for the abolition of slavery.[68] He married Mary Catlett in 1750, with whom he raised a niece, Elizabeth Catlett. Mary died in 1790, and Newton followed in 1807.[69]

Newton met John Ryland on January 17, 1768,[70] when Ryland traveled to Olney with a Mr. Jones and a Mr. Key.[71] Newton journeyed to Northampton in August of that year, and Ryland went to hear him preach on August 11.[72] Seventeen days later, Ryland began a one-week stay with Newton in Olney. By the date of Newton's first known letter to Ryland (October 17, 1771), the two had been friends for almost four years. That first letter is worth considering, as it encapsulates the catholicity to which Newton held and which he sought to inculcate in his young friend. Newton wrote to rebuke Ryland, a young man who, in Newton's opinion, was in danger of falling to the temptation of pride, which Newton understood to be the enemy of catholicity. Ryland had published a book of poetry and was gaining public acclaim for it.[73] Newton saw in both the book and its reception significant issues that could lead to defects in Ryland's character. Newton's problems with the book itself were twofold. First, though Newton said that Ryland's writings "bear evident marks of genius," he also informed the budding writer that they were "too inaccurate and

---

66. Newton, *Authentic Narrative*, 206.

67. He was ordained a deacon on April 29, 1764 and priest on June 17 of the same year.

68. Newton, *Thoughts on the African Slave Trade*, passim.

69. For more information on John Newton, see the full-length works by Bull, Martin, and Hindmarsh. Hindmarsh also deals more specifically with Ryland's catholicity in examining Newton's role as a "broker of consensus" among evangelicals of differing theological commitments (Hindmarsh, "I Am a Sort of Middle Man," 29–55).

70. Newton had met Ryland's father several years earlier (Bull, *John Newton*, 138).

71. Ryland Jr., "Autograph Reminiscences," 31. Ryland mentions that they were after this time expelled from Oxford. It is likely, then, that this was Thomas Jones and Benjamin Key (also spelled "Kay"), who, along with Thomas Grove, James Matthews, Erasmus Middleton, and Joseph Shipman were expelled from Oxford in March 1768 for public praying and preaching. For more information on their expulsion and the furor it raised in the press, see Firman, "Footnote on Methodism in Oxford," 161–66.

72. Ryland Jr., "Autograph Reminiscences," 35.

73. The book is entitled *Serious Essays on the Truths of the Glorious Gospel*. Ryland had published shorter works prior to this, but this was his first "major" work.

hasty."[74] Second, Newton told Ryland that his writings "savour of vanity."[75] For example, Newton took note of Ryland's hard stance with regard to a particular understanding of justification (e.g., his support of John Gill's doctrine of eternal justification). Ryland had pronounced that the error of those who oppose the doctrine appeared to him "in a great meaſure to ariſe from the want of making proper diſtinctions, without which it will be impoſſible to reconcile, many apparently oppoſite, but really conſonant paſſages in the Bible."[76] Newton responded, "But for a young man under 18, to pronounce *ex cathedra* upon a point in which a great majority of the most learned, spiritual and humble divines, are of another opinion, was such an offence against decency as grieved me."[77] He counseled Ryland, "Upon the whole I would wish you to let a few years more pass over your head, before you take the chair in controversial matters, especially those, in which the life of faith and the power of religion is no way concerned."[78]

With regard to the attention Ryland was getting in the press, Newton urged caution and wrote, in part, to provide it: "I mention these things, partly because there is too much confidence in your manner, and partly to balance the exaggerated encomium in the *Magazine*."[79] He, therefore, wrote to Ryland to warn him of his course. Though the letter was brutally honest,[80] Newton assured Ryland that he wrote out of love, "My reasons for

---

74. Newton, "Letter to John Ryland Jr.," October 17, 1771; cf. Gordon, *Wise Counsel*, 12. Of one of Ryland's poetic lines, Newton commented, "Indeed it is not easy to preserve a serious face in reading it" (Newton, "Letter to John Ryland Jr.," October 17, 1771; cf. Gordon, *Wise Counsel*, 13).

75. Newton, "Letter to John Ryland Jr.," October 17, 1771; cf. Gordon, *Wise Counsel*, 12.

76. Ryland Jr., *Serious Essays*, xiii; cf xv–xvi.

77. Newton, "Letter to John Ryland Jr.," October 17, 1771; cf. Gordon, *Wise Counsel*, 14. Newton's use of "*ex cathedra*" would have been especially biting as a rebuke to Ryland, considering his vehement opposition to the pope.

78. Newton, "Letter to John Ryland Jr.," October 17, 1771; cf. Gordon, *Wise Counsel*, 14–15. Newton also took issue with Ryland making much of not having any help in his writing, as though he needed no help in his journey (see Ryland Jr., *Serious Essays*, xxi). Newton said to his young correspondent, "[Y]ou must have been indebted for it, more to the persons you have conversed with and the books which have fallen in your way than to your own skill in making distinctions" (14).

79. Newton, "Letter to John Ryland Jr.," October 17, 1771; cf. Gordon, *Wise Counsel*, 13. "The *Magazine*" referred to the *Gospel Magazine*, in which Ryland was lauded: "Young as the author is, yet, like a scribe well instructed unto the kingdom of God, he bringeth forth, out of his treasury, things new and old" (*Gospel Magazine* 6 [April 1771], 191, cited in Gordon, *Wise Counsel*, 10).

80. Such honesty marks all the letters of Newton to Ryland. He was never afraid to rebuke his friend. In another letter, he warned Ryland, "I have occasionally heard sad tales of you—that by the loudneſs length and frequency of your public discourses you

writing are two, first because I love you, and secondly because I have a good opinion of you."[81]

The catholicity Newton taught his young friend was a catholicity rooted in humility and a desire to maintain peace, seen in Newton's gentle rebuke to his young friend for his harshness toward those who differ from him. In his book *Serious Essays*, Ryland had written, "I have aimed to displease Arminians."[82] Newton chided Ryland for this, adding, "I had rather you had aimed to be useful to them, than to displease them."[83] He continued with his instruction by showing Ryland the manner of being useful to opponents, which consisted not of aiming at their displeasure or offense but in winning them, writing, "Now these should not be displeased, by our endeavouring to declare the truth in terms the most offensive to them which we can find, but we should rather seek out the softest and most winning way of encountering their prejudices."[84]

Newton's letter had its intended effect. While Ryland's exact reply to Newton's letter is not known,[85] Newton's next letter to Ryland shows that the overall response was favorable.[86] One exact effect of the letter is known to posterity: in Ryland's personal copy of his book, the line that Newton

---

are lighting your candle at both ends. I cannot blame your zeal, you serve a good master—who is well worthy you should spend and be spent for his sake" (Newton, "Letter to John Ryland Jr.," undated; cf. Gordon, *Wise Counsel*, 30). His honesty also went the other way, as Newton did not refrain from expressing his love for Ryland, sometimes in surprisingly humorous fashion: "I think I love you no lefs than I should do, if you were an Episcopalian" (Newton, "Letter to John Ryland Jr.," December 9, 1795; cf. Gordon, *Wise Counsel*, 325).

81. Newton, "Letter to John Ryland Jr.," October 17, 1771; cf. Gordon, *Wise Counsel*, 11. In the same letter, he said that he wrote because "I love you and wish your prosperity" (16).

82. The full sentence is even more bracing: "As to manner, I have not aimed to please critics; as to matter, I have aimed to displease *Arminians*" (Ryland Jr., *Serious Essays*, xxi).

83. Newton, "Letter to John Ryland Jr.," October 17, 1771; cf. Gordon, *Wise Counsel*, 15.

84. Newton, "Letter to John Ryland Jr.," October 17, 1771; cf. Gordon, *Wise Counsel*, 15. It is possible that Ryland was imitating the manner of his father, who was known to be abrasive in manner. For the older Ryland, however, the manner was, as Newton would say, "constitutional." That is to say, it was simply his nature. For the younger Ryland, Newton seems to insinuate that such abrasiveness was not in his nature and that he should cease trying to be someone he was not.

85. None of Ryland's letters to Newton have been preserved.

86. Newton, "Letter to John Ryland Jr.," January 16, 1772; cf. Gordon, *Wise Counsel*, 19. Ryland's response was, to Newton, a commendation of his character: "I am pleased with the spirit you discover, and your bearing so well to be told of the mistakes I pointed out to you, endears you more to me than if you had not made them."

found so objectionable ("I have aimed to displease *Arminians*") is modified. Ryland has himself completely blacked out "aimed" and written in his unmistakable script above the word "not feared."[87] The young Ryland whom Newton rebuked in this first letter would eventually give way to a very different man,[88] no doubt through the continued influence of Newton's friendship and counsel.

The correspondence between Ryland and Newton continued until April 23, 1803, the date of the last extant letter that Ryland received from Newton,[89] and it varied based on the seasons of life. Newton counseled Ryland several times on the choice of a wife,[90] how to handle sensitive issues

---

87. Ryland Jr., *Serious Essays*, Ryland's personal copy in Bristol Baptist College Archives, xxi. This change is reflected in all future editions of the work (see Ryland Jr., *Serious Essays*, viii).

88. In a later letter from Ryland to Newton, Ryland had apparently disagreed with something Newton had said, and Newton commented that he had done so "in your modest & friendly manner" (Newton, "Letter to John Ryland Jr.," November 6, 1790; cf. Gordon, *Wise Counsel*, 237). In counsel Ryland would later give to John Saffery, he echoes some of Newton's own advice, saying, "I am sure I have no prejudice ag^t. you my dear Bro^r. I have always highly esteemed you. I fully approved of your object in your sermon at Frome, but I really think you w^d. succeed in it better, if you could be somewhat gentler in your manner" (Ryland Jr., "Letter to John Saffery," undated [1819–1824?]).

89. Newton did not die until four years later, so it is possible that they continued to write, but it is unlikely given Newton's declining health during that period. Even if no other letters passed between them, their relationship was a long and fruitful one. Reflecting on the changes that had happened in their lives throughout their friendship, Newton comments, "We began when you were a Lad and I a Curate & we have gone on till you are grown into a Doctor & I am dignified with the title of Rector. Our friendship, now grown old, will I hope continue to the end, whatever changes may yet await us—yea, & subsist & flourish in a better world" (Newton, "Letter to John Ryland Jr.," July 28, 1795; cf. Gordon, *Wise Counsel*, 317).

90. Newton wrote, "I doubt not but it is very lawful at your age to think of marriage, and, in the situation you describe, to think of money likewise" (Newton, "Letter to John Ryland Jr.," February 3, 1775; cf. Gordon, *Wise Counsel*, 73). Thus began a long series of counsels regarding potential mates, money, and Ryland's desperate desire to marry. After Ryland expressed frustration at not finding a wife, Newton wrote, "Worldly people expect their schemes to run upon all-fours," adding, "You were sent into the world for a nobler end than to be pinned to a girl's apron-string" (92). He also encouraged Ryland: "If [God] sees the marriage state best for you, he has the proper person already in his eye; and though she were in Peru or Nova-Zembla, he knows how to bring you together. In the mean time, go thou and preach the Gospel" (92). After Ryland's marriage to Elizabeth Tyler, Newton wrote, "I cordially rejoice that my two friends are at length happily brought together" (137). After the death of Elizabeth, Ryland again turned to Newton for help. Newton wrote to him, "You are still a young man; there are circumstances about you that make you uneasy, and to pair yourself to another gracious suitable partner, seems the easiest and most effectual way of deliverance from your thralldom" (205). After Ryland found a suitable woman, he seems to have had

related to Ryland's father,[91] and whether or not to accept the call from Broadmead.[92] Catholicity continues to be a major theme throughout the

---

some misgivings about her, for Newton wrote to him, "As matters seem to have gone too far for receding with honour and propriety, and as you mean to marry in the Lord, I think you may trust him to give you such feelings as may suffice to make your relation comfortable" (214).

91. These issues seemed to come from two different fronts. First, J. C. Ryland was not known as a wise handler of money, and it appears as though he found himself in financial straits. Ryland Jr. was then expected, both by his father and College Lane Baptist Church, to meet his father's financial needs, which he did, giving his father half of his salary. This is reflected in Newton's words to Ryland: "If you have engaged to allow for your father half your salary *durante vita*, I am not quite sure he will relinquish his claim, so readily as you suppose" (Newton, "Letter to John Ryland Jr.," May 17, 1788; cf. Gordon, *Wise Counsel*, 209). It seems as though J. C. Ryland also expected his son to continue to contribute half of his salary to J. C. Ryland's widow, Ryland Jr.'s stepmother. Newton believed this to be too much for Ryland Sr. to ask of his son: "It appears to me, that what your father expects from you, or from any of his children, after his death, is not reasonable. And that what you contribute towards his comfortable subsistence, during his life, ought to satisfy him" (209). The second issue is even more opaque. However, the evidence indicates that there was a personal rift between father and son, owing perhaps to some indiscretion on the father's part. Newton makes reference to J. C. Ryland's "imprudencies and improprieties" (228) and "eccentricities and failures" (241). These failures Newton attributed to Ryland's constitution: "He acts according to the impetus of his spirits, is hurried away, and I believe he cannot help it" (256). At one point, Newton says that he will not mourn the death of J. C. Ryland, since it means that he will no longer live to sully his own reputation (242). When J. C. Ryland spoke against his own son and his theological commitments (specifically with regard to the "Modern Question"), Ryland Jr. was tempted to respond in kind, a move against which Newton counseled his younger friend: "I hope you will long live to be useful and increasingly so, in Northampton. But I agree with you, that you had better quit the town, or even the kingdom, than write against your father" (256). In every case, Newton spoke well, though honestly, of J. C. Ryland and urged Ryland Jr. toward peace.

92. Ryland's move from Northampton to Bristol was a long affair (see Gordon, "Call of Dr. John Ryland Jr.," 214–27), and Newton gave continual counsel to his friend during it. While Newton would say, "I neither advise nor dissuade" (Newton, "Letter to John Ryland Jr.," April 30, 1792; cf. Gordon, *Wise Counsel*, 268), he made his opinion known with undeniable clarity. He told Ryland, plainly, "I cannot say that I wish you may be induced to leave Northampton" (261). He warned his young friend, "If the Lord really calls you to Bristol, go in his name, and he will be with you. But I advise you to be very sure of the *if* before you stir" (264). He disapproved of ministers moving from place to place, though he himself moved from Olney to London in 1780: "I am always afraid of the transplanting of ministers from places where they are useful and acceptable. It seems like transplanting a full grown tree" (262). After Ryland's first refusal to Broadmead, Newton wrote, "If more and more honourable messages should be sent, and more silver and gold, and greater honour be proposed, I hope you will still be enabled to abide by your late determination" (271). When it was clear that Ryland would leave Northampton, Newton wrote, "Had I been one of your church I should have voted for nailing your ear to the door of College Lane Meetinghouse" (283). However, when Ryland was settled in Bristol, Newton assured him of his support: "I am glad you are

correspondence of Newton with Ryland. Newton's doctrine of catholicity[93] was fairly simple: if a person belongs to Christ, then they are his brother or sister. He wrote, "So far I am of the Establishment, but not much farther. I own to be of no sect or party, high or low, in Church or State. A Dissenter who holds the Head, and walks in love, is as dear to me, as if he were dressed in prunella."[94] The doctrine of sin, the necessity of the cross, the deity of Jesus, and simple faith in him were Newton's uniting doctrines. From the first known letter, Newton stressed this sort of simplicity to Ryland: "Let me advise you to aim at plain and experimental things, and endeavour rather to affect your hearers' hearts with a sense of the evil of sin, and the love of Jesus, than to fill their heads with distinctions."[95] In a later letter, he returned to a similar theme, saying, "There are other truths, important in their places, but unless beheld through the medium of the cross, they have but a faint effect."[96] As he grew older, Newton seemed to focus even more closely on

satisfied with your removal, and hope you will be so more and more. I am satisfied, likewise, because as I believe your views and motives were right" (299).

93. For the purposes of expediency, this section will focus on Newton's doctrine of catholicity as expressed to Ryland. This is so for two reasons. First, to go further afield into Newton's own writings would involve more information than is necessary for this section. Second, the purpose of this section is to show Newton's influence on Ryland and his understanding of catholicity. It is most expedient to achieve this end by focusing on Newton's doctrine and practice of catholicity as expressed directly to Ryland in their correspondence.

94. Newton, "Letter to John Ryland Jr.," March 15, 1794; cf. Gordon, *Wise Counsel*, 304. In their early correspondence, Newton took Ryland to task for his writing on eternal justification. Ryland's response seems to indicate that he desired to debate the issue with Newton (at least, through correspondence). Newton refused to do so, saying, "If we hold the *Head* and love the Lord, we *agree* with him, and I think my time ill employed in disputing the point with you" (19). His basic understanding of Christian fellowship remained the same: if a person is united to Christ, then Newton believed that he should be united to them.

95. Newton, "Letter to John Ryland Jr.," October 17, 1771; cf. Gordon, *Wise Counsel*, 15. This would be his main contention with American Divinity: "Most of the New England divines I have met with have in my judgment one common fault: they abound with distinctions and refinements in experimental matters, which are suited to cast down those who the Lord would have comforted" (119). This is not to say that he rejected the Edwardseans. He believed that they were "good men, and I hope I am not too wise yet, to sit at their feet and receive instruction from them; but not implicitly" (236). He was willing to learn from them, but he was not willing to be led by them.

96. Newton, "Letter to John Ryland Jr.," August 30, 1790; cf. Gordon, *Wise Counsel*, 232. Newton was no fan of systems of theology. At least, he did not put much stock into them, warning Ryland, "It would be well if both preachers and people would keep more closely to what the scripture teaches of the nature, marks and growth of a work of grace instead of following each other in a track (like sheep) confining the Holy Spirit to a system; imposing at first the experience and sentiments of others as a rule to themselves, and afterward dogmatically laying down the path in which they themselves have been

those doctrines: "My views seem collecting to a few points: the need and worth of a Saviour, the hidden life, consistent walk, and sure supports, and happy prospects of a true believer."[97] This aligns with Ryland's understanding of union with Christ through the Spirit as a major unifying factor of Christian fellowship.[98]

Newton lamented the divisions of Christians into parties "too often squabbling about non-essentials," despite the fact that they "are all one in him."[99] Newton himself despised parties and party labels. Referring to the host of Protestant denominations, he said:

> I belong to none of these churches exclusively; but I am connected with them all, because I believe there are among them all, members of the one true church, the spiritual body of Christ, of which I trust I, through grace, am, however unworthy, a member also. If they love the Lord Jesus Christ in sincerity, I care not a button, by what name they are called, nor to what party they are joined. They are as my mother, and my sisters, and my brethren. In other things we shall not be all of a mind till we meet above. Till then let us love and pity and pray for one another.[100]

---

led, as absolutely necessary to be trodden by others" (120). Around the same time, he wrote, "We may be very orthodox, skilled in defence of the five points, satisfied that our constitution of church order is the very best in the world, and yet be lamentably cold and formal in the feelings of our hearts towards him. Indeed the Congregationalists and Baptists, who are both equally satisfied that they possess the perfect model of the tabernacle to a single loop or pin, need a double portion of grace to prevent their over admiring the supposed excellency of their forms" (128). Correct theology was no guarantee of spiritual vitality nor did Newton see it as necessarily uniting one person to another.

97. Newton, "Letter to John Ryland Jr.," November 26, 1796; cf. Gordon, *Wise Counsel*, 335. He understood his calling in London to be of that stripe, saying, "So far as I can judge, my call in this city, besides preaching the salvation of God to sinners is twofold. 1. To inculcate peace and love among those who are upon the one foundation, though in some points they are not all of a mind. 2. To insist much upon the life of God in the soul, and to show that the power of religion is something different, from an attachment to systems, or modes or forms. These principles draw together a motley sort of assembly, and Church folks and Dissenters of different names—Methodists from Tabernacle [and] from Foundery, Moravians, and if I mistake not sometimes Quakers, gather round me and sit as quiet as so many lambs" (144).

98. Ryland Jr., *Dependance of the Whole Law and Prophets*, 41.

99. Newton, "Letter to John Ryland Jr.," September 20, 1797; cf. Gordon, *Wise Counsel*, 345–46.

100. Newton, "Letter to John Ryland Jr.," January 9, 1796; cf. Gordon, *Wise Counsel*, 323–24. This was a repeated refrain in his letters to Ryland. In one letter, he writes, "My part is only to say with the Apostle, 'Grace be with all that love the Lord Jesus Christ in sincerity.' I hope my heart is with them all, whether Episcopalians, Presbyterians, Independents, Baptists, Methodists, Seceders, Relief-Men, Moravians, etc. etc.; Nay if a Papist gave me good evidence that he loved my Saviour, I would beg leave of men, and

This last quote leads to another point about Newton's catholicity: it had a distinctly eschatological focus. He hoped that "the Spirit which animates the church triumphant, were more diffused amongst his militant members upon earth, and that all who love Jesus in sincerity could learn to love and acknowledge one another."[101] He looked forward to the day that all party labels would die: "When the great trumpet sounds (and perhaps not before) all party walls will fall like the walls of Jericho."[102]

As the missionary movement began to take shape, Newton introduced a missionary element to his catholicity. He welcomed William Ward, Joshua Marshman, Daniel Brundson, and William Grant to London on their way to India.[103] He prayed fervently and longed for the success of Baptist missionary efforts, saying, "May they be instrumental in making many Christians and I shall have no objection to their being all Baptists."[104] He was afraid of the damage that preaching denominational distinctions could do to the

---

ask grace of the Lord, that I might love such Papists likewise, with a pure heart fervently. We shall be known by none of these names of party and prejudice when we meet in the kingdom of glory" (345). Newton consistently held out hope that he might find brothers and sisters in Christ among Roman Catholics, saying, "In the mean time I pray the Lord to grant me two things—First that with respect to doctrines he will be pleased to preserve me in a settled attachment to the great truths as he has taught me, and give me to feel the power and influence of them all in my own soul—Secondly, that with respect to persons, he would enlarge and dilate my heart, that it may have room to embrace all without exception who love our Lord Jesus Christ in sincerity, whether they are called Churchmen or Baptists or Independents or Methodists or Calvinists or Arminians or Moravians, yea though they should happen to be shuffled among the Papists" (Newton, "Letter to John Ryland Jr.," April 16, 1774; cf. Gordon, *Wise Counsel*, 66).

101. Newton, "Letter to John Ryland Jr.," January 22, 1774; cf. Gordon, *Wise Counsel*, 49. Speaking of a Mrs Place, a woman whose theological commitments were less than ideal and perhaps not quite orthodox ("her judgment in spiritual things is not so established as some"), Newton wrote, "Be that as it may, I trust the Lord will guide and bless her and that you and I shall meet her one day, where they are neither Methodists or Dissenters, Baptists or Moravians, Arminians or Calvinists, but are freed from all names, parties and distinctions, and intimately united in Jesus the common object of their adoration and love" (48–49).

102. Newton, "Letter to John Ryland Jr.," April 16, 1774; cf. Gordon, *Wise Counsel*, 66. As he neared the end of his life, Newton wrote, "I am of no party; and I hope soon to be where there are no parties" (324).

103. Newton, "Letter to John Ryland Jr.," May 14, 1799; cf. Gordon, *Wise Counsel*, 354. Newton also held William Carey in high regard, offering a prayer for the Lord to raise up one hundred like him: "Oh that the Lord would raise up and send forth (for only He who made the world can make a true missionary) a hundred such men as I believe Dr. V[an der Kemp] and Mr. C[arey] to be. I would not care whether they were called Baptists or Methodists, Calvinists or Lutherans" (366).

104. Newton, "Letter to John Ryland Jr.," January 9, 1795; cf. Gordon, *Wise Counsel*, 325.

mission field. While some today may find his language condescending, one cannot mistake the concern shown in the following quote for the people to whom the missionaries were going: "If Clergymen, Baptists and Methodists preach the same gospel in Africa, it is to be feared, that when the poor blacks find them differing among themselves in points confessedly of a secondary importance, they will suppose that they are endeavouring to propagate three different religions."[105] He appreciated the work of Moravian missionaries and, later in his life, what money he gave to missionary causes, he gave to the *Unitas Fratrum*.[106]

Ryland's catholicity and Newton's catholicity share some important similarities. Most notably, they both place an emphasis on union with Christ and on shared missionary activity as uniting factors. However, there are significant differences in their theological justifications for their practice of catholicity. First, the eschatological element of Newton's catholicity, while not absent in Ryland, does not play as prominent a role in his thinking. Newton's later letters, especially, make the eschatological element a major factor in why Newton sought communion with those outside the Anglican tradition. Second, the pneumatological aspect of Ryland's catholicity is missing in Newton's catholicity as expressed to Ryland. What this suggests is that Newton influenced Ryland not so much in his theological and philosophical understanding of catholicity but, rather, in its practice.

The letters of Newton to Ryland show that Newton pressed Ryland to a kind of catholicity that is less concerned with theological conviction than it is with peace and concord. This is seen most clearly in how Newton counseled Ryland through controversy. Newton's advice was not to aim for the truth no matter the cost, but was, rather, to seek after unity and not to disturb the peace of the church. If Ryland would refrain from feeding the fire of controversy, it would soon extinguish its own fuel and go out. His advice during the controversy over the Modern Question is indicative of this: "The embers at Northampton will soon go out, if you do not keep them alive, and blow them up. I have such a love for you and for peace, that, if money would prevent it, I would give something out of my pocket rather than see you degrade yourself, and perplex your people, by answering a performance which

---

105. Newton, "Letter to John Ryland Jr.," July 28, 1795; cf. Gordon, *Wise Counsel*, 319.

106. Newton, "Letter to John Ryland Jr.," November 26, 1796; cf. Gordon, *Wise Counsel*, 334. In several letters, Newton lauded the Moravians. He was not in complete agreement with them ("I can sit in a whole skin by the fire-side and find fault with some things in the system of the Brethren as they are called"), but he recognized the righteousness of their zeal: "I must honour such faithful labourers whatever name they bear" (66).

deserves no other treatment than silent contempt."[107] Newton's counsel was not necessarily along theological lines, nor did he give Ryland hints as to how to win an argument; rather, he sought always to keep the peace.

Conclusion

The previous chapter showed one source of Ryland's catholicity in his theological reflection; this chapter has shown a more personal source in his relationships with his biological father and his spiritual father.[108] The life and writings of both John Collett Ryland and John Newton were examined to show the similarities between their thinking and practice and that of John Ryland Jr. While certainty is not possible, it seems that these two men and their catholicity shaped the younger Ryland's thought on the subject in profound ways. Indeed, it is difficult to conceive of Ryland having the same outlook without those two influences.

These personal influences are vital to an understanding of Ryland. While his theological foundations were no doubt important, he did not come to those convictions in a vacuum. There were people in his life that led him down that path. Though it is not possible to pinpoint exactly how Ryland Sr. and Newton impacted precise aspects of Ryland Jr.'s theology and practice, the similarities between their catholicity and his, combined with his own words as to their personal influence, are impossible to ignore.

These two men provided Ryland with a practical template for his practice of catholicity. John Collett Ryland showed his son the possibility of breaching the wall of the Baptist garden in his friendships with the Anglicans George Whitefield and James Hervey. The young Ryland's fire for truth, however, had to be tamed, and it was left to Newton to tame it. From his first letter until his last, Newton showed Ryland Jr. what catholicity requires: humility, a basic commitment to Christ and the doctrine of the gospel, and the desire to maintain peace rather than stir up controversy.

---

107. Newton, "Letter to John Ryland Jr.," January 31, 1792; cf. Gordon, *Wise Counsel*, 258. Newton confessed not to be terribly informed about the issues surrounding the Modern Question (257), but he understood that Ryland had "changed sides," which he thought was "much for the better" (257).

108. After Newton's death, Ryland wrote to Levi Hart, "Dear Father Newton is entered into rest" (John Ryland Jr., "Letter to Levi Hart," January 18, 1808).

7

Conclusion

In a letter to an Anglican friend, John Ryland Jr. writes, "The articles in which we are agreed, are far more numerous, and far more important, than those in which we differ, and ought to do more to unite us, than the latter to divide us. I so believe 'the communion of saints,' as to feel myself much more closely united to every one who is sanctified by the truth, than I can be to any one who is unrenewed in the spirit of his mind."[1] When Ryland appealed to the Apostles' Creed, it was quite often the line about the communion of saints which drew his attention.[2] While he would not retreat on any of his theological convictions, and would defend the particularities of his system to the very last, he would not allow those convictions to divide him from others who loved the same Jesus as he (Eph 6:24). Such was the catholicity of John Ryland Jr.

Summary of Findings

The present work has sought to demonstrate the sources, nature, and context of the catholicity of John Ryland Jr., which was defined in the opening chapter as visible unity in Christ and in intimate fellowship, expressed in life and service together for Christ. The work first explained the importance of Ryland and his catholicity as a subject of serious academic study. Until recently, not only had he not been the subject of any lengthy academic work,

---

1. Ryland, "Letter to a Person of the Establishment," *Pastoral Memorials*, 2:28.
2. Cf. Ryland, "Letter to Stephen West," March 31, 1814, 180–81; "Sermon Notes: Philippians 4:21," *Original Manuscript Sermons: Old Testament, Vol. II.*

the articles and chapters in which he was featured tended merely to emphasize his role in larger organizations and movements, such as the BMS, Bristol Baptist Academy, Broadmead, and the rise of a moderate, missionary Calvinism within the Particular Baptist denomination. Few researchers dealt with Ryland on his own. Those who gave attention to Ryland would at least make reference, even if fleetingly, to his catholicity. However, several things are lacking in these treatments. First, while many recognized the importance of his catholicity, none gave extended attention to it nor did any of them singularly pursue it.[3] Second, there was very little work done on Ryland's correspondence, in which much of his catholic practice is demonstrated, an important aspect of a catholicity that is expressed in life and service together. Third, while Ryland's theology had been briefly studied, and while his catholicity had been noted, no study had pursued Ryland's theology of catholicity. A person of Ryland's stature and importance deserves a fuller explication of his theology and practice with regard to something that others have noted as so central to his thought and life. The present work fills the gap in Ryland studies by singularly treating Ryland's catholicity, showing how he practiced it not only in his correspondence but in his broader ministerial practice, and explaining its theological and personal foundations. In so doing, a fuller picture of Ryland emerges, a portrait of a complex man thoroughly committed to twin convictions: the promulgation of Particular Baptist doctrines, and partnership across denominational and theological lines.

This research project has also sought to situate Ryland's catholicity in the context of other and earlier Baptist catholicities.[4] Henry Jessey, John Bunyan and the Bedford church, Broadmead, and the 1644 and 1677 *Confessions* were all studied with a special focus on their catholicities as seen in either their mixed communionism (as in the case of Jessey, Bunyan, and Broadmead) or their desire to be seen in connection and communion with other traditional and theological movements (the *Confessions*). Ryland was shown as both inhabiting that stream of catholicity and diverging from it. He fits into that context in his broad-minded, catholic embrace of others outside of his tradition. Jessey and Bunyan's commitment to communion with saints as saints; Broadmead leader Robert Purnell's inveighing against division among Christians along denominational lines; and the 1677 *Confession*'s stated desire to be seen in agreement with the broader English

---

3. The most in-depth work on Ryland's catholicity prior to the present research was that of Crocker, "Life and Legacy," 331–59.

4. The caveat is again offered that having a catholic view does not necessitate open communionism, but open communionism does necessitate some form of a catholic understanding. It is with that in mind that earlier catholicities were studied.

Reformed community are all seen, in some form, in Ryland's catholicity.[5] However, Ryland does not sit wholly comfortably in the earlier streams of catholicity. Most notably, Ryland places an emphasis on the experience of the individual as a key component of his catholicity,[6] which emphasis, while not necessarily absent from the earlier streams, is unique to Ryland.

This research project has also done much to demonstrate the catholic practice of Ryland. As was argued earlier, Ryland's catholicity is a fundamentally deed-oriented concept,[7] which means that the actions of catholicity are equally as important as the reasons for it. Ryland showed his catholic sentiments in his correspondence with Presbyterians, Congregationalists, Anglicans, and the Russian Orthodox; his partnerships with Wesleyan Methodists and Congregationalists; and ministerial cooperation with General Baptists and others of differing theological commitments. These have been amply demonstrated, many for the first time.

The theological foundations of Ryland's catholic practice have also been pursued. Like those who went before him, Ryland roots his understanding and practice of catholicity in the doctrine of union with Christ: all those who "hold to the head" are worthy of his Christian love and fellowship. However, across his published and unpublished works, Ryland expounds his understanding of that union with emphases not found in his predecessors. It is accomplished by the work of the Spirit, so that Ryland's catholicity may be seen as both christological as well as pneumatological.[8] However, the most important aspect of his theology of catholicity is his epistemology of catholicity, or how he determines whether or not to treat a person as a fellow Christian. In his epistemology of catholicity, experience is determinative: does a person exhibit the presence of Christ in their lived experience? His theology of catholicity, then, is christological, pneumatological, and experiential. All three are important, and all three play a vital role in his overall theology, but, in practice, the experiential aspect has the highest priority, as that is the one that is demonstrable. It is on the experiential aspect that Ryland leans in practice, as evidenced in his continuing friendships with Robert Hall Jr. and John Foster, as well as his partnership with those of diverse theological commitments, such as the Emperor of Russia and the Wesleyan Methodists.

Ryland came to his convictions through theological reflection, as evidenced by his works, as well as personal influences, which were his father,

---

5. See chapter 3.
6. See chapter 5.
7. See chapter 4.
8. See chapter 5.

John Collett Ryland, and his mentor, John Newton.[9] John Collett Ryland practiced a similar kind of catholicity, forming and maintaining friendships with those outside of his tradition, including George Whitefield and James Hervey, both Anglicans. The younger Ryland would have seen this practiced during his childhood and would have had the chance to form friendships with such people. The catholicity he practiced was in many important ways inherited from his father. The other important influence in Ryland's development was Newton, who counseled Ryland and showed him a more broad-minded way than even Ryland's father did. It was through Newton that Ryland learned to moderate his words toward concord, and Newton counseled Ryland in the way of peace in several controversies throughout Ryland's life, including one with John Collett Ryland. It may be said, then, that from his father, Ryland Jr. learned the general shape of catholicity, and from Newton, Ryland learned the spirit required to maintain catholic friendships and partnerships.

This work has offered a unique account and interpretation of Ryland in general and his catholicity in particular. It is unique in at least two aspects. First, it has utilized sources not found in other works on Ryland. For example, Ryland's handwritten sermon notes held in the archives of Bristol Baptist College have been used in this work but are not found elsewhere.[10] In addition, while it has been quoted in previous works, much of Ryland's correspondence found in this work has either been unused or underused. That is, when his correspondence has been utilized, it has merely been quoted and not used as a means of discerning his theological understanding. Moreover, contemporary newspaper accounts of Ryland that have been overlooked in previous works have been utilized in this project not only to set Ryland in his context but also to reveal an important aspect of his catholic practice.

The second way in which the present work makes a unique contribution to studies of John Ryland is in the depth of study provided. This is seen in four areas. First, whereas previous studies have made mention of Ryland's open communion beliefs, none of them have set his overall catholicity in its theological and denominational context.[11] Second, previous studies, with Christopher Crocker's work excepted, have typically asserted rather than demonstrated Ryland's catholic correspondence. Chapter 4 of the present

9. See chapter 6.

10. Bristol Baptist College holds most of these sermon notes; however, it does not possess them all. The Angus Library, the American Baptist Historical Society archive, and the Northamptonshire Record Office all have some of the sermon notes, though none of these institutions holds more than a dozen of them.

11. See chapter 3.

work demonstrates it through copious quotations of Ryland's actual letters to those outside of his tradition. Third, Ryland's work with the Wesleyans has been missed in previous studies. In light of his theological opposition to Arminianism, his missionary partnerships are enlightening and revealing of his catholicity. Finally, the theological and personal foundations of Ryland's catholic practice have not been covered in previous studies as they have here. The christological, pneumatological, and, ultimately, experiential nature of Ryland's catholicity have not been expounded in prior studies of Ryland.

It remains now to summarize some broader considerations stemming from the foregoing research and point out some potential avenues for future research. Three areas are worth exploring briefly.

The Enclosed Garden Opened: Ryland's Catholic Influence on Particular Baptist Life

During Ryland's lifetime and after his death, the walls of the "enclosed garden" of the Particular Baptists continually lowered. The Baptist Union was founded in 1813 as a Particular Baptist denomination, but, by 1833, General Baptists were allowed to be admitted. In 1891, the Baptist Union and the General Baptists of the New Connexion amalgamated, formally bringing the Particular and General Baptists together into one denomination. While Ryland died in 1825, his influence continued to be felt and impacted the course of union among Baptists in the nineteenth century.

This is seen clearly in one of the last major denominational activities of Ryland's life, which consisted of the reorganization of the Western Baptist Association. The Association had grown too large and unwieldy; thus, in 1823, the original Association held its last meeting and sent its last circular letter.[12] In 1824, the first meeting of the Bristol Baptist Association was held. Ryland was tasked with writing the first circular letter of the new association, which is unsurprising considering that he was the senior minister in the area and exercised the widest influence. What is interesting is that two versions of Ryland's 1824 circular letter exist: the one that was published and a handwritten version that is held in the Bristol Baptist College Archives.

---

12. Ryland was elected moderator for the last Association meeting (Western Baptist Association, *Circular Letter*, 1823, 14). The minutes of the meeting record the decision to discontinue the association: "It was determined by a considerable majority, that this Association, at the close of its present meeting, be dissolved" (15). An association would continue under the same name, but it was not the same organization. It bore the marks of catholicity, however, as, in its 1824 meeting, three Independent ministers attended and participated.

CONCLUSION

Both are instructive for the kind of catholicity that Ryland sought for the new Association.

The published version is an exposition of Prov 4:23, in which Ryland exhorts the people of the churches to look well to themselves and keep their own hearts with all diligence.[13] Prior to the exposition itself, however, Ryland speaks to the basis of their union in comparison with the previous Association. It is worth quoting at length:

> It appears necessary to a comfortable Associate Connection, that we should not only agree in our sentiments respecting the scriptural administration of the ordinance of baptism, but still more so that we should be nearly of one mind with regard to the most important doctrines of revealed religion: but instead of the systematical detail of Articles, which were prefixed to our Letters from the year 1798, or the earlier reference to the Confession of our Forefathers in their Assembly in 1689, (of which we generally approve,) we would, in a more practical and experimental manner, state our deep conviction of the infinite glory and excellency of the every blessed God, who has revealed himself in his word as subsisting in a trinity in unity; the perfection of his moral character as delineated in the scriptures; the absolute dependance of all created beings on him; the importance of his moral government over all rational creatures; their obligations to reverence, love, and obey him; the spirituality, equity, and immutability of his holy law; the guilt and depravity of all the race of man since the fall, and their just exposure to the curse of the divine law; the impossibility of a sinner's establishing his own righteousness, or justifying himself in the sight of God; the riches of divine grace, as the only source of salvation; the sovereign love of God, displayed in the gift of his only-begotten Son; the absolute necessity of Christ's mediation, and the sufficiency of his obedience unto death, for the pardon and justification of every sinner that shall return unto God in his name; the happiness of all that are interested in his great salvation, and the glorious harmony of the divine perfections in the plan of redemption; with the necessity of the efficacious influence of the Holy Spirit, to regenerate the soul, to carry on the work of progressive sanctification, and enable believers to persevere to the end. We are well convinced that the salvation of sinners is altogether of grace, through faith, and that not of ourselves, it is the gift of God; and while we confess that it is not by works of righteousness which we have done, but according to divine

---

13. Ryland, *Circular Letter*, 1824, 3.

mercy that we are saved, we are satisfied that all true believers are God's workmanship, created anew in Christ Jesus unto good works, which God has before ordained that we should walk in them; we are fully convinced that our blessed Lord has not, by his redeeming us from the curse of the law, released us from personal obedience; but has increased our obligations to regard his law as the unalterable standard of duty. We rejoice that God will be eternally glorified in the everlasting happiness of all who repent and believe the gospel, while we are convinced that the ungodly will be consigned to everlasting destruction.[14]

While this is a lengthy quotation, it represents the whole of their confessional union. It is much shorter than any previous doctrinal statement, but nothing more is required of partnering churches than is stated here. It is a statement with which a Calvinist would surely agree, but its Calvinistic affirmations are softened: there is no mention of the elect or predestination. Rather, the statement speaks of "divine grace, as the only source of salvation." Indeed, more is done in this statement to exclude antinomians than Arminians: emphasis is placed on the necessity of repentance and believing the gospel, and adherence to God's moral law as the standard of duty is upheld.[15] The 1824 reorganization of the Bristol Association could have been a time to recommit the Western Baptists to previous confessional standards of faith, but it was, instead, used as an opportunity to distance them from those standards, for, despite the "general approval" given to them in the statement, they come to have less influence on the life of the Bristol Baptist Association after 1824 rather than more.

The second version of Ryland's letter is even more explicit in its catholic emphases. It is an exhortation to Christian unity in which Ryland urges the Bristol Baptists to adopt a broad-minded charity toward one another and "all the genuine followers of Christ."[16] He begins with a note about true Religion, which says, "While true Religion tends to expand the foul with genuine Benevolence towards all Mankind, it leads those who pofsefs it to take a peculiar Complacency in all them that wear the same divine Image."[17] He then rehearses his general ideas about catholicity: it is founded on union

---

14. Ryland, *Circular Letter*, 1824, 2–3.

15. To be sure, Arminians would undoubtedly take issue with the idea of perseverance to the end present in the statement, but, even in that part of the statement, there is room for Arminians to find comfort: perseverance is the product of the work of the Spirit enabling the believer to persevere, rather than a gift received at the time of salvation.

16. Ryland, "Letter to Churches about the New Association," 12.

17. Ryland, "Letter to Churches about the New Association," 3.

with Christ through the influence of the Spirit, and it is proven through "the internal feelings of pious persons."[18] These general ideas are expected, given the foregoing exposition of Ryland's catholicity. It is still interesting, however, that Ryland, in a letter to churches of a Baptist Association, emphasizes union with those of other denominations. He writes, "We are indeed far from wishing to confine our Christian Affection to one Denomination, but would sincerely esteem all the genuine followers of Christ, and rejoice in seeing the power of Godliness prevail, and the salvation of souls promoted, among Christians who may differ from us, on various religious subjects of minor importance."[19] Ryland sought to inculcate his catholicity into the new Bristol Baptist Association, and, while he would not live to see it, his catholic propensity would continue not only in the new association but also through the students he taught at the Bristol Baptist Academy, who are worth considering briefly.

A list of students who attended the Academy under Ryland's Presidency includes dozens of ministers, tutors, missionaries, and denominational leaders. These would form the backbone of the movement of British Particular Baptists in the nineteenth century. Francis Augustus Cox learned under Ryland from 1798 until 1800. He later exercised leadership across a variety of institutions: he was a minister at Clipstone, Cambridge, and Hackney; helped found the *Baptist Magazine* in 1809; was a member of the Baptist Board; was Tutor at the Baptist College at Stepney from 1813 until 1822; co-founded the University of London; and served on the General Body of Dissenting Ministers of the Three Denominations. Micah Thomas, a Welshman, attended the Academy from 1800 until 1802; he would later serve as Tutor and President of the Baptist College at Abergavenny from 1807 until 1836. Solomon Young began his time at the Academy in 1805, and he would remain there until 1807. He later served as Tutor at the Baptist College at Stepney from 1814 until 1826, becoming President of that institution in 1827. John Howard Hinton was a student at the Academy from 1811 until 1813. He would later serve as a minister as well as secretary of the Baptist Union (1841–1866). Joshua Tinson came to Bristol in 1818 and was a student until 1822. He went from Bristol to Jamaica as a BMS missionary. He became President of the Baptist College at Calabar in 1843, in which position he served until 1850. Further research into the work of Ryland's students and their influence on Baptist life in the nineteenth century would, no doubt, prove enlightening and fruitful.

---

18. Ryland, "Letter to Churches about the New Association," 4. That is, it is experiential. See chapter 5 for more on Ryland's experiential catholicity.

19. Ryland, "Letter to Churches about the New Association," 12.

Baptist Catholicity

This work began with reference to the movement called Baptist catholicity. As was mentioned in the opening chapter, this project is not a work "*on* Baptist Catholicity" but is, rather, "*from* Baptist Catholicity."[20] One of the ways that this is true is found in a consideration of one of the foundational impulses of the Baptist catholicity movement, which is to listen to, learn from, and partner with non-Baptists.[21] Ryland is a helpful guide in doing so. He demonstrates the possibility of robust critique of those who differ while maintaining deep friendships and partnerships with those critiqued. In this arena, he is also a model for the broader Christian world as to how we might navigate deep differences while maintaining real unity. The inner logic and feeling of Ryland with regard to criticism, and how he understood critique to take place within the context of relationships, is seen clearly in a line he writes to Levi Hart, "I never offer to teize an honest man on subjects on which we differ, but if a new argument strikes me, I make no scruple of mentioning it, to any very candid friend, and so leave it, without further debate."[22] He does not want merely to belittle or denounce a person over differences they have, as that would not demonstrate love for that person or a love for peace. However, he does not hesitate to mention an argument against a "candid friend." Debate was not a strike against friendship, nor was it prohibited by close friendship. Indeed, it may well be a mark of friendship. He would mention a new argument, but then he would leave it, if his friend had no desire to engage, with no damage done to the friendship. This encapsulates the open-hearted, open-minded, conversant catholicity that Ryland practiced, and he is a model for modern-day Baptists, and other Christians, as we listen to and learn from those who are different, seeking unity in the face of an ever-growing diversity.

This work may also be seen as part of a general *ressourcement* for Baptists exploring their history and tradition. This is so in a couple of ways. First, for Baptists who have rediscovered their history and appreciate those who have gone before, Ryland is an important figure.[23] It is important, however, truly to understand him for who he was and how he was situated in his own context. He and the Particular Baptists which he helped to lead must not be read as modern Reformed Baptists. They had their own context, cultural

---

20. James, *Analogous Uses of Language*, 24.

21. Harmon, *Towards Baptist Catholicity*, 218–19: "We affirm that there is much the believers church can and must learn from other Christian traditions."

22. Ryland, "Letter to Levi Hart," January 18, 1808.

23. See, for example, Gordon, "John Ryland," 2:77–95; Haykin, "Sum of All Good," 332–53; Crocker, "Life and Legacy," *passim*.

and theological assumptions, and practices. This work has sought to understand and present Ryland in his historical, theological, and denominational context. Second, Ryland shows that it is possible for someone to remain a person of particular theological commitments while also welcoming and cooperating with those who differ. Indeed, he demonstrates not only the possibility of such but also a way forward in a catholic spirit that is christocentric, pneumatological, and experiential. In a fractured Christian world, the catholicity of Ryland could prove to be beneficial.

Importance of Personal Narrative in Theological Formation and Expression

The formation of Ryland's catholicity demonstrates the influence that personal narratives play in theological, philosophical, and ministerial development and practice. In the present work, one may see Ryland's own theological foundations for his belief and practice, which shows that he thought through his reasons and made them his own, but one may also see just as readily the personal influences that led him to his conclusions.

An important aspect of this study has been to examine not only the published words of Ryland but also to investigate his actions. A perusal of Ryland's published writings could lead a person to believe that he was merely a staunch Calvinist who came to support mission work. Such a summation of Ryland misses the broader picture of the man and the movement he helped to lead. He not only wrote; he lived. Indeed, Ryland's was not chiefly a publishing ministry. He exercised leadership and influence in ways that typically went unpublished. For example, during his lifetime, the Particular Baptists were undergoing a transition. They were moving from the high Calvinism of Gill and Brine to a more moderate, evangelical Calvinism. Part of this movement included the theological shift toward an affirmative answer to the Modern Question begun by Hall Sr., given theological impetus by Fuller, and spearheaded by Carey. Ryland was a leader in this transition as well, as he both helped to promulgate the theology of his friend Fuller as well as found and direct the Baptist Missionary Society. Champion summarizes Ryland's unique place in the history of this period of Particular Baptist life, "If Fuller the powerful apologist and controversialist and Carey the practical visionary both understood Christian faith and life in terms of obligation and duty it was John Ryland whose many sermons present perhaps the most systematic and integrated statement of this total theological position."[24] A reading of Ryland's "Text Book" gives indications of the

24. Champion, "Evangelical Calvinism," 199.

nature and breadth of his influence upon the Particular Baptists: it was done chiefly through preaching, and it spread throughout England, Scotland, and Wales.[25] Ryland's leadership, then, differed from that of Fuller and Carey; his was of a more pastoral, relational type. Therefore, a study of Ryland, especially one that concerns his catholicity, should take into account the fullness of the man in his published works, unpublished writings, and deeds.

The importance of Ryland's personal narrative for understanding his theology in general and catholicity in particular is seen in several ways. For example, while Ryland wrote a defense of the Baptist position with regard to baptism and held tenaciously to his conviction, his practice was to befriend and even partner with non-Baptists as far as possible. His published writings reveal that he was an open communionist,[26] but a study of his practice shows the depth of his open-communion ideals: he preached in non-Baptist churches hundreds of times, helped non-Baptist missionary societies in their work, and carried on an extensive and intimate correspondence with non-Baptists on both sides of the Atlantic. The breadth of his catholicity with non-Baptists is not seen in his published writings alone. Additionally, Ryland said very harsh things about Arminians, which could lead the historian to believe that his strict opposition is the only side of the story of Ryland and non-Calvinists.[27] However, a careful study of Ryland's life and practice finds that he partnered with Arminians in a variety of ways throughout his life, from preaching in their churches to helping raise money for their missionaries. The harshness of his words against Arminian theology is mitigated somewhat by his work alongside them. Again, the picture is more complicated than his published writings might show. It is a picture of a man with firm theological convictions who did not allow those convictions to erect dividing walls between him and those with whom he differed. His words against Arminians, as severe as they might have been, were, in the end, intramural critiques rather than broadsides against an enemy. While Ryland maintained his Calvinism until the end of his life, it was not Calvinism that bound him to other Christians.[28] It was a basic commitment to what he called "evangelical truth."[29] Though he could argue for Calvinism against other understandings of theology, Ryland, nevertheless, believed

---

25. In addition to the two churches of which he was the pastor, Ryland is found preaching at over 250 others throughout his life (Ryland, "Text Book").

26. Even in those instances in which he discusses his open communionism, he assumes that his readers know more about it than he reveals (Ryland, *Candid Statement*, xi).

27. Cf. Crocker, "Life and Legacy," 352.

28. *Pace* Crocker, "Life and Legacy," 331–32.

29. Ryland, *Practical Influence*, 6. See chapter 5 for an explanation of what Ryland means by this phrase.

that non-Calvinists can also hold to evangelical truth. His cooperation with other "evangelical" ministers and organizations demonstrates this.[30] The breadth of his catholicity would only be hinted at in his published writings and is only revealed fully in his practice of catholic friendships and ministerial partnerships seen largely in his unpublished writings.

While noting Ryland's catholicity is no innovation, little of his actual catholic practice has been uncovered. Champion includes some of the unpublished material found in the Bristol Baptist College Archives and at College Lane. Haykin also utilizes some of Ryland's correspondence, particularly that found in the American Baptist Historical Society archives. Crocker makes the most use of unpublished material and the deeds of Ryland, including many of the letters found in various archives all over the world. However, in each case, the material adduced, whether much of it or little of it, does not materially impact the conclusions drawn. That is, his actual practice of catholicity is not integrated into his overall theology of catholicity. If catholicity is a fundamentally deed-oriented concept, as this work has argued, then the practice of it must be a central element used in understanding it. It is hoped that future studies of Ryland, whether of his catholicity or other aspects of his life and thought, will include more research into his actions as a minister.

This is important for historical and theological research in general, as it shows that convictions are not merely the natural outcome of intellectual enquiry. Without discounting that aspect of Ryland's, or any person's theological development, Ryland's life narrative shows that his catholicity was not merely the result of his study of scripture and theology. Rather, his father and John Newton, in very particular ways, impacted and even determined the shape of his catholic belief and practice. Theological formation and expression are complex processes. The published writings of an individual tell only one part of their story. Historical and theological research cannot be content with only part of the story. It must delve into all aspects of extant material. It is only in so doing that a fuller, more complex picture of the person, their beliefs, and their practice may come into view.

Every person lives in a context, and that context plays a large role in their development and lives. Paying attention to that contextuality is key for understanding the whole of people and even institutions under study. Vast potential exists for research into the broader context, actions, and influences upon the Particular Baptists, research that could ultimately help all of us better understand not only the people of the past but also ourselves and our situation in the world.

30. See chapter 4 for Ryland's cooperation with non-Calvinists and non-Baptists.

Bibliography

John Ryland—Unpublished Correspondence

American Baptist Historical Society Archives

"Letter to Daniel Sutcliff." August 12, 1818.
"Letter to John Sutcliff." August 26, 1774.

Angus Library and Archive

"Letter to John Dyer." 1824(?).
"Letter to John Saffery." September 9, 1796.
"Letter to John Saffery." Unknown date.
"Letter to John Saffery." May 29, 1815.
"Letter to John Saffery." January 12, 1818.
"Letter to John Sutcliff." January 26, 1807.
"Letter to John Sutcliff." September 23, 1802.

Beinecke Rare Book and Manuscript Library, Yale University

"Letter to Jonathan Edwards Jr." June 29, 1787.
"Letter to Jonathan Walter Edwards." August 31, 1807.

Bristol Baptist College Archives

"Letter to Churches about the New Association." In *A Discourse on the Gospel Offer by a Minister of the Reformed Church Translated from the Dutch by the Rev. William Carey...Transcribed with a Few Corrections (by John Ryland): Hints and Queries on Theological Subjects: Sundry Transcripts of Letters, etc.*
"Letter to the Editors of the Baptist Magazine." In *A Discourse on the Gospel Offer.*
"Letter to John Harris." In *A Discourse on the Gospel Offer.*
"Letter to Unknown about Broadmead." In *A Discourse on the Gospel Offer.*

"Letter to William Adam." 1821[?]. In *A Discourse on the Gospel Offer*.
"Letter to William Wilberforce." June 1, 1812. In *Letters to John Ryland (1807–1824)*.

Herman Witsius Ryland and Family Fonds, National Archives of Canada

"Letter to William Ryland." October 25, 1808.

Isaac Mann Collection, National Library of Wales

"Letter to John Sutcliff." June 1796.

National Library of Wales

"Letter to the Emperor of Russia." 1815–1825.

Samuel Miller Papers, Princeton University Library

"Letter to Samuel Miller." Unknown date.
"Letter to Samuel Miller." November 25, 1800.
"Letter to Samuel Miller." 1799.
"Letter to Samuel Miller." May 13, 1806.
"Letter to Samuel Miller." May 8, 1802.

Silliman Family Papers, Yale University Library

"Letter to Unknown Recipient." February 26, 1806.

Simon Gratz Collection, The Historical Society of Pennsylvania

"Letter to Edward Dorr Griffin." May 12, 1807.
"Letter to Levi Hart." January 18, 1808.
"Letter to Levi Hart." 1805.
"Letter to Levi Hart." August 10, 1805.
"Letter to Samuel Hopkins." March 13, 1798.
"Letter to Samuel Hopkins." 1797.

William Wilberforce Papers, David M. Rubenstein Rare Book and Manuscript Library, Duke University

"Letter to William Wilberforce." March 26, 1821.

Yale University Library

"Letter to Jonathan Edwards Jr." August 28, 1801.

John Ryland—Books

Advice to Young Ministers, Respecting Their Preparatory Studies: A Sermon Preached June 25, 1812, in the Meeting-House in Devonshire-Square, London: Before the Subscribers to the Academical Institution at Stepney, for the Education of Candidates for the Ministry of the Baptist Denomination: Published at the Request of the Managers, Tutor, and Students. Bristol: E. Bryan, 1812.

A Candid Statement of the Reasons Which Induce the Baptists to Differ in Opinion and Practice from Their Christian Brethren. London: W. Button, 1814.

The Certain Increase of the Glory and Kingdom of Jesus: A Sermon Preached at Chard, in Somersetshire, on Wednesday Evening, July 11th, 1794, at the Annual Meeting of the Baptist Association. Bristol: John Rose, 1794.

Christ Manifested, and Satan Frustrated. A Sermon, Preached at the Meeting-House, in College-Lane, Northampton, December 25, 1781. Northampton: Thomas Dicey, 1782.

Christ, the Great Source of the Believer's Consolation; and the Grand Subject of the Gospel Ministry. London: J. Buckland and J. P. Lepard, 1788.

A Compendious View of the Principal Truths of the Glorious Gospel of Christ. For the Use of Youth. London: Printed by T. and J. W. Pasham, 1769.

The Dependance of the Whole Law and the Prophets on the Two Primary Commandments: A Sermon Preached before the Ministers and Messengers of the Baptists Churches Belonging to the Western Association, at Their Annual Meeting Held in Salisbury; on Thursday. Bristol: Briggs and Cottle, 1798.

The Difficulties and Supports of a Gospel Minister; and the Duties Incumbent on a Christian Church. A Charge, by J. Ryland, and a Sermon by J. Hinton, Delivered Nov. 17, 1801 at the Ordination of T. Coles. Bristol: Harris and Bryan, 1801.

The Earnest Charge, and Humble Hope of an Affectionate Pastor: Being the Substance of Three Discourses. Addressed to the Church, and Congregation, in College-Lane, Northampton, December 1, 1793. Bristol: W. Pine, 1794.

The Efficacy of Divine Grace Explained and Defended: In a Sermon Preached before the Ministers and Messengers of the Baptist Churches, Belonging to the Western Association, at Their Annual Meeting, Held in Bath, on Thursday, June the 6th, 1816, and Published at Their Request. Bristol: Button and Son, 1816.

Eight Characteristics of the Messiah, Laid Down by the Prophet Zechariah; and All Found in Jesus of Nazareth, Evinced in a Sermon Preached on Dec. 26, 1810, at the Jews' Chapel, Church Street, Spitalfields. London: B. R. Goakman, 1810.

The Faithfulness of God in His Word Evinced: Or, the Fulfilling of the Scriptures in the Believer's Own Experience. London: J. W. Pasham, 1773.

Hymns and Verses on Sacred Subjects: The Greater Part of Which Are Now Published for the First Time from the Originals. London: Daniel Sedgwick, 1862.

The Indwelling and Righteousness of Christ No Security against Corporeal Death, but the Source of Spiritual and Eternal Life. London: Button and Son, 1815.

Memoirs of the Rev. Robert Hall of Arnsby: With a Brief History of the Baptist Church at Arnsby, Leicestershire. Rev. ed. London: James Paul, 1850.

The Necessity of the Trumpet's Giving a Certain Sound. Bristol: E. Bryan, 1813.

Pastoral Memorials. 2 vols. Edited by J. E. Ryland. London: B. J. Holdsworth, 1826–28.

The Practical Influence of Evangelical Religion. Bristol: J. G. Fuller, 1819.

Seasonable Hints to a Bereaved Church; and, the Blessedness of the Dead Who Die in the Lord Being the Substance of 2 Discourses. . .Occasioned by the Death of the Rev. William Guy. Northampton: Thomas Dicey, 1783.

Serious Essays on the Truths of the Glorious Gospel: And the Various Branches of Vital Experience. For the Use of True Christians. London: J. Pasham, 1771.

Serious Essays on the Truths of the Glorious Gospel, and the Various Branches of Vital Experience, for the Use of True Christians. 3rd ed. London: John Bennett, 1829.

Serious Remarks on the Different Representations of Evangelical Doctrine by the Professed Friends of the Gospel. 2 vols. Bristol: J. G. Fuller, 1817–18.

The Work of Faith, the Labour of Love, and the Patience of Hope, Illustrated, in the Life and Death of the Reverend Andrew Fuller, Late Pastor of the Baptist Church at Kettering, and Secretary to the Baptist Missionary Society. London: Button and Son, 1816.

John Ryland—Articles and Other Short Works

"Circular Letter, Bristol Baptist Association." 1824. Bristol Baptist College Archives.

"Extracts from the Diary of the Late Rev. Dr. Ryland." *New Baptist Miscellany* 6 (January 1832) 1–5.

"A Hint Respecting Efficacious Grace." *Evangelical Magazine* 4 (August 1796) 315–17.

"A Letter from Dr. Ryland." *Baptist Quarterly* 12 (April–July 1947) 221–22.

"Letter to Joseph Kinghorn." In *Joseph Kinghorn of Norwich*, edited by Martin Hood Wilkin, 183–85. Norwich: Fletcher and Alexander, 1855.

"Letters of Dr. John Ryland to Dr. Stephen West." *Bibliotheca Sacra* 30 (January 1873) 178–87.

"Mursell's Preparation for College." *Transactions of the Baptist Historical Society* 2 (October 1911) 74–76.

"The Nature, Evidences, and Advantages of Humility, Part 1." *Baptist Magazine* 19 (November 1827) 497–502.

"The Nature, Evidences, and Advantages of Humility, Part 2." *Baptist Magazine* 19 (December 1827) 556–59.

"On the Alledged Impiety of Calvinism." *Baptist Magazine* 17 (July 1825) 277–86.

"On the Connection of the Doctrine of the Trinity, with Other Scriptural Truths." *Baptist Magazine* 17 (January 1825) 1–4, 59–63.

"On the Divine Decrees." *Baptist Magazine* 14 (September 1822) 365–68.

"Preface." In *Help to Zion's Travellers*, by Robert Hall Sr., v–xii. London: Whittingham and Rowland, 1815.

"Ryland's Poetical Letter." *Baptist Quarterly* 6 (July 1933) 327–29.

"Salutations of Hell, or the Greetings of the Damned." *Baptist Memorial and Monthly Record* (1845) 36–42, 68–75.

"The Zeal of the Lord of Hosts." In *Missionary Sermons: A Selection from the Discourses Delivered on Behalf of the Baptist Missionary Society on Various Occasions*, 21–27. London: Carey, 1924.

[as Eleutherides]. "An Inquiry Concerning the Events to Be Accomplished by the Three Angels, Mentioned, Rev. XIV.6–11." *Evangelical Magazine* 4 (October 1796) 412–14.

John Ryland—Unpublished Material

Angus Library and Archive

"An Account of the Rise and Progress of the Two Society's at Mr Rylands and Mrs Trinders Boarding School in Northampton."
[as Pacificus]. "Queries to Praying Proffessors of Every Denomination Respecting Political and Imprecatory Prayer." n.d.

Bristol Baptist College Archives

"Autograph Reminiscences." 1807.
"A Confession of Faith Delivered by John Ryland Junr of Northampton at His Ordination to the Pastoral Care of the Church in College Lane." In *Original Manuscripts (c. 1770-1824)*.
Discourses on the Book of Psalms (c. 1771-1824).
"Hints and Queries on Theological Subjects: The Necessity of the Atonement." In *A Discourse on the Gospel Offer*.
"Letter in Rhyme by Rev. John Ryland, M.A., Addressed to Mr. Christian, of Sheepshead, a Few Days after an Association Meeting Held There in 1774."
"Marginalia." In *An Account of the Life of the Late Reverend David Brainerd*. Edinburgh: Jon Gray, 1765.
"Material Related to the Departure of Joseph Hughes." In *Original Manuscripts (c.1770-1824)*.
"Material Relating to the Departure of Henry Page." In *A Discourse on the Gospel Offer*.
[with Caleb Evans]. "Notebook of Caleb Evans, with Details of Broadmead Members and Personal Notes, Including Details of His Library. With Some Entries by John Ryland."
"On the Free Offer of the Gospel." In *Remains: A Collection of Historicall Sentences and Practices 1693, etc., Vol I*.
Original Manuscript Sermons: Old Testament, Vol. I (c.1771-1823).
Original Manuscript Sermons: Old Testament, Vol. II (c.1773-1822).
Poems by John Ryland Junr, Vol. 1 (1778-1821).
Poems by John Ryland Junr, Vol. 2 (1783-1795).
"Respecting Written Experiences." In *A Discourse on the Gospel Offer*.

Northamptonshire Record Office

"Text Book." 1825.

Primary Sources—Books

Anonymous. *An Account of the Bristol Education Society: Began Anno 1770*. Bristol: W. Pine, n.d.

Anonymous. *A Confession of Faith Put Forth by the Elders and Brethren of Many Congregations of Christians (Baptized Upon Profession of Their Faith) in London and the Country*. London: n.d., 1677.

Anonymous. *The Confession of Faith, of Those Church Which Are Commonly (Though Falsly) Called Anabaptists*. London: n.d., 1644.

Beddome, Benjamin. *A Scriptural Exposition of the Baptism Catechism by Way of Question and Answer*. 2nd ed., corrected ed. Bristol: W. Pine, 1776.

Bellamy, Joseph. *True Religion Delineated: Or, Experimental Religion, as Distinguished from Formality on the One Hand, and Enthusiasm on the Other, Set in a Scriptural and Rational Light*. Boston: S. Kneeland, 1750.

Blyth, Thomas Allen. *The History of Bedford and Visitor's Guide*. London: Longmans, Green, Reader, and Dyer, 1873.

Booth, Abraham. *An Apology for the Baptists. In Which They Are Vindicated from the Imputation of Laying an Unwarrantable Stress on the Ordinance of Baptism; and against the Charge of Bigotry in Refusing Communion at the Lord's Table to Paedobaptists*. London: Dilly, 1778.

———. *The Reign of Grace from Its Rise to Its Consummation*. 4th ed. London: L. Wayland, 1790.

Brine, John. *The Solemn Charge of a Christian Minister Considered*. London: John Ward, 1750.

Bunyan, John. *A Confession of My Faith and a Reason of My Practice, or, with Who, and Who Not, I Can Hold Church-Fellowship, or the Communion of Saints*. London: Francis Smith, 1672.

———. *Differences in Judgment About Water-Baptism, No Bar to Communion; or, to Communicate with Saints, as Saints, Proved Lawful*. London: Wilkins, 1673.

———. *The Heavenly Foot-man: Or, a Description of the Man That Gets to Heaven*. London: Charles Doe, 1698.

———. *Peaceable Principles and True*. In *The Works of That Eminent Servant of Christ Mr. John Bunyan* 1:107–17. London: W. Johnston, 1767.

Calamy, Edmund, and Samuel Palmer. *The Nonconformist's Memorial: Being an Account of the Lives, Sufferings, and Printed Works of the Two Thousand Ministers Ejected from the Church of England, Chiefly under the Acts of Uniformity, Aug 24, 1662*. 3 vols. London: Button and Son, 1803.

Cox, Benjamin. *An Appendix to a Confession of Faith, or a More Full Declaration of the Faith and Judgement of Baptized Believers*. London: n.d., 1646.

Dwight, Timothy. *The Nature and Danger of Infidel Philosophy Exhibited in Two Discourses Addressed to the Candidates for the Baccalaureate in Yale College, September 9th, 1797*. 3rd ed. Cambridge: B. Flower, 1804.

Edwards, Jonathan. *A Careful and Strict Enquiry into the Modern Prevailing Notions of That Freedom of Will, Which Is Supposed to Be Essential to Moral Agency, Vertue and Vice, Reward and Punishment, Praise and Blame*. London: Thomas Field, 1762.

———. *The Excellency of Christ*. 2nd ed. Northampton: Thomas Dicey, 1780.

———. *The Life of the Late Reverend, Learned and Pious Mr Jonathan Edwards*. Boston: S. Kneeland, 1765. Copy held at the Bristol Baptist College Archives.

———. *A Treatise Concerning Religious Affections*. Edinburgh: John Gray, 1772.

Edwards, Jonathan, Jr. *The Faithful Manifestation of the Truth, the Proper and Immediate End of Preaching the Gospel*. New Haven, CT: Thomas and Samuel Green, 1783.

———. *The Necessity of Atonement: And the Consistency between That and Free Grace, in Forgiveness: Illustrated in Three Sermons, Preached before His Excellency the Governor, and the Legislature of the State of Connecticut at New-Haven, in October, A.D. M.DCC.LXXXV.* New Haven, CT: Meigs, Bowen, and Dana, 1785.
Ely, Ezra Stiles. *A Contrast between Calvinism and Hopkinsianism*. New York: S. Whiting, 1811.
Foster, John. *Critical Essays Contributed to the Eclectic Review*. 2 vols. London: Henry G. Bohn, 1857.
———. *Lectures Delivered at Broadmead Chapel*. Edited by J. E. Ryland. 2 vols. London: Henry G. Bohn, 1845.
———. *The Life and Correspondence of John Foster*. Edited by J. E. Ryland. 2 vols. New York: Wiley and Putnam, 1846.
———. *The Life and Correspondence of John Foster*. Edited by J. E. Ryland. 2 vols. London: Henry G. Bohn, 1861.
Fuller, Andrew. [as Agnostos]. *The Reality and Efficacy of Divine Grace*. London: Lepard, 1790.
———. *Strictures on Sandemanianism*. 2nd ed. London: Thomas Williams, 1811.
Gill, John. *The Dissenter's Reasons for Separating from the Church of England*. London: n.d., 1760.
———. *An Exposition of the Old Testament*. 9 vols. London: Mathews and Leigh, 1810.
Griffin, Edward Dorr. *An Humble Attempt to Reconcile the Differences of Christians Respecting the Extent of the Atonement*. New York: Stephen Dodge, 1819.
———. *The Kingdom of Christ: A Missionary Sermon*. Philadelphia: Jane Aitken, 1805.
Hall, Robert, Sr. *Help to Zion's Travellers*. Bristol: William Pine, 1781.
Hall, Robert, Jr. *On Terms of Communion*. Philadelphia: Anthony Finley, 1816.
———. *The Works of the Rev. Robert Hall, A.M.: With a Memoir of His Life*. Edited by Olinthus Gregory. 3 vols. New York: Harper, 1832–33.
Hardcastle, Thomas. *Christian Geography and Arithmetick, or a True Survey of the World: Together with a Right Art of Numbring Our Dayes Therein*. London: Richard Chiswel, 1674.
Hopkins, Samuel. "A Dialogue between a Calvinist and a Semi-Calvinist." In *Sketches of the Life of Samuel Hopkins, D.D.* Edited by Stephen West. Hartford: Hudson and Goodwin, 1805.
———. *An Inquiry into the Nature of True Holiness*. Newport: Solomon Southwick, 1773.
———. *The System of Doctrines Contained in Divine Revelation, Explained and Defended*. 2 vols. Boston: Isaiah Thomas and Ebenezer T. Andrews, 1793.
———. *Two Discourses*. Boston: William McAlpine, 1768.
———. *The Works of Samuel Hopkins, D.D.* 3 vols. Boston: Doctrinal Tract and Book Society, 1854.
Ivimey, Joseph. *A History of the English Baptists*. 4 vols. London: Holdsworth, 1823.
———. *Letters on the Serampore Controversy, Addressed to the Rev. Christopher Anderson*. London: George Wightman, 1831.
Jacob, Henry. *A Declaration and Plainer Opening of Certain Points, with a Sound Confirmation of Some Other, Contained in a Treatise Intituled, the Divine Beginning and Institution of Christes True Visible and Ministeriall Church*. n.d.: n.d., 1612.
Jessey, Henry. *Miscellanea Sacra*. London: T. M., 1665.

———. *A Storehouse of Provision to Further Resolution in Severall Cases of Conscience, and Questions Now in Dispute*. London: Charles Sumpter, 1650.

Jurieu, Pierre. *The Practice of Devotion; or, a Treatise of Divine Love*. London: James Woodward, 1710.

Keach, Benjamin. *The Glory of a True Church, and Its Discipline Display'd*. London: n.d., 1697.

———. *Gold Refin'd; or, Baptism in Its Primitive Purity*. London: Nathaniel Crouch, 1689.

———. *Gospel Mysteries Unveiled: Or, an Exposition of All the Parables, and Many Express Similitudes, Spoken by Our Lord and Savior Jesus Christ*. 4 vols. London: E. Justins, 1815.

Kiffin, William. *A Briefe Remonstrance of the Reasons and Grounds of Those People Commonly Called Anabaptists, for Their Seperation*. London: n.d., 1645.

———. *A Sober Discourse of Right to Church-Communion*. London: George Larkin, 1681.

Mather, Cotton. *Manuductio Ad Ministerium; or, Directions for a Candidate of the Ministry*. London: Charles Dilly, 1781.

Miller, Samuel. *An Essay on the Warrant, Nature, and Duties of the Office of the Ruling Elder in the Presbyterian Church*. Philadelphia: Presbyterian Board of Education, 1832.

———. *Infant Baptism Scriptural and Reasonable: And Baptism by Sprinkling or Affusion, the Most Suitable and Edifying Mode*. Philadelphia: Presbyterian Board of Education, 1834.

———. *Presbyterianism, the Truly Primitive and Apostolical Constitution of the Church of Christ*. Philadelphia: Presbyterian Board of Education, 1835.

Miller, Samuel, Jr. *The Life of Samuel Miller, D.D., LL.D., Second Professor in the Theological Seminary of the Presbyterian Church, at Princeton, New Jersey*. 2 vols. Philadelphia: Claxton, Remsen and Haffelfinger, 1869.

Miller, William. *The Paedobaptist Mode of Administering the Baptismal Ordinance Defended*. London: T. Chapman, 1794.

Newman, William. *The Principles of Nonconformity Sanctioned by the New Testament. A Sermon Delivered at Dr. Rippon's Meeting-House, March 20, 1817*. London: Button and Son, 1817.

Newton, John. *An Authentic Narrative of Some Remarkable and Interesting Particulars in the Life of John Newton*. 3rd ed. London: S. Drapier, 1765.

———. *Thoughts on the African Slave Trade*. London: J. Buckland, 1788.

Owen, John. *Discourses Concerning Evangelical Love, Church-Peace and Unity*. London: n.d., 1672.

Purnell, Robert. *Good Tydings for Sinners, Great Ioy for Saints*. London: Giles Calvert, 1652.

———. *A Little Cabinet Richly Stored with All Sorts of Heavenly Varieties, and Soul-Reviving Influences*. London: Thomas Brewster, 1657.

Rippon, John. *A Brief Essay Towards an History of the Baptist Academy at Bristol; Read before the Bristol Education Society, at Their Anniversary Meeting, in Broadmead, August 26th, 1795*. London: Dilly and Button, 1796.

———. *The Gentle Dismission of Saints from Earth to Heaven: A Sermon Occasioned by the Decease of the Rev. John Ryland, Senior, A.M.* London: Dilly, 1792.

———, ed. *A Selection of Hymns from the Best Authors, Intended to Be an Appendix to Dr. Watt's Psalms and Hymns*. London: Longman, n.d.

Ryland, Frances Barrett. "The Diary of Frances Barrett Ryland." In *Nonconformist Women Writers, 1720-1840*, edited by Timothy Whelan, 8:307-97. London: Pickering and Chatto, 2011.

Ryland, John Collett. *The Character of the Rev. James Hervey, M.A.* London: W. Justins, 1790.

———. *Contemplations on the Divinity of Christ, Evinced from His Names Jehovah, God, and Sovereign Lord; His Attributes and Actions, the Beauties of Creation, Providence, and Redemption; and the Acts of Worship Paid to Him in Scripture.* 3 vols. Northampton: Thomas Dicey, 1782.

——— [as Pacificus]. *A Modest Plea for Free Communion at the Lord's Table; between True Believers of All Denominations.* June 15, 1772. Typeset copy. Northamptonshire Central Library Archives.

Scott, Thomas. *The Force of Truth: An Authentic Narrative.* Boston: J. Belcher, 1814.

Scraggs, George Glyn. *Instructive Selections: Or, the Beauties of Sentiment.* 2 vols. London: H. D. Symonds, 1802.

Spring, Samuel. *Moral Disquisitions.* Exeter: Charles Norris, 1815.

Turner, Daniel. *Charity the Bond of Perfection.* Oxford: J. Buckland, 1780.

——— [as Candidus]. *A Modest Plea for Free Communion at the Lord's Table; Particularly between the Baptists and Poedobaptists.* London: Johnson, 1772.

Venning, Ralph. *Milke and Honey, or a Miscellaneous Collation of Many Christian Experiences, Sayings, Sentences, and Several Places of Scripture Improved.* London: John Rothwel, 1653.

Warham, Francis. *Free Grace Alone Exalted in Man's Conversion.* London: Edward Archer, 1658.

West, Stephen. *Essay on Moral Agency.* Salem, Massachusetts: Thomas C. Cushing, 1794.

Westminster Assembly. *The Confession of Faith and the Larger and Shorter Catechisme.* Amsterdam: Luice Elsever, 1649.

Whiston, Edward. *The Life and Death of Mr. Henry Jessey, Late Preacher of the Gospel of Christ in London.* London: n.d., 1671.

Whitefield, George. *A Select Collection of Letters of the Late Reverend George Whitefield, M.A.* 3 vols. London: Edward and Charles Dilly, 1772.

Primary Sources—Articles

Anonymous. "Public Meetings." *Baptist Magazine* 1 (June 1809) 241-47.

Anonymous. "Public Meetings." *Baptist Magazine* 5 (June 1813) 262-63.

Anonymous. "New Chapels Opened." *Baptist Magazine* 6 (June 1814) 263-64.

Booth, Abraham. "Mr. Booth on Village Preaching." *Baptist Magazine* 2 (May 1810) 282-85.

Edminson, Robert. "Association. Wilts and Somerset." *Baptist Magazine* 12 (May 1820) 207.

Fuller, Andrew. "The Final Consummation of All Things." In *The Complete Works of Andrew Fuller*, edited by Andrew Gunton Fuller, 843. Boston: Lincoln, Edmands, 1833.

Hart, Levi. "A Discourse, Delivered at Newport Rhode-Island, at the Funeral of the Rev. Samuel Hopkins, D.D." In *Sketches of the Life of the Late Rev. Samuel Hopkins, D.D.*, edited by Stephen West, 217-40. Hartford: Hudson and Goodwin, 1805.

Jessey, Henry. "Essay." In *Differences in Judgment About Water-Baptism, No Bar to Communion; or, to Communicate with Saints, as Saints, Proved Lawful*, edited by John Bunyan, 101–22. London: Wilkins, 1673.

Johnson, Samuel. "Complacency" and "Vital." In *A Dictionary of the English Language*. 3rd ed. Dublin: W. G. Jones, 1768.

Ryland, John Collett. "To the Gentlemen and Other Several Christians, in London and in the Country." In *Manuductio Ad Ministerium; or, Directions for a Candidate of the Ministry*, edited by Cotton Mather, iii–xvi. London: Charles Dilly, 1781.

———. "Preface." In *The Excellency of Christ*, by Jonathan Edwards, 3–6. Northampton: Thomas Dicey, 1780.

Wesley, John. "Catholic Spirit." In *The Works of John Wesley, A.M.*, edited by John Emory, 1:346–55. New York: Emory and Baugh, 1831.

———. "Salvation by Faith." In *The Works of John Wesley, A.M.*, edited by John Emory, 1:13–19. New York: Emory and Baugh, 1831.

Whitefield, George. "Christ the Believer's Refuge." In *Eighteen Sermons Preached by the Late Rev. George Whitefield, A.M.*, edited by Joseph Gurney and Andrew Gifford, 21–42. New Brunswick: A. Blauvelt, 1802.

———. "A Faithful Minister's Parting Blessing." In *Eighteen SermonsPreached by the Late Rev. George Whitefield, A.M.*, edited by Joseph Gurney and Andrew Gifford, 1–20.

———. "The Folly and Danger of Being Not Righteous Enough." In *The Christian's Companion*, 269–97. London: n.d., 1739.

Primary Sources—Newspapers

Anonymous. "The Anniversary of the Bristol Missionary Society." *Bristol Mirror*, September 30, 1820, 3.

Anonymous. "Baptist Home Missionary Society." *Bristol Mercury*, November 5, 1842, 6.

Anonymous. "Baptist Missionary Society." *Bristol Mercury*, May 16, 1840, 7.

Anonymous. "Bristol Missionary Society." *Bristol Mirror*, October 17, 1812, 3.

Anonymous. "The Late Rev. Dr. Ryland." *Bristol Mirror*, June 4, 1825, 3.

Anonymous. "Mission in India." *Caledonian Mercury*, June 20, 1811, 3.

Anonymous. "On Tuesday Last." *Northampton Mercury*, June 21, 1823, 3.

Anonymous. "To the Friends of Christianity in Scotland. Baptist Missionary Society." *Caledonian Mercury*, July 25, 1816, 3.

Anonymous. "The Wesleyan Methodists." *Bristol Mirror*, May 12, 1821, 3.

Silvester, James. "Two Famous Bath Preachers: William Jay and Archbishop Magee." *Bath Chronicle and Weekly Gazette*, February 9, 1899, 6.

Primary Sources—Correspondence

Brine, John. "Letter to John Collett Ryland." April 15, 1755. Isaac Mann Collection, National Library of Wales.

Edwards, Jonathan, Jr. "Letter to John Ryland." May 28, 1785. Beinecke Rare Book and Manuscript Library, Yale University.

———. "Letter to John Ryland." April 23, 1793. Beinecke Rare Book and Manuscript Library, Yale University.
Hall, Robert, Jr. "Letter to John Ryland." May 1, 1815. Cadbury Research Library, University of Birmingham.
Hopkins, Samuel. "Letter to John Ryland." October 17, 1799. Andover-Newton Miscellaneous Personal Papers Collection, Yale University Divinity School Library.
Newton, John. "Letters of John Newton to John Ryland." Bristol Baptist College Archives.
Ryland, John Collett. "Letter to James Hervey." October 10, 1758. Bristol Baptist College Archives.
Scott, John. "Letter to John Ryland." April 13, 1821. In *A Discourse on the Gospel Offer*.
———. "Postscript to John Scott Letter." April 17, 1821. In *A Discourse on the Gospel Offer*.
Scott, Thomas. "Letter to John Ryland." February 15, 1821. In *A Discourse on the Gospel Offer*.

Primary Sources—Circular Letters

Anonymous. "Breviates." *Northamptonshire Baptist Association, Circular Letter* (1779) 14–15.
Anonymous. "Breviates." *Northamptonshire Baptist Association, Circular Letter* (1774) 8.
Anonymous. "Breviates." *Northamptonshire Baptist Association, Circular Letter* (1780) 9.
Anonymous. "Copy of the Preliminaries, Annually Read, at the Meeting of the Western Association of Baptist Churches." *Western Baptist Association Circular Letter* (1798) 14–15.
Strict Baptist Churches of the United Kingdom. "Circular Letter." *The Primitive Church (or Baptist) Magazine* 231 (March 2, 1863) 68–69.

Primary Sources—Church Record Books

"College Lane Baptist Church: Church Book, 1737–1781." Northamptonshire Record Office.
"College Lane Baptist Church: Church Book, 1781–1801." Northamptonshire Record Office.
"Records of the Independent Church at Broadmead, 1757–1818." Bristol Archives.
"Records of the Independent Church at Broadmead, 1830–1853." Bristol Archives.
"Warwick Church Book, 1714–1759." Warwickshire Record Office.

Primary Sources—Unpublished Material

Anonymous. "England and Wales, Non-Conformist and Non-Parochial Registers, 1567–1970." National Archives of the United Kingdom.
Anonymous. "Northampton, College Street (Baptist), 1786–1837, Record of Non-Conformist and Non-Parochial Registers." Northamptonshire Record Office.

Anonymous. "Northamptonshire, England, Church of England Baptisms, Marriages and Burials, 1532–1812." Northamptonshire Record Office.

Anonymous. "Northamptonshire, England, Church of England Marriages, 1754–1912." Northamptonshire Record Office.

Foster, John. "Record by John Foster of His Last Conversation with Dr John Ryland, Dated 20 May 1825." Bristol Baptist College Archives.

Hall, Robert Sr. "Letter to John Ryland Jr." March 8, 1787. Bristol Baptist College Archives.

Ryland, John Collett. "Diary: April 1745." Angus Library and Archive.

———. "Sermons: January 1791." Northamptonshire Record Office.

Ryland, John Collett, and John Ryland. "M.S. Note Book of John Ryland." Angus Library and Archive.

Secondary Sources—Books

Anonymous. *Dutch Tiles: Being the Narratives of Holy Scripture*. London: John Mason, 1842.

———. *Historical Catalogue of the First Church in Hartford, 1633–1885*. Hartford: First Church in Hartford, 1885.

Armitage, Thomas. *A History of the Baptists: Traced by Their Vital Principles and Practices, from the Time of Our Lord and Saviour Jesus Christ to the Year 1886*. New York: Bryan, Taylor, 1887.

Ball, Bryan. *A Great Expectation: Eschatological Thought in English Protestantism to 1660*. Leiden: Brill, 1975.

Batalden, Stephen K. *Russian Bible Wars: Modern Scriptural Translation and Cultural Authority*. Cambridge: Cambridge University Press, 2013.

Bebbington, David. *Baptists through the Centuries: A History of a Global People*. Waco, TX: Baylor University Press, 2010.

Belcher, Joseph. *Historical Sketches of Hymns, Their Writers, and Their Influence*. Philadelphia: Lindsay and Blakiston, 1859.

Belcher, Richard, and Anthony Mattia. *A Discussion of the Seventeenth Century Particular Baptist Confessions of Faith*. Southbridge: Crown, 1990.

Betteridge, Alan. *Deep Roots, Living Branches: A History of Baptists in the English Western Midlands*. Leicester: Matador, 2010.

Birch, Ian. *To Follow the Lambe Wheresoever He Goeth: The Ecclesial Polity of the English Calvinistic Baptists, 1640–1660*. Eugene, OR: Pickwick, 2017.

Brackney, William H. *A Genetic History of Baptist Thought: With Special Reference to Baptists in Britain and North America*. Macon, GA: Mercer University Press, 2004.

Brooks, Thomas. *Pictures of the Past: The History of the Baptist Church, Bourton-on-the-Water*. London: Judd and Glass, 1861.

Brown, John. *John Bunyan: His Life, Times, and Work*. London: William Isbister, 1885.

Bull, Josiah. *John Newton of Olney and St. Mary Woolnoth*. 2nd ed. London: Religious Tract Society, 1870.

Bustin, Dennis L. *Paradox and Perseverance: Hanserd Knollys, Particular Baptist Pioneer in Seventeenth-Century England*. Milton Keynes: Paternoster, 2006.

Carty, T. J. *A Dictionary of Literary Pseudonyms in the English Language*. 2nd ed. Milton Park: Routledge, 2000.

Chadwick, Rosie. *A Protestant Catholic Church of Christ: Essays on the History and Life of New Road Baptist Church, Oxford*. Oxford: New Road Baptist Church, 2003.

Chapman, Joseph Miller. *Brief Memorials of Departed Saints*. London: J. Haddon, 1842.

Child, R. L., and C. E. Shipley. *Broadmead Origins: An Account of the Rise of Puritanism in England, and of the Early Days of Broadmead Baptist Church, Bristol, Issued for the Tercentenary*. London: Kingsgate, 1940.

Christie, Robert. *A History of the Late Province of Lower Canada: Parliamentary and Political, from the Commencement to the Close of Its Existence as a Separate Province*. Vol. 6. Montreal: Richard Worthington, 1866.

Coleman, Thomas. *Memorials of the Independent Churches of Northamptonshire*. London: John Snow, 1853.

Conforti, Joseph. *Samuel Hopkins and the New Divinity Movement: Calvinism, the Congregational Ministry, and Reform in New England between the Great Awakenings*. Grand Rapids: Eerdmans, 1981.

Cox, F. A. *History of the Baptist Missionary Society, 1792–1842*. Boston: William S. Damrell, 1845.

Crisp, Oliver D., and Douglas A. Sweeney. *After Jonathan Edwards: The Courses of the New England Theology*. Oxford: Oxford University Press, 2012.

Cross, Anthony R. *"To Communicate Simply You Must Understand Profoundly": Preparation for Ministry among British Baptists*. Didcot: Baptist Historical Society, 2016.

———. *Useful Learning: Neglected Means of Grace in the Reception of the Evangelical Revival among English Particular Baptists*. Eugene, OR: Pickwick, 2017.

Culross, James. *The Three Rylands: A Hundred Years of Various Christian Service*. London: Elliot Stock, 1897.

Dexter, Franklin Bowditch. *Biographical Sketches of the Graduates of Yale College, with Annals of the College History: July, 1778–June, 1792*. 6 vols. New York: Henry Holt, 1907.

Dray, Stephen. *A Proper Old Confloption Down Penzance: An Account and Interpretation of the "Tucknet" Controversy of 1824 within the History of the Baptist Movement in Cornwall*. n.d.: Carn Brea Media, 2013.

Dresser, Madge. *Slavery Obscured: The Social History of the Slave Trade in an English Provincial Port*. New York: Bloomsbury, 2016.

Ellis, William. *History of the London Missionary Society*. 2 vols. London: John Snow, 1844.

Ferm, Robert. *Jonathan Edwards, the Younger, 1745–1801: A Colonial Pastor*. Grand Rapids: Eerdmans, 1976.

Flynn, James T. *The University Reform of Tsar Alexander I, 1802–1835*. Washington, DC: Catholic University of America Press, 1988.

Fowler, Stanley K. *More Than a Symbol*. Milton Keynes: Paternoster, 2002.

Foster, Frank Hugh. *A Genetic History of the New England Theology*. Chicago: University of Chicago Press, 1907.

Fyfe, Christopher. *A History of Sierra Leone*. 2 vols. Oxford: Oxford University Press, 1962.

Garrett, James Leo. *Baptist Theology: A Four-Century Study*. Macon, GA: Mercer University Press, 2009.

Gordon, Grant. *Wise Counsel: John Newton's Letters to John Ryland, Jr*. Carlisle, PA: Banner of Truth Trust, 2009.

Greaves, Richard L. *Glimpses of Glory: John Bunyan and English Dissent*. Stanford: Stanford University Press, 2002.

Guelzo, Allen C. *Edwards on the Will: A Century of American Theological Debate*. Eugene, OR: Wipf & Stock, 1989.

Hague, William. *William Wilberforce: The Life of the Great Anti-Slave Trade Campaigner*. London: Harper, 2007.

Hall, Catherine. *Civilising Subjects: Metropole and Colony in the English Imagination 1830–1867*. Chicago: Chicago University Press, 2002.

Hall, C. Sidney, and Harry Mowvley. *Tradition and Challenge: The Story of Broadmead Baptist Church, Bristol from 1685 to 1991*. Bristol: Broadmead Baptist Church, 1991.

Harmon, Steven R. *Baptist Identity and the Ecumenical Future: Story, Tradition, and the Recovery of Community*. Waco, TX: Baylor University Press, 2016.

———. *Towards Baptist Catholicity: Essays on Tradition and the Baptist Vision*. Milton Keynes: Paternoster, 2006.

Hatfield, Edwin Francis. *The Poets of the Church*. New York: Anson D. F. Randolph, 1884.

Hayden, Roger, ed. *The Records of a Church of Christ in Bristol, 1640–1687*. Bristol: Bristol Record Society, 1974.

Haykin, Michael A. G. *One Heart and One Soul: John Sutcliff of Olney, His Friends and His Times*. Durham: Evangelical, 1994.

Hindmarsh, D. Bruce. *The Evangelical Conversion Narrative: Spiritual Autobiography in Early Modern England*. Oxford: Oxford University Press, 2008.

———. *John Newton and the English Evangelical Tradition: Between the Conversions of Wesley and Wilberforce*. Grand Rapids: Eerdmans, 2001.

Hinton, John Howard. *Memoir of William Knibb*. 2nd ed. London: Houlston and Stoneman, 1849.

James, Aaron. *Analogous Uses of Language, Eucharistic Identity, and the Baptist Vision*. Milton Keynes: Paternoster, 2014.

Jay, William. *The Autobiography of William Jay*. Edited by George Redford and John Angell James. 2 vols. New York: Robert Carter, 1855.

Julian, John. *A Dictionary of Hymnology, Setting Forth the Origin and History of Christian Hymns of All Ages and Nations*. New York: Dover, 1957.

Kling, David William, and Douglas A. Sweeney. *Jonathan Edwards at Home and Abroad: Historical Memories, Cultural Movements, Global Horizons*. Columbia, SC: University of South Carolina Press, 2004.

Leonard, Bill. *Baptist Ways: A History*. Valley Forge, PA: Judson, 2003.

Long, Edwin McKean. *Illustrated History of Hymns and Their Authors*. Philadelphia: Joseph F. Jaggers, 1875.

Marsden, George M. *Jonathan Edwards: A Life*. New Haven, CT: Yale University Press, 2003.

Marshman, John Clark. *The Life and Times of Carey, Marshman, and Ward: Embracing the History of the Serampore Mission, Volume 1*. London: Longman, Brown, Green, Longmans, and Roberts, 1859.

Martin, Bernard. *John Newton*. London: Heinemann, 1950.

McBeth, Leon. *The Baptist Heritage*. Nashville: Broadman, 1987.

McDermott, Gerald R., and Michael J. McClymond. *The Theology of Jonathan Edwards*. New York: Oxford University Press, 2012.

Moon, Norman S. *Education for Ministry: Bristol Baptist College, 1679–1979*. Bristol: Bristol Baptist College, 1979.

Morris, John Webster. *Biographical Recollections of the Rev. Robert Hall, A.M.* London: George Wightman, 1833.
Nash, Ansel. *Memoir of Edward Dorr Griffin, D.D.* New York: S. W. Benedict, 1842.
Naylor, Peter. *Calvinism, Communion, and the Baptists: A Study of English Calvinistic Baptists from the Late 1600s to the Early 1800s.* Eugene, OR: Wipf & Stock, 2006.
Newman, William. *Rylandiana: Reminiscences Relating to the Rev. John Ryland, A.M. Of Northampton, Father of the Late Rev. Dr. Ryland, of Bristol.* London: George Wightman, 1835.
Nott, Helena Elizabeth, and Elizabeth Ralph, eds. *The Deposition Books of Bristol.* Vol. 13. Bristol: Bristol Record Society, 1948.
Paterson, John. *The Book for Every Land: Reminiscences of Labour and Adventure in the Work of Bible Circulation in the North of Europe and in Russia.* London: John Snow, 1858.
Payne, Ernest A. *College Street Church, Northampton, 1697–1947.* London: n.d., 1947.
Peggs, James. *A History of the General Baptist Mission Established in the Province.* London: John Snow, 1846.
Pollock, John. *Wilberforce.* New York: St. Martin's, 1997.
Post, Stephen. *Christian Love and Self-Denial: An Historical and Normative Study of Jonathan Edwards, Samuel Hopkins, and American Theological Ethics.* Lanham: University Press of America, 1987.
Rey, Marie-Pierre. *Alexander I: The Tsar Who Defeated Napoleon.* DeKalb: Northern Illinois University Press, 2012.
Riddell, Peter G., and Peter Cotterell. *Islam in Context: Past, Present, and Future.* Grand Rapids: Baker Academic, 2003.
Seelye, Julius Hawley. *Christian Missions.* New York: Dodd and Mead, 1875.
Slim, Cornelius. *My Contemporaries of the Nineteenth Century: Brief Memorials of More Than Four Hundred Ministers of the Gospel of Various Denominations Who Have Lived, Laboured, and Entered into Rest, from A.D. 1800 to 1869.* London: Elliot Stock, 1870.
Spurgeon, Charles H. *Farm Sermons.* London: Passmore and Alabaster, 1882.
———. *Feathers for Arrows; or, Illustrations from My Note Book.* New York: Sheldon and Company, 1870.
———. *My Sermon-Notes, a Selection from Outlines of Discourses Delivered at the Metropolitan Tabernacle with Anecdotes and Illustrations, from Ecclesiastes to Malachi.* New York: Funk and Wagnalls, 1891.
———. *Sermons of Rev. C. H. Spurgeon of London.* Second Series. New York: Robert Carter, 1883.
———. *Spurgeon's Sermons on Prayer.* Peabody: Hendrickson, 2007.
———. *The Treasury of David.* 6 vols. New York: Funk and Wagnalls, 1882–83.
Stanley, Brian. *The History of the Baptist Missionary Society, 1792–1992.* Edinburgh: T. & T. Clark, 1992.
Starr, Edward C. *Baptist Bibliography.* 25 vols. Rochester: American Baptist Historical Society, 1974.
Steane, Edward. *Address Delivered at the Funeral of the Rev. Thomas Steffe Crisp, by the Rev. Edward Steane, D.D.; Together with the Funeral Sermon, Preached by the Rev. Frederic William Gotch, LL.D.* London: Hodder and Stoughton, 1868.
Stiles, Ezra. *The Literary Diary of Ezra Stiles.* New York: Charles Scribner's Sons, 1901.
Stott, Anne. *Wilberforce: Family and Friends.* Oxford: Oxford University Press, 2012.

Swaine, Stephen Albert. *Faithful Men; or, Memorials of Bristol Baptist College, and Some of Its Most Distinguished Alumni*. London: Alexander and Shepheard, 1884.

Sweeney, Douglas A., and Allen C. Guelzo. *The New England Theology: From Jonathan Edwards to Edwards Amasa Park*. Grand Rapids: Baker Academic, 2006.

Taylor, John. *History of College Street Church, Northampton: With Biographies of Pastors, Missionaries and Preachers; and Notes of Sunday Schools, Branch Churches and Workers: Illustrated with Portraits and Drawings*. Northampton: Taylor and Son, 1897.

Tolmie, Murray. *The Triumph of the Saints: The Separate Churches of London 1616-1649*. Cambridge: Cambridge University Press, 1977.

Underhill, Edward Bean, ed. *The Records of a Church of Christ: Meeting in Broadmead, Bristol, 1640-1687*. London: J. Haddon, 1847.

van Vlastuin, Willem. *Catholic Today: A Reformed Conversation about Catholicity*. Göttingen: Vandenhoeck and Ruprecht, 2020.

Vedder, Henry Clay. *A Short History of the Baptists*. Rev. ed. Philadelphia: American Baptist Publication Society, 1897.

Waddington, John. *Congregational History, 1700-1800*. London: Longman, Green, and Company, 1876.

Waldron, Samuel. *A Modern Exposition of the 1689 Baptist Confession of Faith*. Darlington: Evangelical, 1989.

Walker, Michael J. *Baptists at the Table: The Theology of the Lord's Supper Amongst English Baptists in the Nineteenth Century*. Didcot: Baptist Historical Society, 1992.

Waterbury, J. B. *Sketches of Eloquent Preachers*. New York: American Tract Society, 1864.

Whelan, Timothy D., ed. *Baptist Autographs in the John Rylands University Library of Manchester, 1741-1845*. Macon, GA: Mercer University Press, 2009.

White, Barrington Raymond. *The English Baptists of the Seventeenth Century*. London: The Baptist Historical Society, 1983.

Whyte, Iain. *Zachary Macaulay 1768-1838: The Steadfast Scot in the British Anti-Slavery Movement*. Liverpool: Liverpool University Press, 2011.

Wright, Stephen. *The Early English Baptists, 1603-49*. Martlesham: Boydell and Brewer, 2006.

Yeager, Jonathan. *Early Evangelicalism: A Reader*. Oxford: Oxford University Press, 2013.

———. *Enlightened Evangelicalism: The Life and Thought of John Erskine*. Oxford: Oxford University Press, 2011.

———. *Jonathan Edwards and Transatlantic Print Culture*. Oxford: Oxford University Press, 2016.

Secondary Sources—Articles and Chapters

Anderson, Philip J. "Letter of Henry Jessey and John Tombes to the Churches of New England, 1645." *Baptist Quarterly* 28 (January 1979) 30-40.

Anonymous. "The Life and Character of Dr. Edwards." In *The Works of President Edward*, edited by Edward Williams and Edward Parsons, 1:103-19. Leeds: Edward Baines, 1806.

Anonymous. "Memoir of Mrs. Dent." *Baptist Magazine* 13 (1821) 185-88.

Anonymous. "Memoir of Richards and Ryland." *The Christian Review and Clerical Magazine* 2 (1828) 205–24.
Anonymous. "Memoir of the Late Rev. John Ryland, D.D." *The American Baptist Magazine* 6 (1826) 221–30.
Anonymous. "Memoir of the Late Rev. John Ryland, D.D." *Baptist Magazine* 18 (1826) 1–9.
Anonymous. "Minutes of the Congregational Missionary Society." *The Panoplist, and Missionary Magazine* 10 (1809) 482–84.
Anonymous. "Obituary." *The American Baptist Magazine* 5 (1825) 256.
Anonymous. "Obituary: Rev. John Ryland, D.D. LL.D." *The American Baptist Magazine* 5 (1825) 317.
Anonymous. "Records of the Jacob-Lathorp-Jessey Church, 1616–1641." *Transactions of the Baptist Historical Society* 1 (1910) 203–25.
Anonymous. "Review of a Sermon, Occasioned by the Death of the Rev. John Ryland, D. D., Preached at the Baptist Meeting, Broadmead, Bristol, June 5, 1825." *The Monthly Repository of Theology and General Literature* 21 (1826) 172–77.
Anonymous. "Review of a Sermon, Occasioned by the Death of the Rev. John Ryland, D. D., Preached at the Baptist Meeting, Broadmead, Bristol, June 5, 1825." *The Spiritual Magazine; or, Saint's Treasury* 2 (1825) 216–23.
Anonymous. "Rise of Particular Baptists in London, 1633–1644." *Transactions of the Baptist Historical Society* 1 (1910) 226–36.
Anonymous. "Ryland, John, D.D." In *Baptist Encyclopedia*, edited by William Cathcart, 1018. Philadelphia: Louis H. Everts, 1883.
Anonymous. "Story of the Jacob-Jessey Church, 1616–1678." *Transactions of the Baptist Historical Society* 1 (1910) 246–50.
Axon, William. "Canne, John." In *Dictionary of National Biography: Brown-Chaloner*, edited by Sidney Lee, 863–65. London: Smith, Elder, 1908.
Ban, Joseph D. "Was John Bunyan a Baptist?" *Baptist Quarterly* 30 (1984) 367–76.
Belyea, Gordon Lansdowne. "Origins of the Particular Baptists." *Themelios* 32 (2007) 40–67.
Bogue, David. "To the Evangelical Diſſenters Who Practiſe Infant Baptiſm." *Evangelical Magazine* 2 (1794) 378–80.
Brachlow, Stephen. "The Elizabethan Roots of Henry Jacob's Churchmanship." *Journal of Ecclesiastical History* 36 (1985) 228–54.
———. "Lathrop, (or Lothrop, Lathorp), John (1584–1653)." In *Biographical Dictionary of British Radicals in the Seventeenth Century: G–O*, edited by Richard L Greaves and Robert Zaller, 173–74. Brighton: Harvester, 1982.
Briggs, John H. Y. "Evangelical Ecumenism: The Amalgamation of General and Particular Baptists in 1891." *Baptist Quarterly* 34 (1991) 99–115.
Burrage, Champlin. "Lost Prison Papers of Henry Jacob." *The Review and Expositor* 4 (1907) 489–513.
———. "Was John Canne a Baptist? A Study of Contemporary Evidence." *Transactions of the Baptist Historical Society* 3 (1913) 212–46.
Burton, N. J. "The North Congregational Church." In *The Memorial History of Hartford County Connecticut 1633–1884*, edited by James Hammond Trumbull, 1:389–91. Boston: Edward L. Osgood, 1886.
Bustin, Dennis L. "Hanserd Knollys and the Formation of Particular Baptist Identity in Seventeenth-Century London." In *Baptist Identities: International Studies from*

the Seventeenth to the Twentieth Centuries, edited by Ian M. Randall et al., 3–21. Eugene, OR: Wipf & Stock, 2006.

Carnahan, James. "Letter to William Buell Sprague." In *Annals of the American Pulpit; or Commemorative Notices of Distinguished American Clergymen of Various Denominations, from the Early Settlement of the Country to the Close of the Year Eighteen Hundred and Fifty-Five*, 3:607–10. New York: Robert Carter and Brothers, 1858.

Carr, Rosalind. "A Polite and Enlightened London?" *The Historical Journal* 59 (2016) 623–634.

Champion, L. G. "Evangelical Calvinism and the Structures of Baptist Church Life." *Baptist Quarterly* 28 (1980) 196–208.

———. "The Letters of John Newton to John Ryland." *Baptist Quarterly* 27 (1977) 157–63.

———. "The Theology of John Ryland: Its Sources and Influences." *Baptist Quarterly* 28 (1979) 17–29.

Conforti, Joseph. "Joseph Bellamy and the New Divinity Movement." *The New England Historical and Genealogical Register* 87 (1983) 126–38.

———. "The Rise of the New Divinity in Western New England." *Historical Journal of Western Massachusetts* 3 (1980) 37–47.

———. "Samuel Hopkins and the New Divinity: Theology, Ethics and Social Reform in Eighteenth Century New England." *William and Mary Quarterly* 34 (1977) 572–89.

Courtney, W. P. "Ryland, John." In *Dictionary of National Biography*, edited by Sidney Lee, 55–56. London: Smith, Elder, 1897.

Crisp, Oliver D. "The Moral Government of God: Jonathan Edwards and Joseph Bellamy on the Atonement." In *After Jonathan Edwards: The Courses of the New England Theology*, edited by Oliver D. Crisp and Douglas A. Sweeney, 78–90. Oxford: Oxford University Press, 2012.

Cross, Anthony R. "The Early Bristol Tradition as a Seedbed for Evangelical Reception among British Baptists, C.1720–C.1770." In *Pathways and Patterns in History: Essays on Baptists, Evangelicals, and the Modern World in Honour of David Bebbington*, edited by Anthony R. Cross et al., 50–77. Didcot: The Baptist Historical Society, 2015.

———. "'To Communicate Simply You Must Understand Profoundly': The Necessity of Theological Education for Deepening Ministerial Formation." *Journal of European Baptist Studies* 19 (2019) 54–67.

Dear, J. "Elegiac Lines on the Late Rev. Dr. Ryland." *Baptist Magazine* 17 (1825) 352.

Dunan-Page, Anne. "Bunyan and the Bedford Congregation." In *The Oxford Handbook of John Bunyan*, edited by Michael Davies and W. R. Owens, 53–68. Oxford: Oxford University Press, 2018.

Everts, William Wallace. "The Life, Character, and Writings of John Foster." In *The Life and Thoughts of John Foster*, edited by J. E. Ryland, 5–53. New York: Edward H. Fletcher, 1849.

Fiddes, Paul S. "Daniel Turner and a Theology of the Church Universal." In *Pulpit and People: Studies in Eighteenth Century Baptist Life and Thought*, edited by John H. Y. Briggs, 112–27. Eugene, OR: Wipf & Stock, 2009.

Finn, Nathan A. "The Renaissance in Andrew Fuller Studies: A Bibliographic Essay." *Southern Baptist Journal of Theology* 17 (2013) 44–61.

Firman, Catherine K. "A Footnote on Methodism in Oxford." *Church History* 29 (1960) 161–66.
Foster, John. "Ryland's Pastoral Memorials." *Eclectic Review* 30 (1828) 537–44.
Freeman, Curtis W. "A Confession for Catholic Baptists." In *Ties That Bind: Life Together in the Baptist Vision*, edited by Garry Furr and Curtis Freeman, 83–97. Macon, GA: Smyth and Helwys, 1994.
Gordon, Grant. "The Call of Dr John Ryland Jr." *Baptist Quarterly* 34 (1992) 214–27.
———. "John Ryland (1753–1825)." In *British Particular Baptists*, edited by Michael A. G. Hayken, 2:77–95. Springfield, Missouri: Particular Baptist, 1998.
———. "A Revealing Unpublished Letter of George Whitefield to John Collett Ryland." *Baptist Quarterly* 47 (2016) 65–75.
Graham, Lon. "'The Dearest of Women Is Gone': A Historical Study of Grief in the Life of John Ryland Jr." *Journal of European Baptist Studies* 19 (2019) 66–83.
———. "John Collett Ryland, Daniel Turner, and *A Modest Plea*." *Baptist Quarterly* 52 (2021) 34–42.
———. "'A Union of Sentiments in Apostolical Doctrines': The Catholicity of Andrew Fuller." *Journal of European Baptist Studies* 21 (2021) 105–22.
Greaves, Richard L. "Conscience, Liberty, and the Spirit: Bunyan and Nonconformity." In *John Bunyan: Conventicle and Parnassus*, edited by N. H. Keeble, 21–43. Oxford: Clarendon, 1988.
Griffin, Edward Dorr. "Letter X: Revival of Religion in New-Hartford." *Connecticut Evangelical Magazine* 1 (1800) 217–23.
———. "Letter XI: Revival of Religion in New-Hartford." *Connecticut Evangelical Magazine* 1 (1800) 265–68.
Harmon, Steven R. "'Catholic Baptists' and the New Horizon of Tradition in Baptist Theology." In *New Horizons in Theology*, edited by Terrence W. Tilly, 117–43. Maryknoll, NY: Orbis, 2005.
———. "Dei Verbum § 9 in Baptist Perspective." *Ecclesiology* 5 (2009) 299–321.
———. "Free Church Theology, the Pilgrim Church, and the Ecumenical Future." *Journal of Ecumenical Studies* 49 (2014) 420–42.
———. "Scripture in the Life of the Baptist Churches: Openings for a Differentiated Catholic-Baptist Consensus on Sacred Scripture." *Pro Ecclesia* 18 (2009) 187–215.
———. "Why Baptist Catholicity, and by What Authority?" *Pro Ecclesia* 18 (2009) 386–92.
Hayden, Roger. "Broadmead, Bristol in the Seventeenth Century." *Baptist Quarterly* 23 (1970) 348–59.
———. "John Tyler Ryland, 1786–1841: A Further Assessment." *Baptist Quarterly* 46 (2015) 120–27.
Haykin, Michael A. G. "'A Garden Inclosed': Worship and Revival among the English Particular Baptists of the Eighteenth Century." https://repository.sbts.edu/bitstream/handle/10392/6318/2008-02-28-Haykin02.EnclosedGardensFULL.pdf.
———. "The Baptist Identity: A View from the Eighteenth Century." *Evangelical Quarterly* 67 (1995) 137–52.
———. "John Ryland Jr.—'O Lord, I Would Delight in Thee': The Life and Ministry of John Ryland, Jr. Appreciated on the 250th Anniversary of His Birth." *Reformation Today* 196 (2003) 13–20.

———. "John Ryland, Jr. (1753–1825) and Theological Education." *Nederlands Archief voor Kerkgeschiedenis* 70 (1990) 173–91.

———. "Review of *The Life and Thought of Andrew Fuller*." *Church History and Religious Culture* 97 (2017) 149–52.

———. "'The Sum of All Good': John Ryland, Jr. and the Doctrine of the Holy Spirit." *Churchman* 103 (1989).

Helm, Paul. "A Different Kind of Calvinism? Edwardsianism Compared with Older Forms of Reformed Thought." In *After Jonathan Edwards: The Courses of the New England Theology*, edited by Oliver D. Crisp and Douglas A. Sweeney, 91–104. Oxford: Oxford University Press, 2012.

———. "Jonathan Edwards and the Parting of the Ways?" *Jonathan Edwards Studies* 4 (2014) 42–60.

———. "Turretin and Edwards Once More." *Jonathan Edwards Studies* 4 (2014) 286–96.

Hindmarsh, D Bruce. "'I Am a Sort of Middle Man': The Politically Correct Evangelicalism of John Newton." In *Amazing Grace: Evangelicalism in Australia, Britain, Canada, and the United States*, edited by George A. Rawlyk and Mark A. Noll, 29–55. Grand Rapids: Baker, 1993.

Jauhiainen, Peter. "Samuel Hopkins and Hopkinsianism." In *After Jonathan Edwards: The Courses of the New England Theology*, edited by Oliver D. Crisp and Douglas A. Sweeney, 107–17. Oxford: Oxford University Press, 2012.

Jones, John Andrews. "Editor's Preface." In *Serious Essays on the Truths of the Glorious Gospel*, by John Ryland, edited by John Andrews Jones, iii–xii. London: John Bennett, 1829.

Julian, John. "John Ryland." In *Dictionary of Hymnology*, edited by John Julian, 984. New York: Charles Scribner's Sons, 1892.

Kling, David William. "Edwards in the Second Great Awakening: The New Divinity Contributions of Edward Dorr Griffin and Asahel Nettleton." In *After Jonathan Edwards: The Courses of New England Theology*, edited by Oliver D. Crisp and Douglas A. Sweeney, 130–41. Oxford: Oxford University Press, 2012.

Lucas, Sean Michael. "'He cuts up Edwardsism by the roots': Robert Lewis Dabney and the Edwardsian Legacy in the Nineteenth-Century South." In *The Legacy of Jonathan Edwards: American Religion and the Evangelical Tradition*, edited by D. G. Hart et al., 200–214. Grand Rapids: Baker, 2003.

McClendon, James. "What Is a Southern Baptist Ecumenism?" *Southwestern Journal of Theology* 10 (1968) 73–78.

McClendon, James, and John Howard Yoder. "Christian Identity in Ecumenical Perspective." *Journal of Ecumenical Studies* 27 (1990) 561–80.

McGlothlin, W. J. "The Sources of the First Calvinistic Baptist Confession of Faith." *Review and Expositor* 13 (1916) 502–05.

Morden, Peter J. "Andrew Fuller and the Baptist Missionary Society." *Baptist Quarterly* 41 (2005) 134–57.

Muller, Richard A. "Jonathan Edwards and the Absence of Free Choice: A Parting of Ways in the Reformed Tradition." *Jonathan Edwards Studies* 1 (2011) 3–22.

———. "Jonathan Edwards and Francis Turretin on Necessity, Contingency, and Freedom of Will. In Response to Paul Helm." *Jonathan Edwards Studies* 4 (2014) 266–85.

Nelson, Stanley A. "Reflecting on Baptist Origins: The London Confession of Faith of 1644." *Baptist History and Heritage* 29 (1994) 33–46.
Noll, Mark. "The Founding of Princeton Seminary." *Westminster Theological Journal* 42 (1979) 72–110.
Nuttall, Geoffrey F. "Letters from Robert Hall to John Ryland 1791–1824." *Baptist Quarterly* 34 (1991) 127–31.
———. "Northamptonshire and 'the Modern Question': A Turning-Point in Eighteenth-Century Dissent." *The Journal of Theological Studies* 16 (1965) 101–23.
Oliver, Robert W. "John Collett Ryland, Daniel Turner and Robert Robinson and the Communion Controversy, 1772–1781." *Baptist Quarterly* 29 (1981) 77–79.
Park, Edwards Amasa. "Introduction to Letters of Dr. John Ryland to Dr. Stephen West." *Bibliotheca Sacra* 30 (1873) 178.
———. "Introductory Essay." In *The Atonement. Discourses and Treatises*, edited by Edwards Amasa Park, vii–lxxx. Boston: Congregational Board of Publication, 1859.
Paul, Robert. "Henry Jacob and Seventeenth-Century Puritanism." *The Hartford Quarterly* 8 (1967) 92–113.
Post, Stephen. "Disinterested Benevolence: An American Debate over the Nature of Christian Love." *The Journal of Religious Ethics* 14 (1986) 356–68.
Priest, Gerald L. "Andrew Fuller, Hyper-Calvinism, and the 'Modern Question.'" In *'At the Pure Fountain of Thy Word': Andrew Fuller as an Apologist*, edited by Michael A. G. Hayken, 43–73. Milton Keynes: Paternoster, 2004.
Rathel, David Mark. "A Case Study in Baptist Catholicity: The Scriptures and the Tradition in the Theology of John Gill." *Baptist Quarterly* (2017) 1–9.
———. "Was John Gill a Hyper-Calvinist? Determining Gill's Theological Identity." *Baptist Quarterly* 48 (2017) 47–59.
Read, Stella. "Further Information on the Ryland Family." *Baptist Quarterly* 36 (1995) 202–3.
Rennie, Ian S. "William Wilberforce: The Rise and Decline of Progressive Evangelical Anglicanism." *Didaskalia* 11 (2000) 1–18.
Robinson, H. Wheeler. "The Experience of John Ryland." *Baptist Quarterly* 4 (1928) 17–26.
Ryland, J. E. "Memoir." In *Pastoral Memorials*, edited by J. E. Ryland, 1–61. London: B. J. Holdsworth, 1828.
Scott, John Thomas. "The Final Effort to Fulfill George Whitefield's Bequest: The Bethesda Mission of 1790–1792." *The Georgia Historical Quarterly* 89 (2005) 433–61.
Shaw, W. A. "Jones, John Andrews." In *Dictionary of National Biography*, edited by Sidney Lee, 135–36. New York: MacMillan, 1892.
Smith, Karen E. "Preparation as a Discipline of Devotion in Eighteenth-Century England: A Lost Facet of Baptist Identity?" In *Baptist Identities: International Studies from the Seventeenth to the Twentieth Centuries*, edited by Ian Randall et al., 22–44. Eugene, OR: Wipf & Stock, 2006.
Sprague, William Buell. "Jonathan Edwards, D.D." In *Annals of the American Pulpit; or Commemorative Notices of Distinguished American Clergymen of Various Denominations, from the Early Settlement of the Country to the Close of the Year Eighteen Hundred and Fifty-Five*, 1:653–60. New York: Robert Carter, 1857.

———. "Levi Hart, D.D." In *Annals of the American Pulpit; or Commemorative Notices of Distinguished American Clergymen of Various Denominations, from the Early Settlement of the Country to the Close of the Year Eighteen Hundred and Fifty-Five*, 1:590–94. New York: Robert Carter and Brothers, 1857.

———. "Samuel Miller, D.D." In *Annals of the American Pulpit; or Commemorative Notices of Distinguished American Clergymen of Various Denominations, from the Early Settlement of the Country to the Close of the Year Eighteen Hundred and Fifty-Five*, 3:600–12. New York: Robert Carter and Brothers, 1858.

Spring, David. "The Clapham Sect: Some Social and Political Aspects." *Victorian Studies* 5 (1961) 35–48.

Stanton, Allen. "Princeton's Pastor: A Reconsideration of Old Princeton's View of the Christian Ministry." *Puritan Reformed Journal* 4 (2012) 143–57.

———. "Samuel Miller: The Forgotten Founder and Shaper of Old Princeton." *The Journal of Presbyterian History* 91 (2013) 4–17.

Stassen, Glen H. "Anabaptist Influence in the Origin of the Particular Baptists." *The Mennonite Quarterly Review* 36 (1962) 322–48.

Stephens, Bruce M. "Samuel Miller, 1769–1850, Apologist for Orthodoxy." *The Princeton Seminary Bulletin* 67 (1975) 33–47.

Stuart, J. "Printing Ryland's Funeral Sermon." *Transactions of the Baptist Historical Society* 1 (1909) 145–47.

Summers, Thomas O. "John Ryland, D.D." *Quarterly Review of the Methodist Episcopal Church, South* 17 (1880) 749–52.

Thompson, David. "Baptists in the Eighteenth Century: Relations with Other Christians." In *Challenge and Change: English Baptist Life in the Eighteenth Century*, edited by Stephen L. Copson and Peter J. Morden, 259–79. Didcot: The Baptist Historical Society, 2017.

Thompson, Philip E. "A New Question in Baptist History: Seeking a Catholic Spirit Among Early Baptists." *Pro Ecclesia* 8 (1999) 51–72.

———. "People of the Free God: The Passion of Seventeenth-Century Baptists." *American Baptist Quarterly* 15 (1996) 223–41.

Toon, Peter. "English Strict Baptists." *Baptist Quarterly* 21 (1965) 30–36.

———. "John Brine, 1703–1765." *Free Grace Record* 3 (1965) 557–71.

von Rohr, John. "The Congregationalism of Henry Jacob." *Transactions of the Congregational Historical Society* 19 (1962) 107–17.

Walker, Franklin A. "Enlightenment and Religion in Russian Education in the Reign of Tsar Alexander I." *History of Education Quarterly* 32 (1992) 343–60.

Ward, W. R. "The Baptists and the Transformation of the Church, 1780–1830." *Baptist Quarterly* 25 (1973) 167–84.

Weaver, Daniel T. and Michael Haykin. "A Significant Letter from John Ryland to Samuel Hopkins." *The Andrew Fuller Review* 3 (2012) 29–33.

Wenkel, David. "John Bunyan's Soteriology during His Pre-Prison Period (1656–1659) Amyraldian or High-Calvinist?" *Scottish Journal of Theology* 58 (2005) 333–52.

Whelan, Timothy. "An Evangelical Anglican Interaction with Baptist Missionary Society Strategy: William Wilberforce and John Ryland, 1807–1824." In *Interfaces: Baptists and Others*, edited by David Bebbington and Martin Sutherland, 56–85. Milton Keynes, United Kingdom: Paternoster, 2013.

———. "'For the Hand of a Woman, Has Levell'd the Blow': Maria De Fleury's Pamphlet War with William Huntington, 1787–1791." *Women's Studies* 36 (2007) 431–54.

———. "S. T. Coleridge, Joseph Cottle, and Some Bristol Baptists, 1794–96." In *English Romantic Writers and the West Country*, edited by Nicholas Roe, 99–114. London: Palgrave MacMillan, 2010.

Whelan, Timothy, and Roger Hayden. "John Tyler Ryland, 1786–1841: A Postscript with Two Additional Manuscripts." *Baptist Quarterly* 47 (2016) 120–28.

White, Barrington Raymond. "The Doctrine of the Church in the Particular Baptist Confession of 1644." *Journal of Theological Studies* 19 (1968) 575–82.

———. "Open and Closed Membership among English and Welsh Baptists." *Baptist Quarterly* 24 (1972) 330–34.

Whitley, William Thomas. "Debate on Infant Baptism, 1643." *Transactions of the Baptist Historical Society* 1 (1910) 237–45.

Williams, Thomas. "Edwards, Jonathan W." In *Report of Cases Argued and Determined in the Supreme Court of Errors of the State of Connecticut Prepared and Published in Pursuance of the Statute Law of the State*, edited by Thomas Day. Appendix, 15:26–27. New York: Banks and Brothers, 1869.

Wilson, John F. "Another Look at John Canne." *Church History* 33 (1964) 34–48.

World Council of Churches, Faith and Order Commission. "Appendix 12: By-Laws of Faith and Order as Approved by the WCC Central Committee 2014." In *Minutes of the Commission on Faith and Order Meeting at the Monastery of Caraiman, Busteni, Romania, 17–24 June 2015, Faith and Order Paper No. 222*, 101–8. Geneva: World Council of Churches, 2015.

Yeager, Jonathan. "The Letters of John Erskine to the Rylands." *Eusebia* 8 (2008) 183–95.

———. "A Microcosm of the Community of the Saints: John Erskine's Relationship with the English Particular Baptists, John Collett Ryland and His Son John Ryland Jr." In *Pathways and Patterns in History: Essays on Baptists, Evangelicals, and the Modern World in Honour of David Bebbington*, edited by Anthony R. Cross et al., 231–54. Didcot: The Baptist Historical Society, 2015.

Secondary Sources—Dissertations and Theses

Boersma, Spencer. "The baptist Vision: Narrative Theology and Baptist Identity in the Thought of James Wm. McClendon, Jr." ThD diss., University of Toronto, 2017.

Conforti, Joseph. "Samuel Hopkins and the New Divinity Movement, 1740–1820: A Study in the Transformation of Puritan Theology and the New England Social Order." PhD diss., Brown University, 1975.

Cooley, Daniel W. "The New England Theology and the Atonement: Jonathan Edwards to Edwards Amasa Park." PhD diss., Trinity Evangelical Divinity School, 2014.

Crocker, Christopher W. "The Life and Legacy of John Ryland Jr. (1753–1825), a Man of Considerable Usefulness: An Historical Biography." PhD diss., University of Bristol, 2018.

Daniel, Curt. "Hyper-Calvinism and John Gill." PhD diss., University of Edinburgh, 1983.

Duesing, Jason G. "Counted Worthy: The Life and Thought of Henry Jessey, 1601–1663: Puritan Chaplain, Independent and Baptist Pastor, Millenarian Politician and Prophet." PhD diss., Southwestern Baptist Theological Seminary, 2008.

Griffith, Ryan. "'Promoting Pure and Undefiled Religion': John Ryland, Jr. (1753–1825) and Edwardsean Evangelical Biography." PhD diss., Southern Baptist Theological Seminary, 2017.

Hayden, Roger. "Evangelical Calvinism among Eighteenth Century British Baptists, with Particular Reference to Bernard Foskett, Hugh and Caleb Evans, and the Bristol Baptist Academy, 1690–1791." PhD diss., University of Keele, 1991.

Jorgenson, Cameron H. "Bapto-Catholicism: Recovering Tradition and Reconsidering the Baptist Identity." PhD diss., Baylor University, 2008.

McNutt, Cody Heath. "The Ministry of Robert Hall, Jr.: The Preacher as Theological Exemplar and Cultural Celebrity." PhD diss., Southern Baptist Theological Seminary, 2012.

Renihan, James M. "The Practical Ecclesiology of the English Particular Baptists, 1675–1705: The Doctrine of the Church in the Second London Baptist Confession as Implemented in the Subscribing Churches." PhD diss., Trinity Evangelical Divinity School, 1997.

Thompson, Philip E. "Toward Baptist Ecclesiology in Pneumatological Perspective." PhD diss., Emory University, 1995.

Tillman, Keith. "'He Worked out His Salvation with Fear and Trembling': The Spirituality of John Ryland, Jr." ThM thesis, Southern Baptist Theological Seminary, 2014.

Ward, Matthew. "Pure Worship: The Early English Baptist Distinctive." PhD diss., Southwestern Baptist Theological Seminary, 2013.

Wright, Barbara. "John Collett Ryland (1723–1792) Baptist Minister, Schoolmaster and Writer." Unbound manuscript. Bristol Baptist College Archives.

Yarbrough, Slaydon. "Henry Jacob, a Moderate Separatist, and His Influence on Early English Congregationalism." PhD diss., Baylor University, 1972.

www.ingramcontent.com/pod-product-compliance
Lightning Source LLC
Chambersburg PA
CBHW070255230426
43664CB00014B/2540